LITERATURES,
COMMUNITIES,
AND LEARNING

Indigenous Studies Series

The Indigenous Studies Series builds on the successes of the past and is inspired by recent critical conversations about Indigenous epistemological frameworks. Recognizing the need to encourage burgeoning scholarship, the series welcomes manuscripts drawing upon Indigenous intellectual traditions and philosophies, particularly in discussions situated within the Humanities.

Series Editor

Dr. Deanna Reder (Cree-Métis), Associate Professor of English and Chair of First Nations Studies and English, Simon Fraser University

Advisory Board

Dr. Jo-ann Archibald (Stó:lō), Professor Emeritus, Educational Studies, Faculty of Education, University of British Columbia

Dr. Kristina Bidwell (NunatuKavut), Professor of English, University of Saskatchewan

Dr. Daniel Heath Justice (Cherokee Nation), Professor of First Nations and Indigenous Studies/English and Canada Research Chair in Indigenous Literature and Expressive Culture, University of British Columbia

Dr. Eldon Yellowhorn (Piikani), Associate Professor, First Nations Studies, Simon Fraser University

For more information, please contact:

Dr. Deanna Reder
First Nations Studies and English
Simon Fraser University
Phone 778-782-8192
Fax 778-782-4989
Email dhr@sfu.ca

LITERATURES, COMMUNITIES, AND LEARNING

Conversations with Indigenous Writers

Aubrey Jean Hanson

WILFRID LAURIER
UNIVERSITY PRESS

This book has been published with the help of a grant from the Canadian Federation for the Humanities and Social Sciences, through the Awards to Scholarly Publications Program, using funds provided by the Social Sciences and Humanities Research Council of Canada. Wilfrid Laurier University Press acknowledges the support of the Canada Council for the Arts for our publishing program. We acknowledge the financial support of the Government of Canada. This work was supported by the Research Support Fund.

Library and Archives Canada Cataloguing in Publication

Title: Literatures, communities, and learning: conversations with Indigenous writers / Aubrey Jean Hanson.
Names: Hanson, Aubrey Jean, [1979–] author.
Series: Indigenous studies series.
Description: Series statement: Indigenous studies | Includes bibliographical references.
Identifiers: Canadiana (print) 20200164643 | Canadiana (ebook) 2020016466X | ISBN 9781771124492 (hardcover) | ISBN 9781771124515 (EPUB) | ISBN 9781771124522 (PDF)
Subjects: LCSH: Indigenous authors—Canada—Interviews. | CSH: Native authors—Canada Interviews. | LCGFT: Interviews.
Classification: LCC PS8089.5.I6 H36 2020 | DDC C810.9/897—dc23

Front-cover image by Leah Dorion. Cover design and text design by Angela Booth Malleau, designbooth.ca

This book is printed on FSC˚ certified paper. It contains recycled materials and other controlled sources, is processed chlorine free, and is manufactured using biogas energy.

Printed in Canada

CONTENTS

ACKNOWLEDGEMENTS

I OFFER MY MOST sincere thanks to all those who helped me to carry out this work. To the Killam Trusts, the Métis Education Foundation, the Alberta Network Environments for Aboriginal Health Research (of the Canadian Institutes of Health Research's Institute of Aboriginal Peoples' Health), Indspire, the Government of Alberta, the University of Calgary, and the Werklund School of Education for providing awards and funding that made this project possible. To the Banff Centre for Arts and Creativity, the mountains, and the wintery woods for space and time to assemble it into a bookish shape.

To Siobhan McMenemy for her keen eyes, thoughtful presence, and generous commitment to strong work. To the whole team at Wilfrid Laurier University Press for helping me to strengthen and share this project. To Gail Jardine for her limitless support and advice, and to Catherine Burwell and Phyllis Steeves for their wise and cogent feedback. To Gregory Lowan-Trudeau, Aruna Srivastava, and Vicki Kelly for their guidance, questions, and encouragement.

To all those in the ILSA community who care so deeply for the Indigenous literary arts and are wonderful mentors and comrades. To Daniel Justice for providing me with excellent advice and support during my early conceptual work for this project, and to Sam McKegney for offering me mentorship on making it happen. To Mark Abley for first encouraging me to publish this project and for offering his insights. To all my students, who have pushed me to be a better teacher and learner.

To my institution, the Werklund School of Education and the University of Calgary, for making space for Indigenous people and research and for working to listen to Indigenous communities. To my colleagues and collaborators for being in the work together.

To Kit for always advising, encouraging, reading drafts, and lifting me up. To my girls for all the moments that I spent on this work. To my family, friends, and all my loved ones for supporting me. To the many coffee shops, libraries, airports, and other writing spots and life-sustaining places in the cities of Calgary, Montreal, New York, and Banff where I was able to work on this project. To the land and all its beings, all my relatives, who teach me every day.

And, above all, to every one of the writers and teachers for sharing their time, words, and experiences with me during the course of the bigger project. Respectful relationships are integral here, especially with the people who so generously shared their perspectives with me. Although not all of them are explicitly present in this book, they have all shaped it—thank you to Richard Van Camp, "Angela Varila," "Rachel Baker," "Alice Curtis," "Robin Green," Jesse Archibald-Barber, David Robertson, Katherena Vermette, Warren Cariou, Sharron Proulx-Turner, Lee Maracle, Daniel Justice, "Suzette Williams," "Francesca Rawson," "Danny Bill," Tenille Campbell, and Marilyn Dumont. I am so grateful for your generosity and kindness, as well as for the truths you speak.

Maarsii, merci, thank you!

Introduction

WRITING-IN-RELATION

THIS IS A BOOK of conversations with Indigenous writers about their work: about how their writing intersects with notions of community and with the work of learning. One spark for this project was the disconnect I perceived in the early 2010s between the vibrant artistic practices taking place in Indigenous literary arts and some of the calcified practices, when it came to text selection, that often persisted in English language arts education. That is, while Indigenous writers were busily representing their experiences, resisting colonialisms, reclaiming their histories, languages, and cultures, envisioning brighter futures, and wielding powerful aesthetic sensibilities, English language classrooms were engaging busily in the complex work of teaching and learning in ways that did not usually expose students to Indigenous literatures, let alone teach them to appreciate them or connect to the peoples and politics behind them. I believe that Indigenous literatures have the capacity to draw readers into relationship with Indigenous Peoples, through the intimate nature of story, through the beauty of well-wrought words, and through the experiences and knowledges they share. Literatures can be a way of building understanding and relationships between different peoples as a step toward social and political change. Creating change in the service of Indigenous communities, reckoning with the ongoing impacts of settler colonialism in this place now called Canada, is an immense educational project in which literatures can have a prominent place. However, too often the work required to engage responsibly with Indigenous texts has not been done in educational settings.[1]

Fundamental to the process of building understandings and shifting relationships to precipitate social change, in my view, is the work of learning. That is, when people learn more about a community's history and their own place in it, about why they deserve a sense of pride and belonging, or when they develop a grasp of history and its implications, they may shift their beliefs. Change can take place when people learn something about how things have been or how things could be and then act on that knowledge. Ours is a unique moment in this place we call Canada, as conversations on reconciliation and Indigenous perspectives are occupying public forums; possibly more than ever before, Canadian eyes are focused on Indigenous arts as well. In this context, understandings and relationships between Indigenous and non-Indigenous Peoples have the potential to contribute to meaningful change. The social and political change that communities are hoping for requires deep commitment and immeasurable labour. When I roll up my sleeves to get working on my own tiny contributions, I focus my energies on strengthening connections between the powerful work going on in the Indigenous literary arts and the possibilities for learning that can be opened up.

Whose learning am I thinking of when I talk about learning and change? Different readers of this book will have different investments and assumptions. In talking about learning, I am thinking, first, of Indigenous youth.[2] In part this thinking falls within formal education settings, or *schooling*. Some of my professional experience has involved teaching a few Indigenous students in urban high schools where they were a minority and where the curriculum (as prescribed and as taught) largely did not reflect or validate who they were—either their experiences or their cultures. I want young Indigenous people to be able to learn about themselves and the world in a way that enables them to grow into healthy members of self-determining communities. Much of their learning takes place, of course, through what we think of as *education* in a much broader sense than schooling—that is, outside of institutions dedicated to formal education.[3] I am also thinking of different kinds of education when I talk about Indigenous youth learning from (or with, about, for, or through, etc.) Indigenous literatures. Within the purview of the literary arts is a vast field of possibility for their learning journeys: Indigenous languages and oral storytelling, historical understandings, speculative and creative visioning of futures, culturally informed artistry, personal and collective narratives. While my focus here is youth, adults and families and communities are learners, too, and I am thinking of them as well.

Beyond my central focus on Indigenous communities, I am thinking of non-Indigenous people learning from and with Indigenous people, stepping into understanding in the spirit of building good ways of being together. For non-Indigenous people, this learning means being willing to face the difficult truths of colonial violence, confronting their own positionality within broader social systems, and rolling up their sleeves to dismantle colonial structures and to make way for Indigenous resurgence. The required learning, as allied settler scholar Paulette Regan points out, can be unsettling: "For many non-Native Canadians," confrontation with truths of colonial violence may "provoke powerful feelings of denial, guilt, and shame." Regan argues that "we may resist hearing such stories, partly because they challenge our own identity as a nation of benevolent peacemakers."[4] Along similar lines, Lenape and Potawatomi scholar Susan Dion addresses the issue of resistance to learning, suggesting that many non-Indigenous people claim "perfect stranger" status, in the sense that they claim to know virtually nothing about Indigenous people.[5] This positioning, she argues, is "a form of protection against having to recognize their own attachment to and implication in the history of the relationship between Aboriginal people and Canadians."[6] This distancing enables Canadians to maintain a (mis)understanding of Indigenous Peoples as a "romanticised, mythical, victimised, or militant Other."[7] I acknowledge the emotional difficulty entailed in trying to think differently. It can be difficult for non-Indigenous people to change their understandings of Indigenous people because the terrain is contested, politically charged, ideologically laden, and well-travelled for centuries by people invested in the building and stability of the Canadian nation-state. However, such resistance, whatever its origins, is a barrier impeding the transformation of colonial structures and relationships. I recognize and honour those non-Indigenous folks who are already grappling with this difficult learning and shifting their own understandings, working to earn the title of ally or accomplice to Indigenous Peoples.[8] For all those who are willing to learn, Indigenous literatures offer some beautiful pathways into different perspectives.

Notably, *Indigenous* and *non-Indigenous* are broad umbrella terms that gesture very generally toward unstable categories of people. I use the term *Indigenous* to refer to the First Peoples of this place that is now called Canada, namely the First Nations, Métis, and Inuit Peoples. Many commonalities and many distinctions exist within and between these groups. Likewise, I acknowledge that *non-Indigenous* is a vague term that disguises the differences between and among other groups: settler populations, immigrants fleeing famine or persecution, those whose ancestors were brought to the continent as slaves, recently arrived refugees and new Canadians—diverse clusters of people differing in racial, religious, and cultural backgrounds, as well as in wealth, power, and life experience. Lumping everyone together is problematic; generalizations tend to foster inaccuracies, exclusions, and contention. Other possible terms, like *settler*, might gesture toward a largely Euro-Canadian mainstream, bound up historically and in the present day to the colonization, dispossession, and erasure of Indigenous lands, ways of life, languages, cultures, bodies, and knowledges. However, this description may not be appropriate for all.[9] I use the term *non-Indigenous*, then, as a category that, for all its clumsiness, hopefully leaves a little more space for the spirit of learning and potential solidarities among diverse groups. As a woman of Métis and mixed European heritage, I understand that the Indigenous/ non-Indigenous binary is a problematic one, but I still find these broad terms necessary for my work here.

A key distinction to make between Indigenous and non-Indigenous people in terms of learning and change is that resurgence work can only be done by Indigenous Peoples; by contrast, reconciliation work requires contributions from non-Indigenous Canadians. Similarly, decolonizing work can be done collaboratively with contributions from non-Indigenous people. I develop these guiding frameworks later on, but for now I want to emphasize that, when it comes to Indigenous literatures and creating change for the well-being of Indigenous communities, non-Indigenous people can contribute in necessary ways. This work does not rest solely upon Indigenous people. Based on my own experience—largely in working with teachers—many non-Indigenous people do want to contribute to the work of challenging colonialism in its past and present forms, and of improving understandings and relationships between Canadians and Indigenous Peoples. Indeed, I have met many dedicated educators who are taking risks and working tirelessly to advocate for Indigenous communities and to bring their students into this learning.

This book, then, is about Indigenous literatures, communities, and learning. One spark for this work, as I said above, was the need for better learning about Indigenous literatures in schools, given the richness of what exists in Indigenous literary arts. However, sometimes it takes more than one spark to light a fire; there is more to the origin story of this project, as well, and my own educational journey was another incendiary factor. Before I go any further, I need to tell you who I am.

INTRODUCING MYSELF

My name is Aubrey Jean Hanson. I am a proud member of the Métis Nation of Alberta, and I live in the city of Calgary. This city sits on the place called Moh'kins'tsis by the Blackfoot, within the Treaty 7 region of what is now Southern Alberta. The First Nations in this region include the Kainai, Siksika, and Piikuni Blackfoot Nations, the Tsuut'ina First Nation, and the Stoney Nakoda People, made up of the Bearspaw, Chiniki, and Wesley First Nations. Alberta is also in the homeland of the Métis Nation. My membership in the Métis Nation of Alberta to me represents a commitment to be responsible to that heritage and community. I grew up knowing I was Métis, deeply connected with my big Métis family. Calgary has always been home to me, although I have lived in other cities and towns, often moving and adapting for education, work, or love.

My ancestors were from many places, and have moved between many places over the generations. My mother's mother was of Métis ancestry, with Métis and English-German parents. My maternal great-grandfather's family line stretches back to the historic Red River community. Their lives and migrations spanned the Prairies and followed the unfolding of Métis community histories. My grandmother on that side was a gentle but enduring matriarch, gathering her enormous family together into a tight-knit, rowdy Métis bundle. My mother's father was German, the kind of German that is really from further east, a village that was formerly part of Ukraine but is now lost. On the other side of the family, my father's father was Icelandic, a descendant of those immigrants who escaped devastating volcanic activity in their homeland in the late 1800s and went on to survive difficult years in Manitoba.[10] My great-grandfather was apparently a runner and dogsled racer of legendary status. My father's mother also came from Manitoba, and my relatives tell me that her ancestral roots were in Acadian, Scottish, and Cree communities. I never met her, and the fullness of her story is not something I can share here, but she is part of me, too. I am named after my two grandmothers. My parents met in Calgary in the late 1970s, and, although they divorced when I was little, they managed an admirable friendship over time. I grew up loved, with a huge extended family on both sides. I am proud of my family heritage, with all its complexities. I love to hear any stories of where we come from, of how the people before us survived through adversity, how they built futures together across memory-laden landscapes. These widespread family roots hold me up.

My intent in this book is to foreground the words of the remarkable writers with whom I held conversations over the past few years, but it is important to me to explain how I personally came to this project of gathering and sharing those words. I need to describe not only how I am located in relation to the considerations and conversations that follow, but also the inspirations, beliefs, experiences, and hopes that shape them. Before I move on to introducing the conversations, then, I will share some of the background behind them.

I did not grow up with Indigenous literatures.[11] It was not until roughly my third year of university that I can recall having a piece of literature by an Indigenous author assigned to me in my formal education. Thankfully, my undergraduate studies in English introduced me to Indigenous writing—enough to spark a deep desire to read more. I was hungry to connect to others who were learning, thinking, and writing around Indigenous perspectives—whether they were Métis writers or from other Indigenous

Nations. I began to read Indigenous books voraciously—everything I could get my hands on—out of a desire to learn more about other Indigenous people, to understand my own story in relation to theirs, and to foster a sense of connection. What began as a solitary and personal activity grew into a commitment to community and a foundation for my scholarship. Over time, I found space to connect my own identity-making work to that of others, and to think about the bigger picture of how Indigenous literatures relate to Indigenous communities. My own, so far insatiable, hunger for Indigenous writing is a primary motivator for the project that led to this book.

This work also emerges from my sense of responsibility and community as a Métis scholar. Growing up Métis (and everything else that I was, because of course my cultural heritage is just one aspect of who I am), I had a range of ideas about my identity and what I was supposed to do. Formal education has been a powerful influence on my self-understanding, in part because I have often taken refuge in academic work. Developing my proficiency through my various schooling experiences imbued me with a sense of responsibility. I learned that the skills and knowledge that I was developing had to be practised in a good way. I came to feel the same way about being Métis: that whatever doubts I had about who I was—thanks to colonial processes of erasure and assimilation—my responsibility overpowered my uncertainty. I learned that there was urgent and satisfying work to do in Indigenous scholarship: decolonizing education; sustaining Indigenous knowledges and perspectives; sharing and interpreting innovative Indigenous arts; helping non-Indigenous Canadians to understand colonialism and racism; working for social justice. If I could contribute to these collective endeavours, it was my responsibility to do so.

My background as an educator is another strong motivator for this project. I currently teach in a faculty of education at a Canadian university. My students include future teachers in undergraduate teacher education programs, as well as graduate students, practising teachers, educational leaders, and a range of professionals and community members who choose to take graduate studies in education. A substantial portion of my teaching is in Indigenous education for non-Indigenous educators. That is, I support them in developing their capacity to engage respectfully with Indigenous people and perspectives in their professional contexts. Some of my teaching also entails supporting Indigenous educators in developing their ability to serve their own communities. I am very aware that the arts have a power to draw people into these kinds of learning. Creative work can inspire, motivate, and teach in exciting ways.

Before I joined my current university, I worked as a secondary school teacher in both Calgary and Toronto. As I came to this project, I thought of the young people I had seen thriving and building a sense of empowerment, but I thought (more fretfully) about the many young people who had negative experiences at school—who faced systemic oppression, institutional barriers, and a range of threats to their well-being, or who were simply not engaged. While I went to teach every day with the conviction that we educators were working relentlessly in the service of our students, there were too many days where I felt that schooling, in the big picture, was not sufficiently enabling all students to learn or flourish.

When it comes to Indigenous students, there is an urgent need for transformation in schooling. Mi'kmaw scholar Marie Battiste describes the legacy of assimilative education for Indigenous people as follows: "Aboriginal peoples in Canada and Indigenous peoples throughout the world are feeling the tensions created by a Eurocentric education system that has taught them to distrust their Indigenous knowledge systems, their elders' wisdom, and their own inner learning spirit. Neither the assimilative path of residential schools and day schools in the first half of the last century, nor the integrative approaches of the second half of that century in Canada, have succeeded in nurturing many Aboriginal students beyond high school. Most consider education an ongoing failure."[12] I agree with Battiste's assessment here and with her call for decolonizing education: she is right to say that "education can be liberating, or it can domesticate and maintain domination."[13] I maintain that transforming schooling can lead to beneficial change for Indigenous people.

Seeing the rapid growth of and powerful work toward self-determination in Indigenous literatures and literary studies, I came to this project with a determination to bring these two worlds—literatures and learning, stories and schools—into conversation with each other. Such conversations are, for me, always in the service of young people and better Indigenous futures. Creative texts can be powerful. They can change what people think, how people think, and how people treat each other. Stories matter. My work on this project arises from my desire to generate something useful and beautiful out of the relationships between Indigenous literatures, communities, and learning. Part of how I have chosen to engage meaningfully in my own learning on these relationships, and to share that learning with others, is to attend to Indigenous writers' perspectives on their own work.

LITERATURES AND LEARNING

While this book is an Indigenous literary studies project, it is also an Indigenous education project. Under the term *Indigenous education* I bundle together a range of endeavours related to Indigenous people and perspectives within educational theory and practice. It is illustrative to look back nearly twenty-five years to Chickasaw scholar Eber Hampton's essay "Towards a Redefinition of Indian Education," in which he sets out five meanings of "Indian Education": "(1) traditional Indian education, (2) schooling for self-determination, (3) schooling for assimilation, (4) education by Indians, and (5) Indian education *sui generis*."[14] Hampton sets these concepts out through chronological progressions, or as phases. He is interested particularly in the final definition, "Indian education *sui generis*," meaning "a self-determined Indian education using models of education structured by Indian cultures."[15] To move toward this vision, he proceeds to identify twelve "standards for Indian education,"[16] including spirituality, culture, respect, and transformation. In his writing, Hampton identifies the still oppressive nature of contemporary education for "Indian children": he is clear that "education, as currently practised, is cultural genocide."[17] Writing in 2013, Battiste contends that "Aboriginal peoples' invisibility continues to be ignored under modern educational curricula and theory, and psychic disequilibrium continues."[18] In other words, while change may be underway, things have not substantially changed since Hampton's 1995 assessment. With this background in mind, I want to unpack what I mean by *Indigenous education*, and identify the various endeavours that comprise contemporary Indigenous education as I understand it. In so doing, I see education systems as continuing to strive for the kind of self-determining education Hampton was envisioning in the 1990s.[19]

One endeavour of contemporary Indigenous education is the transformation of education to better serve Indigenous students. For instance, Indigenous education includes the ongoing work of educators to decolonize schooling and to provide learning experiences for First Nations, Métis, and Inuit youth that are respectful of Indigenous ways of being, knowing, and doing. Research consistently shows that education is not serving Indigenous students well, and is still at the point of contending that any deficit (deficit discourse is persistent) should be located in the education system, not in the Indigenous student.[20] Responding to the continued call for better educational experiences entails not only addressing these deficits and improving educational outcomes, but also critically considering what constitutes success and even education itself.[21]

Another key endeavour is teaching and learning related to Indigenous subject matter. This dimension includes initiatives to ensure that Indigenous communities, perspectives, histories, and so on are part of school curricula. This is about ensuring that Indigenous people and perspectives are present and validated throughout students' formal education. In theory, this teaching of Indigenous content ripples outward to ensure that knowledge about Indigenous Peoples is present in mainstream consciousness. Ideally, such work does not manifest as token inclusion or superficial change: scholars of Indigenous education work to ensure that Indigenous perspectives are woven into education in meaningful ways that do not perpetrate further harm against Indigenous Peoples.

A related step is teaching content through Indigenous pedagogies—moving from *what* to teach to *how* to teach it. Pedagogies shaped by Indigenous knowledge systems might include land-based learning, learning through story, using talking circles, and so on. My colleagues and I have had success adapting Māori scholar Linda Tuhiwai Smith's twenty-five Indigenous projects into pedagogical approaches in our teacher education classrooms, for instance.[22] Notably, Indigenous pedagogical approaches focus on the individual learner and the meaningful experiences that foster learning rather than mere teacher-centred transmission of knowledge. As Okanagan scholar Jeannette Armstrong puts it, traditional Indigenous education is "a natural process" deeply embedded within "the practice of everyday living."[23] Indigenous pedagogies do not set the teacher up as an "autocratic" leadership figure, according to the Nehinuw (Cree) education model described by Linda and Keith Goulet, but rather involve the building of "respect and reciprocity" between teachers and students.[24]

In many cases, Indigenous education involves the provision of education by Indigenous educators. This teaching may take place at the structural level of Indigenous school authorities, at the community level—as in learning experiences shaped and offered in community—or at the level of individual Indigenous teachers working in any context. While many may agree that having more Indigenous teachers increases the representation of Indigenous perspectives in education systems, the history of "imperialism, colonialism, and racist policies" mean that "many educated First Nations, Métis, and Inuit teachers [have] little knowledge of the traditions and languages of their ancestors": Indigenous educators, too, require support in developing their knowledge and pedagogical expertise.[25]

A broad endeavour within Indigenous education is building societal responsibility in relation to Indigenous Peoples, such as through the education required at a national level for the project of reconciliation. That is, Indigenous education also includes educational initiatives that bring the population as a whole to grapple with the truths of colonialism. For instance, allied settler scholar Paulette Regan suggests the scale of this undertaking when she writes of the Truth and Reconciliation Commission (TRC): "much remains to be done to address settler denial, particularly through educating not only the Canadian public but negotiators, policy makers, and bureaucrats who work in Indigenous contexts" in order to challenge "widespread ignorance about Canada's colonial history."[26] In this sense, Indigenous education is also about building the public awareness required to foment substantial change in the relationship between settlers and Indigenous Nations. The character, direction, or transformative potential of this social change depends upon the framework in which it takes place and the efforts employed in its service. This endeavour overlaps with, or could be seen as an accumulation or result of, the others I have described.

The final dimension of Indigenous education work that I see is the decolonization of education systems. This endeavour involves identifying, understanding, challenging, and deconstructing those aspects of education that continue to marginalize, assimilate, or harm Indigenous students. In other words, decolonizing education means working against any educational structures, systems, practices, spaces, curricula, and so on that continue to posit the superiority of Eurocentric knowledge systems, to invalidate Indigenous knowledge systems, to remain complicit in oppressive racist structures, or otherwise to colonize Indigenous learners. Offering an example of decolonizing work through the humanities, particularly Mi'kmaw humanities, Battiste outlines processes of "naming and examining the mechanisms of Eurocentric colonialism." She understands, for instance, that "First Nations humanities have been systematically excluded in the Eurocentric narratives," and uses that understanding to challenge and change "educational pedagogy and curricula," as well as to build "a more informed base for all teacher candidates."[27] I agree with Battiste here that the humanities—the work of "writers, poets, singers, and dramatists" who "expand Indigenous artistry, creativity, imagination, and dreams"—validate Indigenous knowledge systems and provide a powerful way to transform education.[28] In this way, meaningful work in Indigenous education is intimately tied up with Indigenous literary arts.

I have laid out several understandings of *Indigenous education* here, and it might be helpful to provide a summary before moving on. The following is meant as a quick and simple shorthand of what I see as comprising Indigenous education work today:

Indigenous education as teaching *to* Indigenous students

Indigenous education as teaching *about* Indigenous content

Indigenous education as teaching *with* Indigenous pedagogies

Indigenous education as teaching *by* Indigenous educators

Indigenous education as preparing society *for* social change

Indigenous education as transforming education systems *through* decolonization

These distinct endeavours—or types—of Indigenous education are often more effective when undertaken in combination. For instance, teaching Eurocentric curricula *to* Indigenous students is not as effective as also teaching those students *about* Indigenous content, *with* Indigenous pedagogies. Some of the most inspiring examples that I have witnessed are the result of these undertakings being combined within well-designed, holistic education programs.[29] When they are treated as deeply interconnected parts of a whole, they strengthen each other.

It has been important to set out these conceptions of Indigenous education so that readers of this volume can follow me when I describe the many ways in which Indigenous literatures relate to learning. Indigenous literary arts can enter, inform, shape, or constitute any of the endeavours described above. Indigenous stories can be the content, shape the pedagogy, and help to decolonize the system. Students, teachers, and the Canadian public are potential learners who can read literary texts. Writers in this volume provide real-world illustrations of many of these possibilities. There are many points at which Indigenous education and Indigenous literary arts can intersect and, as Battiste argues, "the Indigenous humanities can become a tremendous step forward in advancing cognitive and knowledge pluralism."[30] In addition to spaces for literatures within contemporary Indigenous education, Indigenous literary arts themselves continue to grow when people learn that their stories as worth telling—as many authors within this volume point out. Indigenous education may be any educational undertaking that involves Indigenous people, topics, and/or perspectives; however, this more complex bundle of understandings helps to highlight how the work of teaching and learning with Indigenous literatures can hold profound significance for Indigenous Peoples.

My work on literatures and learning seeks to align with Indigenous communities' pursuit of self-determination and well-being. For instance, in asking how learning takes place through the complex relationships that encompass artists, communities, texts, formal schooling, educators, students, and reading publics, my concern for Indigenous Peoples centres on how communities are shaped, created, sustained, represented, or affected by those relationships. Focusing on the well-being of Indigenous Peoples and communities, I look for ways in which literatures and learning may contribute to processes of self-understanding and self-determination. I do also feel the strong pull to consider non-Indigenous people—their reading, their teaching, their learning—because of my accompanying focus on education systems in Canada and on Canadian society. This pull toward Indigenous/non-Indigenous relationships accompanies my focus on education and on social change, as I discuss below. Before moving on to those questions, though, I need to engage with the notion of *Indigenous literatures.*

STORIES AND LITERATURES

Indigenous literatures have expanded remarkably over the past decades. I use the term *Indigenous literatures* fairly broadly to refer to creative writing (or literary texts) authored by Indigenous people. This broad sense is frequently used across Indigenous literary studies. I appreciate the consideration of this term offered by the Indigenous Literary Studies Association (ILSA) in its Governing Code:

> "Indigenous Literary Studies" is an expansive term that includes the study of literatures by Indigenous people and the use of Indigenous literary critical methods. While the root of the word "literature" refers etymologically to letters—or to alphabetic written language—we use the term to refer much more broadly to "arts in the medium of language." Although Indigenous literary studies sometimes focuses on written texts, it remains inclusive of and connected to the study of a wide range of textual and rhetorical productions, including oral traditions, film, music, graphic novels, and many other forms of creative expression. Likewise, we welcome and encourage engagement with Indigenous literatures composed not only in English and French, but also in Indigenous languages.[31]

As a scholarly and community-engaged association (one with which I have been quite involved), ILSA sets out strong practices for engaging with Indigenous literatures, and I wish to take up the above understanding of what the terms *Indigenous literary studies* and *Indigenous literatures* comprise. I use the plural *literatures* to indicate that there is no singular body or category of Indigenous literature.[32]

First Nations, Métis, and Inuit Peoples originate in numerous distinct communities across what is now Canada, and their literatures are diverse across Nations, geographies, time periods, and genres. Critical movements such as Indigenous literary nationalisms—which explore literatures in relation to their particular Nations, knowledge systems, cultures, aesthetics, and community concerns—have demonstrated that generalizing across Indigenous literatures can be problematic. For instance, Labrador Métis scholar Kristina Bidwell (previously Fagan) has stated that "Indigenous literary nationalism aims to understand Indigenous literature within its Indigenous contexts," or "to understand how stories work within communities."[33] Such understandings call for specificity. I take up this insistence by encouraging relationship building with particular texts and writers. I hope that this volume, for instance, will enable readers to get to know writers a little, to be introduced to who they are and where they are coming from, and to see some of the complexities that shape their writing. I hope that even a small collection like this will enable readers to see that, for all their commonalities, differences exist between these writers.

Written literatures are both distinct from oral stories and related in important ways. Oral and traditional storytelling are central to Indigenous cultures and communities. It is important to know that oral storytelling is alive and well, occupying significant positions within Indigenous and arts-based communities. Métis scholar Warren Cariou argues that "in the present moment we have to find ways of preserving or encouraging the *practice* of telling our most important stories"[34] so as to ensure that oral storytelling has an active presence in communities and classrooms—not only in archives. The continuance of oral stories is particularly important given the traditional role of storytelling within Indigenous education.[35] Because of how integral it is to Indigenous knowledge systems, storytelling is inseparable from culturally responsive ways of engaging in teaching and learning. As Māori scholar Linda Tuhiwai Smith has said, "the story and the story teller both serve to connect the past with the future, one generation with the other, the land with the people and the people with the story."[36] Given the significance of storytelling for Indigenous knowledges, and given the close relationship between Indigenous stories and literatures, it is important to examine the connections between Indigenous literary writing and the work of education.

With its focus on literatures and learning, this project fosters considerations of the pedagogical dimensions of stories, of how literatures shape people's understandings and affect the world in which texts are read. This focus emerges in relation to the traditional and cultural ways in which learning and stories are intertwined. However, it also emerges in relation to the work already being done in contemporary classrooms at all levels: the significant work of reading texts, understanding them, and responding to them. When young people read and engage with literatures, they are learning—drawing out threads of understanding and weaving them into the fabric of their lives. Literatures can influence how people think about themselves, about what their responsibilities are, about other people, and about how to live. It is in this complex, relational space—between literatures, writers, readers, and their contexts—that this project takes shape.

More than asking writers about their inspirations and their craft, the conversations in this volume ask writers to reflect on how their work exists in the world. They ask writers to think about learning in relation to literatures. Given this emphasis, it is particularly significant that every one of these writers has some kind of pedagogical background—for instance, having taught in schools or in post-secondary institutions, having worked in educational organizations, or having taught creative writing. These experiences inform the conversations, which shift between the worlds of literature and education. These writers speak insightfully about the interconnections between teaching, learning, reading, and writing as they consider their own creative work and their understandings of community. These interconnections make for high stakes when it comes to engaging with Indigenous stories, as the following section suggests.

COMMUNITY AND CONTROVERSY

A couple of recent controversies point to the significance of the questions examined within this collection, including the urgency of certain critical issues that surround Indigenous literatures. Being attentive to these critical contexts will enrich the learning sought by readers of Indigenous literatures. These controversies are very much related to the topics and issues that I consider with writers in this volume. I am not raising them in order to provide my own ruling: such judgment needs to be undertaken carefully and collectively, and I am not equipped to fulfil those needs here. Rather, I raise these controversies in order to suggest that the critical and public discussion they have generated demonstrate the importance of the underlying issues. Indigenous literatures matter, and these conversations with writers matter as well: it is necessary to listen to the perspectives of Indigenous artists on their own work and communities—on how they are writing-in-relation.

The first controversy is that surrounding the writer Joseph Boyden. Gathering critical acclaim with his award-winning and best-selling novels, Boyden grew in prominence as a public figure and Indigenous writer between 2005 and 2015. The controversy around Boyden entered the public eye late in 2016, when his Indigenous heritage was called into question. Allegations that his claims to Indigenous identity were unfounded damaged his repute as a spokesperson for Indigenous people in Canada, on matters ranging from art to colonial histories to the epidemic of violence against Indigenous women. The allegations generated a great deal of controversy, with condemnations, support, and ambivalence peppering social, digital, and print media for several months.

Many in the Indigenous literary studies community had been examining Boyden's practices well before this controversy reached its public peak. For example, some community members had critiqued Boyden's portrayals of the Haudenosaunee people in his 2014 novel *The Orenda*, and some controversy accompanied that novel's inclusion in that year's Canada Reads competition.[37] In the fall of 2015, ILSA organized a panel in Haudenosaunee territory, inviting Boyden to engage in discussion with community members about his role as an artist in portraying another community's history.[38] My interview with Cherokee scholar Daniel Heath Justice included in this volume took place a few hours after that panel discussion. (I was a member of the ILSA Council that organized the gathering.)

The initial volleys targeting Boyden's ancestry appeared on Twitter, followed by an *APTN News* investigation published on December 23, 2016.[39] In that piece, Jorge Barrera wrote that "Boyden has never publicly revealed exactly from which earth his Indigenous heritage grows.... Over the years, Boyden has variously claimed his family's roots extended to the Metis, Mi'kmaq, Ojibway and Nipmuc peoples."[40] Barrera proceeded to delineate APTN's research into Boyden's family lines, suggesting that any links to Indigenous ancestors are "difficult to pin-point."[41] This story called into question Boyden's legitimacy as a "spokesperson on Indigenous issues,"[42] and indeed his positioning as an Indigenous author at all.

The numerous responses that appeared in the wake of this story both directly took up Boyden's situation and connected more broadly to questions of voice, identity, representation, responsibility, and community. Anishinaabe performer Ryan McMahon, for example, wrote a critical piece: "Before you step back in the circle, show us your beadwork, Joseph, so the people inside the circle can know who you are because you haven't told us yet. You haven't earned your place here yet, Joseph, this is why the community is taking that place back from you."[43] By contrast, Anishinaabe artist, performer, and politician Wab Kinew spoke up in favour of Boyden and directed some critical questions at "the indigenous community"—namely, "why did we so quickly embrace someone who has long said he has little biological connection to us?" And further, "what does it say that many of us have so quickly turned on him?"[44] Kinew called on Boyden to "be direct with us about his ancestry,"[45] but ultimately contended that Boyden's ongoing work to build relationships was more important than his heritage or status: "his place among us was built by writing about, giving back to and befriending us.... If he keeps coming back, he will have a place in our circle."[46] Anishinaabe writer Drew Hayden Taylor acknowledged Boyden's culpability but also turned a critical eye to the Canadian public and the media for holding Boyden up as a "literary darling": "Very few of us climb up on a pedestal—most of us are put there."[47]

Discussion roiled over the following weeks. On January 11, 2017, Boyden did a full interview on CBC Radio's *Q* in which he maintained what he had previously said about his heritage: that "a small part of me is Indigenous, but it's a big part of who I am," and in which he apologized for "taking up too much of the airtime."[48] In August of the same year, he authored a lengthy piece in *Maclean's*, sharing his perspectives while also raising questions that got at the heart of the issue: "What does it mean to be Indigenous in this country? Who gets to define it? Who gets to belong? And who gets to say who doesn't belong?"[49]

In the months that followed, it was difficult to discern a definitive outcome of these discussions. As the *BuzzFeed* piece "11 Indigenous Authors You Should Be Reading Instead of Joseph Boyden" suggests,[50] one result has been simply the direction of critical attention elsewhere. As I will elaborate further below, my intent in raising this controversy is to show how important and complex issues of community, representation, and responsibility can be in relation to Indigenous writing.

Another controversy erupted shortly after the Boyden story, again taking place in a range of media—this one around the issue of cultural appropriation. It began with the spring 2017 issue of *Write* magazine, which featured contributions by several emerging Indigenous writers. The issue included an opinion piece by the magazine's editor, Hal Niedzviecki, contending that, in order to diversify Canadian literature, writers need to be given the freedom to portray any and all perspectives beyond their own.[51] In an unsuccessful rhetorical move, he asked whether a cultural appropriation prize could be created to celebrate writers who could appropriate skilfully. The piece precipitated a series of impassioned responses. Some of the Indigenous writers featured in the journal spoke out, objecting to being included in the issue. Some members of the mainstream media, on the other hand, hopped on board with the prize idea, advocating for its creation.[52]

Indigenous artists and community members stepped up to condemn the editorial, expressing dismay, fatigue, and condemnation at having to once again explain why cultural appropriation is harmful. As Ojibwe critic Jesse Wente remarked in an interview on CBC Radio, "These things can't happen again. This absorbs so much energy, it causes so much pain in our community."[53] He also brought the conversation back to the Indigenous writers originally included in the issue of *Write*, saying that theirs "are the voices that should be centred and heard."[54] Anishinaabe writer Kateri Akiwenzie-Damm offered another impactful response, pointing to the long-standing nature of such conversations and directing attention to the well-known 1990 piece by Lenore Keeshig-Tobias entitled "Stop Stealing Native Stories."[55] Akiwenzie-Damm expressed exhaustion at the debate and called for the Indigenous literary community to engage in action toward more significant change: "The appropriation debate needs to end. But not because the war has been won or because our stories are no longer being stolen.... It's time to stop the debate because fighting these battles is getting us nowhere."[56] Such responses pointed, once again, to how such arguments risk trivializing the very real impacts that ongoing misrepresentations and appropriations have on Indigenous communities.

The cultural appropriation controversy led to the resignation of a number of prominent media figures, including Hal Niedzviecki himself, who stepped down from his post as editor of *Write* and issued an apology.[57] This eruption also fostered a great deal of ill will across the Canadian literary scene, with some on social media lamenting the current state of Canadian literature.[58] The events revealed not only a lack of understanding (or perhaps a lack of respect) surrounding the issue of cultural appropriation itself and its impact on Indigenous communities, but also—albeit in complex ways— how important issues of culture, voice, creativity, and community are to writers, critics, and readers across the country. One positive response to the appropriation prize turmoil was the crowd-funded creation, in 2017, of the Indigenous Voices Awards, now an annual event.[59] These awards, which celebrate and support Indigenous creative writers and purposefully include emerging writers, effectively re-centre attention on Indigenous literary arts.

In my view, it is important to recognize the complexity of the issues underlying these debates, and to address them in ways that foster social justice and the self-determination of Indigenous communities. I am not formulating any resolutions for these particular controversies. Working through them involves collective discussion and a great deal of careful and critical thought—more than I can offer here, and certainly more than I can offer on my own. I have invoked these controversies, though, because I think they point to several significant reasons for listening to Indigenous writers' perspectives on their work and on how it affects others. Critical perspectives on Indigenous literatures must be worked out in relation to Indigenous communities, cultures, and knowledge systems. While Indigenous writers do not definitively determine the meaning or significance of their work, they are speaking from their communities and representing Indigeneity for a range of audiences, which puts them in complex positions. Their perspectives are worthy of consideration. Indigenous writers have valuable insights to share on Indigenous writing and how it lives in Indigenous and non-Indigenous communities.

Revealed in and through the two controversies described above is an urgent need to listen to Indigenous Peoples' perspectives on their artistic practices and their significance. This need might be defended through the language of voice, authenticity, identity, responsibility, community, self-determination, or sovereignty. Indeed, in the conversations included in this volume, writers address the significance of their creative practice in a range of ways. For instance, they talk about what kinds of responsibilities they see as inherent to writing, about the possible impacts they recognize their writing can have, and about the role learning plays both in and outside of Indigenous communities. Listening to these considerations will help readers to understand the complexity of these controversies and debates.

Writers in this collection illuminate beautifully some of the contexts surrounding Indigenous literary arts and Indigenous Peoples. I hope, by sharing this volume, to contribute to community-minded, responsible, and responsive critical practices that respect Indigenous arts and their importance to Indigenous communities, Indigenous well-being, and Indigenous self-determination. Conversations, and even controversies, around literary texts and their relationships with Indigenous communities show that Indigenous literatures matter.

READING, WRITING, RESPONSIBILITY, RELATIONSHIP

Indigenous literatures do not exist apart from the real world: creative work connects communities and contexts. Texts and communities affect each other. Communities and contexts—social, political, cultural—shape and contribute to literary writings. Texts influence the communities and contexts from which they arise, as they contribute to readers' understandings of peoples, events, concepts, social dynamics, and histories. Reading Indigenous literatures entails a responsibility to recognize and respond to the relationships between texts and contexts.

The ethical imperative to understand such relationships permeates much of the critical scholarship on Indigenous literatures. Métis scholar Jo-Ann Episkenew, for instance, points out that "Indigenous literature serves a socio-pedagogical function as well as an aesthetic one."[60] While she validates the artistry of Indigenous writing, she also tries to understand "the applications of Indigenous literature as it moves outside the boundaries of the text to affect the material world."[61] Labrador Inuk scholar Kristina Bidwell frames this emphasis in Episkenew's work as a particular way of approaching Indigenous literatures that is founded upon an assumption that "stories *do* things"[62]—namely, that stories "not only reflect reality; they create it."[63] Building upon this assumption means recognizing the responsibility entailed in the work of reading and teaching Indigenous literatures[64]—a topic that many conversations in this collection address.

For Indigenous artists to engage in processes of creation that tell their stories and reflect their communities is a significant and courageous undertaking, one founded upon centuries of colonization and resistance, strengthened by continuity and remembrance, and inspired by change and renewal. "By virtue of their very existence," as Daniel Heath Justice puts it,

"Indigenous literatures affirm Indigenous experiences, presence, and possibility."[65] What does it mean, then, for non-Indigenous audiences to appreciate, respond to, relate to, and respect such creative work? I have known many non-Indigenous people who want to develop their understandings of Indigenous perspectives but are uncertain of how to do so. Perhaps they are afraid of intruding or appropriating, unsure of their own motivations or justifications. Perhaps they are concerned about making mistakes. Perhaps, acknowledging the complex and troubled nature of the histories, contexts, and relationships involved, they feel daunted as to how to begin or proceed. My own experiences have taught me that this discomfort is a challenging but powerful catalyst for learning.

Change can be precipitated by the relationships that form when non-Indigenous people learn from reading Indigenous literatures. When people outside Indigenous communities work to understand Indigenous stories, they can then help to build better ways of being in relation with Indigenous communities. Artistic work can be a call into respectful relationships. This call is a powerful motivation for this book. In gathering together this set of conversations, my aim is to demonstrate the importance of Indigenous literary work for Indigenous communities, as the writers included in this volume see it. These conversations emerge from and speak to Indigenous communities, including those community members who write, read, and teach Indigenous literatures. However, these conversations are also for those beyond those communities who want to learn more, to listen in good ways, and to take up the challenging but rewarding work of building respectful relationships with Indigenous Peoples.

INDIGENOUS LITERATURES AND COMMUNITIES

Understanding relationships and responsibility in this context means understanding the connections between Indigenous literatures and communities. Seeing how literatures and communities are deeply interconnected will help readers to recognize the layers of significance in what writers share in this volume.

In agreement with Episkenew, I find there are many things that Indigenous literatures can do—one of which is to create and sustain communities.[66] Cherokee writer Thomas King suggests that "community ... is one of the primary ideas from which our literature proceeds."[67] The collectivity and peoplehood integral to notions of community are essential for strengthening Indigenous Nations, as that strengthening entails regenerating shared understandings and working together to nourish relationships and collective experiences. Communities are continually shaped through stories, through imaginative work done within relationships. Communities generate stories, but stories in turn generate communities. Writing and reading Indigenous literatures thus entails responsibility: it is not abstract material that is being handled, but rather the imaginative and written being of the communities invested in them.

Along with the notion of community, it is important to voice Indigenous conceptions of kinship. Daniel Heath Justice suggests that kinship is a "delicate web of rights and responsibilities,"[68] and that communities are composed of active, reciprocal relationships. He describes *community* and *kinship* as "interpretive concepts" that enable readers to explore "the relationship of our literatures to our communities—and the role of that relationship in ensuring the continuity of indigenous nations into the future."[69] Through these concepts he contends that stories are "what we do, what we create, as much as what we are."[70] Importantly, kinship in Indigenous knowledge systems is not limited to humans—rather, it extends much more broadly to embrace other-than-human relatives. The term *people* carries more-than-human significance, for instance, and kinship responsibilities extend outward in a relational and ecological manner far beyond humankind. The notion of *people* includes "the people of the animal and plant world," to echo Cree scholar Willie Ermine's words,[71] or, as Justice explains, "The earth speaks in a multitude of voices, only some of which are human. We exist alongside one another, our lives intersecting and overlapping in limitless and often unexpected ways. Other-than-human beings go about their lives as we go about ours; these plants, animals, stones, and other presences are our seen and unseen relatives.... Story, song, poem, and prayer all serve to remind us of our connections to one another, human and other-than-human alike."[72] Our stories can call us to be better relatives to all our kin.

As much as they can create and sustain communities, Indigenous literatures can also influence the health and well-being of Indigenous communities. Stories have the power to combat trauma and violence or to foster healing and resilience.[73] Episkenew argues that Indigenous literature "functions as 'medicine' to help cure the colonial contagion" stemming from destructive government policies.[74] As King points out, recognizing stories as "medicine" means recognizing that they can also be dangerous if used irresponsibly: it means knowing "that a story told one way could cure, [while] that the same story told another way could injure."[75] Responsibility is called for on both sides of the text—from writers and readers—in order to consider whether the impact of the story will be "healing" or "hurtful."[76] Additional layers of responsibility are added when literatures are taught, as educators help to shape the ways in which learners understand and are affected by literary texts.[77]

Indigenous literatures can also resist the ongoing colonialism that threatens the well-being of Indigenous communities today. The long-standing and multi-faceted workings of colonialism on our continent have inspired correspondingly deep and intricate forms of literary resistance. These forms of resistance are intertwined with the other political, social, and cultural ways in which Indigenous people work to assert their continuing presence and to resist the effects of colonialism.[78] Resistance is a pervasive concept in Indigenous literary studies. Cree-Métis scholar Emma LaRocque uses it as a kind of category to characterize (some) Indigenous writing, calling it "resistance literature."[79] Cherokee scholar Jace Weaver describes literature as a space where resistance can take place, as "a critical arena for struggle."[80] Kwakwaka'wakw scholar Laura Cranmer suggests that literatures can teach readers "how to proceed in a de-colonizing process."[81] Many scholars take up Chippewa scholar Gerald Vizenor's notion of *survivance* to describe the work literatures are doing in this regard: for instance allied scholar Renate Eigenbrod describes survivance narratives as "evoking survival, resistance, and continuance of cultures against colonial policies aimed at the annihilation of Indigenous presence."[82] Engaging responsibly with Indigenous literatures necessarily entails engaging with Indigenous communities' struggles to resist colonialism and to work for self-determination.

As Stó:lō scholar Lee Maracle points out, the devaluation of Indigenous literatures is caught up in the struggle against colonialism and for Indigenous self-determination. She argues that "Western literary criticism fails to make any kind of full, fair, or just sense of Indigenous work."[83] This failure is connected to the fact that, "because Canadian society is unable to recognize intelligence among Indigenous societies, it refuses to recognize those aspects of Indigenous society that would force it to value Indigenous people."[84] Many authors in this book insist that the value placed on Indigenous stories connects to the value placed on Indigenous people. Attending to our literatures entails accountability to the kinships and communities that they carry.

COMMUNITIES AND RESURGENCE

When it comes to Indigenous literatures, colonialism and its effects should not always occupy the centre of the critical frame. Colonialism is not the whole story of Indigenous Peoples, nor should it be the starting place for understanding Indigenous communities, Indigenous literary arts, or Indigenous education. Beginning instead with Indigenous ways of being and knowing is more conducive to nourishing healthy Indigenous communities. In the present context, that means placing Indigenous stories and communities themselves at the centre of this critical frame.

One concept I find tremendously useful for keeping Indigenous communities at the core of my critical work is *resurgence*. In the project that led to this book, I used this term as both an organizing and a motivating concept. As part of that project, I worked to understand what resurgence is, how it can be enacted, and why it matters. Focusing on resurgence is different from focusing on decolonization. While it is absolutely necessary to confront and dismantle colonial systems, that process is distinct from the process of nurturing Indigenous communities and revitalizing Indigenous ways of knowing, being, and doing. To be sure, decolonization work and resurgence work both need doing,[85] but it is important to identify the difference between them. In particular, the work of resurgence entails breaking out of what Leanne Simpson calls the "cognitive box of imperialism,"[86] whereas decolonization work entails understanding and taking apart that metaphorical box. Put differently, even if I am talking about how to dismantle the box, focusing on that structure limits the scope of my work.

In thinking through resurgence, I build upon the work of several other scholars. Indigenous education scholars Friedel, Archibald, Head, Martin, and Muñoz, for instance, argue that resurgence is "a concerted demand by Indigenous peoples for the right and responsibility to express their full humanity in the context of a long history of domination that includes being socially and recursively constructed as inferior."[87] In this sense, resurgence is not simply about resisting domination; it is about Indigenous Peoples finding ways to live as Indigenous Peoples without being limited or defined by that colonial context.

Particularly inspiring to me is the work of Leanne Simpson, who is Michi Saagiig Nishnaabeg. Simpson describes resurgence in ways that focus on celebrations of Indigenous existence and on the importance of imaginative and creative work. She writes, for instance, that, "in Nishnaabeg thought, resurgence is ... visioning and dancing new realities and worlds into existence."[88] As Simpson shows, resurgence is culturally specific: it may take shape and be articulated differently in different Indigenous communities.[89] Simpson points to "visioning," along with "intent, collectivization, and action," as necessary elements of resurgence from a Nishnaabeg perspective.[90] That is, working for change—or creating "new worlds"[91]—requires people to envision change and then to be responsible to that vision, collaborating to help it to materialize. I feel that this emphasis on vision and on collectivity is meaningful to understanding the relationship between Indigenous communities' resurgence and their literatures. Simpson not only formulates critical foundations for resurgence but also enacts these processes through her own creative writing. Simpson distinguishes between cultural and radical or political resurgence—warning that "cultural resurgence can take place within the current settler colonial structure of Canada … whereas political resurgence is seen as a direct threat to settler sovereignty"—but also explains that, "within Indigenous thought … the cultural and the political are joined and inseparable."[92] My own thinking in this book may focus more on cultural resurgence than on the political realm, but I hold that cultural resurgence helps to foster political resurgence.

While resurgence is a powerful organizing concept, one that generates and attracts sophisticated theoretical discourse, it is not just a theoretical ideal. Resurgence occurs through the concrete, everyday existence of individuals and communities demonstrating the continuity of Indigenous lifeways. Seemingly small, "daily acts of renewal," such as "prayer, speaking your language, honoring your ancestors,"[93] are significant and sustainable ways of enacting resurgence. Tsalagi (Cherokee) scholar Jeff Corntassel calls such everyday renewals the "foundations of resurgence."[94] Individuals and communities can contribute to the everyday work of resurgence through ceremonies, traditions, gatherings, stories, knowledges, relationships with the land, traditional foods, and kinship systems.[95] Even simple acts like maintaining healthy lifestyles offer possibilities for "embracing a daily existence conditioned by place-based cultural practices."[96] Processes of resurgence are inspired by and emerge from Indigenous words, ways, and wisdom, both old and new.

For my purposes here, I define resurgence as the regrowth of Indigenous communities from strong roots toward strong futures, building upon tradition and heritage through processes of revitalization and reclamation in order to create healthy, vibrant, self-determining Nations. I believe that artistic processes are integral to community resurgence. The strength of Indigenous communities and their artistic processes are deeply interconnected. When I set out to pursue the central question within this project— that is, why Indigenous literatures matter to communities—I began with these understandings of resurgence in mind.

RESURGENCE IN A TIME OF RECONCILIATION

With resurgence as a guiding framework, I often felt in the course of this project that I was negotiating with the differing framework of *reconciliation*. To be clear, when I say *guiding framework*, I mean the rubric under which people engage in work related to Indigenous (and non-Indigenous) people and perspectives: I mean the understanding that motivates that work, or the theoretical aim kept in mind when working for social change. My usage here might compare to what Unangax̂ scholar Eve Tuck calls "theories of change."[97] I think two primary factors have contributed to my gravitation toward reconciliation over the past several years.

One factor is that the educational aspects of my project necessarily focused on the perspectives of both non-Indigenous and Indigenous people. In my broader project, I was speaking with people working in urban public schools and post-secondary institutions, so the populations they worked with were largely non-Indigenous. Our conversations about teaching Indigenous literatures were in fact often about teaching Indigenous literatures to non-Indigenous students. While my central focus was on Indigenous communities, on resurgence, the conversations often came to address the work of building better understandings and relationships between Indigenous and non-Indigenous people. The somewhat fraught concept of reconciliation became a significant concept for that reason.

The second factor that pulled my thinking toward reconciliation was the work of Canada's TRC. The conclusion of the TRC, the release of its *Final Report* and *Calls to Action*, and the ensuing responses have had a large public profile. Reconciliation is a highly prevalent framework now, much more so than when I began this work. Notably, the TRC released its *Final Report* in the same year I started holding these conversations. Public awareness and discourse related to this process have since expanded further. Reconciliation is an energizing framework for many people, and has gathered useful political and institutional momentum.

The term *reconciliation*, however, also carries a slippery range of connotations. In my experience, when used loosely it can invite a sense of letting go of the past, of moving on from troubled relationships into a more positive future. This "moving on" can carry the suggestion that Indigenous people need to "get over" what took place during past generations (and indeed, I find these ways of talking often suggest that colonialism occurred in the distant past).[98] Such usage of the term *reconciliation* comes closer to the colonial notion of "solving the Indian problem,"[99] to use Regan's words. On the other end of the range, *reconciliation* can refer to a collaborative, justice-oriented, and informed rebuilding of reciprocal relationships between Indigenous Peoples and settlers in Canada. The TRC dedicates an entire volume of its six-volume report to the consideration of reconciliation as a framework and process: that volume discusses up front many of the critiques and nuances that have been raised around the term. The commission provides a cogent definition: " 'reconciliation' is about establishing and maintaining a mutually respectful relationship between Aboriginal and non-Aboriginal Peoples in this country. For that to happen, there has to be awareness of the past, acknowledgement of the harm that has been inflicted, atonement for the causes, and action to change behaviour."[100] Notably, the text notes, "we are not there yet."[101] However the term is used, *reconciliation* focuses on relationships between Indigenous and non-Indigenous people. This focus stands in contrast to my use of *resurgence*, which focuses on movements arising from within Indigenous communities.

As a guiding framework, reconciliation is subject to some critique. Before exploring these critiques, it is important to distinguish between reconciliation discourse, or reconciliation as a concept, and the specific work of the TRC, which merits its own respectful consideration.[102] One critique of reconciliation is that it can undermine Indigenous communities' work for regeneration or self-determination by focusing on settler Canadians' desire for social harmony. For instance, allied scholar Keavy Martin has pointed out that the concept of reconciliation can rely upon a form of "amnesia": she suggests that it entails "a fixation upon *resolution* that is not only premature but problematic in its correlation with *forgetting*."[103] This fixation is dangerous, she contends, in that "the discourse of reconciliation—though rhetorically persuasive—can at times be less about the well-being of Aboriginal Peoples and communities than about freeing non-Native Canadians from the guilt and continued responsibility of knowing their history."[104] The kind of continued responsibility she mentions is fundamental to more substantive forms of social change.[105]

Another critique of reconciliation, articulated by Métis scholar and artist David Garneau, highlights the fact that the notion of reconciliation relies upon a problematic assumption about the past: "*Re*-conciliation refers to the repair of a previously existing harmonious relationship."[106] Such a past—characterized by peaceful Indigenous-settler relations, held up by agreements between Canada and all First Nations, Métis, and Inuit Peoples—never existed, Garneau argues. The false premise underlying "*re*-conciliation" obscures the ongoing work required to build respectful relationships. Instead, Garneau offers the term *conciliation*, which calls for ongoing and active processes of relationship through "interpretation, reinterpretation, and renegotiation": in making this contention, he suggests that "the present Reconciliation narrative be recast as a continued struggle for conciliation rather than for the restoration of something lost (that never was)."[107] One aspect of Garneau's critique is the recognition that the TRC is a state-sponsored process, with the accompanying suggestion that Canada is necessarily invested in stifling possible disruptions to order and national identity.[108] Garneau also makes the counterpoint that the TRC "has developed into a complex and responsive organism that has permitted multiple anti- and non-colonial possibilities."[109] However, his enduring priority is to problematize the notion of reconciliation and to call for people to work for conciliation while respecting the spaces occupied by Indigenous Peoples and processes.

Such critiques help to generate discourse around reconciliation that is more nuanced and responsive to Indigenous communities' own processes of self-determination or resurgence. Interrogating reconciliation as a guiding framework may entail pushing further into what is possible for Indigenous communities—in support of their ongoing efforts to live out their own ways of being, knowing, and doing. I contrast reconciliation with resurgence because, while reconciliation is concerned with the relationship between Indigenous and non-Indigenous people, resurgence is about Indigenous communities. Resurgence is a rhetorical and political framework that concentrates on reclamation and regrowth within Indigenous communities. It asserts the value of Indigenous knowledges, cultures, histories, and ingenuity in enabling Indigenous people to survive and continue their lifeways despite centuries of attempted genocide. Resurgence is an Indigenous impulse: it acknowledges colonialism and resistance to domination but it does not focus solely upon those dynamics. Relationships with settler communities affect the well-being of Indigenous communities, but those relationships are not the central focus of a resurgence framework. Instead, resurgence focuses on Indigenous communities as sites of power and regeneration.

RESURGENCE AND RECONCILIATION FRAMEWORKS IN CONVERSATION

The considerations surrounding these two guiding frameworks—namely, resurgence and reconciliation—informed my thinking as I entered into my conversations with Indigenous writers. I wanted to know how my understandings related to their own critical and creative practices. However, it was more important to me to remain open to their perspectives—to make space for the ways in which they were thinking about communities and relationships, about promoting Indigenous Peoples' well-being, and about working for social change or justice. I did not impose this language on our conversations.

I also wanted to resist falling too far into the immediacy of present social circumstances in our conversations. The issues of community, responsibility, decolonization, and resilience, for instance, are much older than contemporary conversations about reconciliation. That continuity deserves ongoing respect as well. Consequently, writers' conversations with me span broader and more varied terrain than I have laid out in the last few pages. Given their influence on my thinking and their potential at present to catalyze social change, however, it is useful to consider these concepts of resurgence and reconciliation and to describe how they relate to the conversations in this volume.

CONVERSATIONS WITH INDIGENOUS WRITERS

With this background in mind, it is time to introduce the conversations themselves. For several years now, I have been exploring how Indigenous literatures connect to Indigenous education, as well as to Indigenous communities' self-understandings, political movements, and well-being.[110] I have outlined many of these concerns over the course of this chapter. This book is one product of that research.

More specifically, this volume emerges from a series of conversations I held with Indigenous writers living and working in the lands claimed by Canada, between 2015 and 2018. These conversations were an opportunity to explore my questions around literatures, communities, and learning in depth with a few great people. I did not select writers with any overarching representative aim in mind, but rather worked step by step to have one conversation after another—responding to relationships, connections, and circumstances of time and place. As a very new scholar when I began, my aims were humble. I did make an intentional choice to feature the voices of newer writers alongside more well-known and established writers, to do my small bit to support the ongoing growth of Indigenous literary arts. I also paid attention to gender. Ultimately, however, this book holds a small set of conversations with people proximal to me, relationally and geographically speaking. It does not attempt or achieve a comprehensive representation of the diversity of Indigenous writers across widespread Nations and territories: most of these writers are in southern and western or central regions of Canada, for instance, not too far from my home city of Calgary. I am nonetheless excited by the range of stories, knowledges, and experiences that resulted from these invitations, and am honoured to have the chance to share them here.

This book features conversations with nine different writers. Each chapter contains its own brief introduction situating the author and their work, but these introductions also help to contextualize the specific issues and topics that emerge in the conversations that follow. However, there are also significant commonalities between the perspectives that the writers raise. For instance, many consider the complexities of what it means for them, as Indigenous authors, to write as representatives of their communities. They explain how their writing is affected by the contexts in which Indigenous literary texts are read and taught—for example, by the ongoing need to challenge colonialism. Many of them explore the educational nature of their work as writers, or make explicit connections to the teaching and learning work they do in schools or post-secondary institutions. Many of them describe how they think about serving future generations of Indigenous youth, and all of them, in their own ways, demonstrate a deep responsibility to their communities. Through their unique and shared perspectives, these authors demonstrate why reading and teaching Indigenous literatures is complex and urgent work.

QUESTIONS AND CONVERSATIONS

In this section, I describe how my conversations with writers took place. The process of meeting with each author entailed an initial respectful dance of connection and explanation, consent and communication, scheduling and organization. Out of respect for the importance of place and situated knowledges, I met with writers in their home cities and at a location of their choice, or at least in person. The conversations are included in the order in which they took place: the first happened in April 2015 and the last in October 2018. Each conversation with a new writer was held in its own particular circumstances. We met in offices, homes, coffee shops, and on campuses. We met over hot beverages and baked goods. Sometimes we caught up on an already-growing relationship and sometimes we started from the beginning with nice-to-meet-yous. It was important to spend time talking, building relationship, before we began. It was also important that I explained my process and investments. Where appropriate, we engaged in cultural protocols out of respect for the gift of words and knowledge that would be shared with me. Writers were generous with their time and experience.

I prepared a set of questions for each writer, but it was important to me that each conversation emerge on its own terms as well. I wanted to respect each conversation partner as contributing knowledge and understanding to the process rather than simply generating content. I wanted us to get "off track" with stories and meanderings, allowing ideas to take us where they would. Approaching each conversation in a relational and respectful manner, to me, meant being open and flexible, allowing others to share what they felt was significant, in their own ways. Recognizing what they were sharing also called for me to reciprocate, I felt, and so I was intentional about sharing in return—stories, experiences, ideas. While I had articulated many of these principles in advance—openness, reciprocity, respect, relationality, dialogue, and so on—what this really meant to me was that the conversation should grow naturally, as conversations do, out of shared company and intersecting interests. This also meant that some of the ideas I was working through in this project would emerge in our discussions. Each conversation, then, has its own particular character and builds its own understandings, as readers will see.

Because I did bring questions to provide some continuity to each conversation, I will explain those briefly here. I came prepared with a central research question and a number of possible questions to ask, depending on how the conversation developed. The central question I had in mind was this: How do Indigenous literatures matter to the resurgence of healthy Indigenous communities? I often posed a simpler and more open version of this question: Why do Indigenous literatures matter?[111] I asked writers a number of different questions in an attempt to explore that central concern. For instance, I asked them about what brought them to their writing—what kinds of things they had read when they were growing up and what they had gained from their experiences in school. I asked them about community—about how they thought about community in their work, or how literatures were connected to communities. I asked them about the impact of their writing, what they hoped their writing might do, or how their work had been important so far. I also asked them about teaching, both to draw out their own experiences and reflections and to encourage them to discuss what they thought about Indigenous literatures being taught in schools or post-secondary institutions.

I also worked to bring different people's perspectives into discussion with each other. For this reason, the conversations are represented here in the order that they occurred; in some ways, they build on each other. One of my reasons for this approach was to enable people to learn from each other and to foster a form of dialogue between their perspectives. This exchange also includes the conversations I was holding with teachers at the same time about teaching Indigenous literatures in their classrooms. Occasionally, then, I introduced comments or questions from other writers or teachers with whom I had previously spoken—particularly when I felt that those perspectives would help to expand our discussion. This kind of interweaving was, for me, a way of enacting what Cree scholar Dwayne Donald calls "ethical relationality,"[112] and it helped to generate understanding as the broader project developed.

I feel a degree of ambivalence about reducing these conversations to a textual form. Translating them onto the page means that they lose much of the vitality inherent to the oral form, not to mention their relational immediacy. As with any book of interviews, much is missing: body language, pauses, interruptions, affective responses, repetitions, incomplete thoughts, verbal mannerisms, wanderings, jokes, overlapping speech, and those little noises or words we use to show or seek agreement, interest, or empathy. Some readers will have had their own experiences with the process of transforming a conversation into an audio recording, then into a transcript, and then into a readable interview: this process is necessarily a kind of translation and reduction. In doing this work, I have tried to retain much of the conversational feel of my discussion with each author. My editorial interventions have therefore been intentionally minimal. I have been very strict in retaining each author's original wording. I have done a fair amount of trimming to focus the texts, but I have not added any content. Because of differences in length, some conversations were edited more than others. In imposing punctuation and sentence or paragraph structure, I have sought simply to convey the original feel of the conversation while ensuring clarity for readers. Authors have had the opportunity to approve these interviews and to make any changes that seemed appropriate to them.

While I see many of the limitations of representing a verbal conversation in a textual medium, I also see how a textual medium opens up possibilities for sharing and revisiting these conversations beyond their original occurrence. The interplay of limitations and possibilities here is not unlike the interplay of limitations and possibilities between oral storytelling and written literatures. By translating these conversations into print, I also want to demonstrate respect for the the ways in which Indigenous writers themselves entrust their stories to the page.

From here, I invite readers to attend to what these writers have shared about writing-in-relation—and, further, to consider their own roles as readers when they are called to respond.

"BEING ABLE TO TELL STORIES FROM THE NORTH"

A Conversation with Richard Van Camp

RICHARD VAN CAMP IS FROM Fort Smith, Northwest Territories, and is Tlicho Dene (Dogrib). Celebrated internationally for his creative gifts, he is both an author and storyteller. Van Camp is widely known and appreciated in the Indigenous literary arts community for his seemingly boundless enthusiasm, positivity, and energy. As a father to a young son, he brings this energy to his family life as well. He and his family make their home in Edmonton but also spend much of their time in the North.

Determined to have a strong foundation in creative writing, Van Camp earned a BFA from the En'owkin Centre at the University of Victoria and an MFA from the University of British Columbia. Van Camp started his breakthrough novel, *The Lesser Blessed*, when he was still in his teens—as he tells me in the following interview. In the years since then, Van Camp has worked as a creative writing instructor and writer-in-residence at a range of programs and institutions, including UBC, the Emily Carr Institute, Yellowhead Tribal College, the University of Alberta, and Athabasca University. He also shares his talents through visiting, residence, and storytelling programs with libraries, schools, and First Nations communities. His commitment to youth and community is evident in our conversation here, as well as in his participation and presence in community initiatives in person and across digital and social media.

Van Camp's boundless energy shows in his publishing history: working across multiple genres, he has published approximately one book per year for the past twenty-three years. *The Lesser Blessed* (1996) was his first novel and remains well known; it was turned into a feature film in 2012, as was his short story "Dogrib Midnight Runners." Another of Van Camp's novels, a shorter young adult book called *Whistle* (2015), was written for Pearson Canada's Well Aware series. With its focus on youth mental health and education, Van Camp's support of this initiative is another sign of his focus on community engagement and social issues. In my view, a deep dedication to community well-being underlies much of this author's creative practice. Along with his novels, Van Camp has also published several short story collections. These include *Angel Wing Splash Pattern* (2004), *The Moon of Letting Go* (2010), *Godless but Loyal to Heaven* (2013), *Night Moves* (2015), and *Moccasin Square Gardens* (2019). Van Camp's stories, as well as some of his comic collaborations, are represented in a range of anthologies, literary journals, magazines, and online venues.

In keeping with his ever-present care for young people, his enthusiasm for popular and diverse genres, and his appreciation for collaborations with visual artists, Van Camp has also published widely in children's books and graphic novels. He has lovely books for babies: *Welcome Song for Baby* (2007), *Nighty Night* (2011), *Little You* (2013), *We Sang You Home* (2016), *Kiss by Kiss/Ocêtôwina* (2018), and *May We Have Enough to Share* (2019). His picture books for children include *A Man Called Raven* (1997) and *What's the Most Beautiful Thing You Know about Horses?* (2003). *Our Stories Help the Northern Lights Dance* (2013) is a picture book created collaboratively with George Littlechild and students from Fort Chipewyan; the book also honours stories from Elders in Fort Chip and Fort McKay. Released in a two-book flip volume called *The Journey Forward: Novellas on Reconciliation*, his story *When We Play Our Drums, They Sing!* (2018) is aimed at youth as well.

An avid consumer of comics, Van Camp has published two comic book projects through the Healthy Aboriginal Network, both of which promote awareness and well-being for teens: *Kiss Me Deadly* (2011) and *The Path of the Warrior* (2009). Similarly, his graphic novel *Spirit* (2016) was published by the South Slave Divisional Education Council as a mental health awareness project. It was also offered in four local languages. His other graphic novels or comic books are *The Blue Raven* (2015), another Pearson/Well Aware project, *A Blanket of Butterflies* (2015), and *Three Feathers* (2016). *Three Feathers* is also being brought to the screen through a film adaptation. Like many of his baby books, *Three Feathers* has been released in multiple Indigenous languages, as Van Camp describes below. Many of his books are also available in Braille. It is important to see that for this author, as for many included in this book, beliefs about responsibility to and engagement with community are enacted in and through his creative process.

Van Camp and his works have received numerous awards, from local to international. He won an award for promising young writers in 1997 from the Canadian Authors' Association at the dawn of his writing career, and a Writer of the Year Award from the Wordcraft Circle of Native Writers and Storytellers in 1999. *The Lesser Blessed*, having been translated into German, won the Youth Literature Prize from the German government for best work in translation in 2001. For his storytelling, Van Camp won the Wordcraft Storyteller of the Year Award for Canada and the US in 2007. *What's the Most Beautiful Thing You Know about Horses?* was recognized with an "Our Choice" recommendation by the Canadian Children's Book Centre in 1999–2000. The Books for B.C. Babies program, which distributes books to newborns in that province, selected his books *Welcome Song for Baby* and *Little You* (in 2008 and 2012, respectively); *Little You* went on to win the R. Ross Arnett Award for Children's Literature in 2015. *Godless but Loyal to Heaven* won the Georges Bugnet Award for Fiction in 2013 from the Alberta Book Awards. *Night Moves* won the Robert Kroetsch City of Edmonton Award and made the ReLit Awards shortlist for 2016. Van Camp also made the shortlist for an Eisner Award in 2016 with *A Blanket of Butterflies*. *We Sang You Home* received a commendation from the Bank Street College of Education for Best Children's Books of the Year and was chosen as one of the best books by the Canadian Children's Book Centre in 2017. Most recently, *The Journey Forward* was awarded the NorthWords Prize for Children's Literature and the Burt Honour Award for First Nations, Inuit and Métis Young Adult Literature in 2018.

Richard Van Camp and I met on April 29, 2015, at his home in Edmonton. I was nervous: it was my first interview for this project and I did not know Van Camp that well, although I had met him before and had read nearly all of his books. However, he set me at ease and got us rolling by telling me a couple of stories—ones I had not heard or read before.[1] Hearing these stories over tea and homemade muffins was a genuine pleasure. We allude back to these stories a couple of times during our conversation.

As with many other interviews in this collection, this conversation begins by tracing Van Camp's path to writing. By way of shaping an origin story for himself as a writer, he shares with me many of his early influences and experiences. I ask him in particular about his engagement with youth and education, knowing that he focuses time and energy on projects, initiatives, visits, and media work for and with young people. Throughout the interview, Van Camp is quick to point to the contributions and successes of other Indigenous artists. For Van Camp, connection to community is not just something that happens off the page. The creation of a text—involving collaborators like writers, translators, illustrators, publishers, and editors—is itself already a site for the creation of community. While Van Camp describes in explicit terms his beliefs about community in this interview, it is important to see these implicit notions at work as well.

OUR CONVERSATION

Richard Van Camp (RVC): Let's start at the beginning. I was raised in a house full of stories. I was raised with some of the greatest storytellers in the world. My parents were taxidermists in the seventies. This was before television. This was a time when families still visited families. Thank goodness, there was only CBC, for four hours every day, most of it in French, black and white. The only thing I remember was *The Edge of Night*. That was Canada's first soap opera. I remember the town used to come to a standstill for about half an hour every day—still does for *The Young and the Restless*. But what I remember most was that we had all day to visit, all day to share, all day to cook, all day to eat, all day to run, all day to play. And our parents read to us. And they told us stories.

We had a great library, Mary Kaeser Library in Fort Smith. Beautiful library. And we had Wally's Drug Store, where they had comic books, the same comic books that the kids were reading in Edmonton and Las Vegas and New York and Vancouver and Toronto. We also had, at Wally's Drugs, *Heavy Metal Magazine* and *Epic Magazine*. I have all mine downstairs, to this day. And I've always worked. I was a paperboy, selling the *Slave River Journal* and the *Edmonton Journal* when I was little. I've always had jobs, whether it was pumping gas at Kelly's, or cleaning the darkroom for the *Slave River Journal*—you name it. I've always had my own money. And I remember saving my money every week for new comic books. As I say that, the new *Walking Dead* is out—right now, today—and I'm going to download it on ComiXology. So, I'm still that little kid that loves to look forward to comic books and great reads. As I became a teenager, I discovered Judy Blume, S. E. Hinton, Stephen King, Pat Conroy, and comic books, comic books, comic books. I can't stress that enough. The comic books gave me the confidence to be a reader for eight-hundred-page Pat Conroys, or seven-hundred-page Stephen Kings.

I have thirteen books out; I have nine coming.[2] I would not be the writer I am today without the stories that I grew up with, learning about medicine power, having grandparents who are medicine people. I would not be the human being that I am today had it not been for those books. Now, when I first published *The Lesser Blessed*—that was twenty years ago next year—

Aubrey Hanson (AH): Is it really?

RVC: *The Lesser Blessed*, the novel, will be twenty years. It came out in 1996. It took me five years to write. Five years. Started when I was nineteen. I couldn't have written *The Lesser Blessed* without Judy Blume and S. E. Hinton and Pat Conroy and Stephen King, and those comic books. Also music. I couldn't have written—you'll see in the back of *Lesser Blessed*, I think, My Bloody Valentine, and Slowdive, and the Sisters of Mercy, and the Cure, and the Mission, and Siouxsie and the Banshees.

AH: That book has a soundtrack.

RVC: And the *Terminator 2* soundtrack. I couldn't have done it without braiding all that medicine power together.

I didn't know that I'd be the first Tlicho Dene to ever publish a novel. I didn't know I'd be the first person from Fort Smith, NWT to ever publish a novel. I had no idea. The greatest joy of my life, in the last twenty years, is seeing northern voices emerge. I leave for Yellowknife next month for the tenth annual NorthWords Writers' Festival. I'm on the board. I'm one of the founding members. During that time—

AH: You helped put that collection out.

RVC: A little bit. There was a huge committee that did that. It's called *Coming Home*. But my greatest joy is not only seeing northern voices grow and become published, but also the Indigenous community. To see someone like Jennifer Storm, who at the age of fourteen wrote *The Boy that Sheldon Killed* in one month. That was her first novel. I was on the selection committee at Theytus Books when that manuscript came in. I'll never forget it. I'll never forget seeing it. It was the most beat-up manuscript I'd ever seen in my life. It was all printed out on a little—I don't know if it was a Commodore 64 or what they were using—but the title, *The Boy that Sheldon Killed*, stole my heart. We had to change that name to *Deadly Loyalties* because there wouldn't be a high school in the nation that would allow a book with a title like *The Boy that Sheldon Killed*. To this day, that's one of my favourite books. It's about Blaze, a young lady trying to get out of an Indian gang in Manitoba.

And then, the beauty of Indigenous literature is that you think you know who somebody is—Drew Taylor has twenty-five books out right now; he comes out with *The Night Wanderer*, a story about a young lady, Tiffany Hunter, sixteen, who meets an Ojibway vampire. Knocked me out of my Indian tuxedo! Knocked me out of my little white mismatched socks!

AH: [*Laughs*] And people talk about that book in the schools—young people take it up.

RVC: Hands down, it's a timeless story. I'm so proud of Drew Taylor, so proud of him. And when you look at what David Robertson's doing with the graphic novel: *7 Generations: Stone*—it's epic, timeless work that he's doing. It's alchemy, what he's capable of. Look at Gregory Scofield. Chrystos. Those are voices of forever. They really, truly are. Continually inspiring.

Haunting. My dear friend Lorne Simon, who wrote *Stones and Switches*. In Indigenous literature we carry each other's joys, like we're excited when Katherena Vermette wins the GG[3] for poetry. We're over the moon when we read something like *Dream Wheels* by Richard Wagamese. I frankly think it's a stronger piece than *Indian Horse*. I think *Indian Horse* hit at a time when Canada was ready to talk about—

AH: People could listen to that.

RVC: Canada was ready. But read *Dream Wheels*. Now that is a riveting novel that is on par with a Pat Conroy. The literature that our mentors, our trail-breakers, are working on right now, the stuff that they're coming out with, is staggering, absolutely staggering in brilliance. Look at Lee Maracle. She's up there with Maria Campbell and Jeannette Armstrong. For her to come out with *Will's Garden*, one of my all-time favourite works—beautiful. She's a trail-breaker, without question. And yet, she comes out with the most elegant, soft-spoken, beautiful story. Just came out of nowhere, in my opinion. I just didn't see it coming until it hit me like a ton of bricks.

My worry is this: Jeannette Armstrong said in '91 that she could count on her fingers the number of people in the Okanagan Nation who read her work. I was always struck by that, hearing that in her classroom at the En'owkin Centre. I was haunted by that. I don't think that we prioritize Indigenous literature as much as we should in our own homes. That's why I'm grateful to organizations like Books for B.C. Babies or the NWT Literacy Council, where they prioritize northern writers for northern homes. I think sometimes that literacy isn't our biggest priority, and it needs to be.

One of the greatest joys as a brand-new dad is reading stories every night to our little boy, together. I think it's the most beautiful thing in the world. He's starting to see that what we're doing is actually on those pages. He's starting to put it together. He looks forward to it. You notice we don't have a TV here. There's no TV upstairs. I wanted the house that I had growing up. Music.

AH: Stories.

RVC: Stories, laughter, feasting, hosting, balloons. I want him to grow up in a time where it's books, music, wonder. It's okay if we have unstructured play time. This is your time to explore. You can do whatever you want. You want to make a pillow fort with blankets? We can do that. You want to go walk in the ravine? We can do that. This is your journey, and it's our journey together. Mind you, we love TV. We love our TV shows. We're hooked on *Downton Abbey, Nashville, Outlander*, but it's once a week. It's after our son goes to bed. It's really important to us that our boy read about the North, read about the world, the works that speak to my heart and my soul, that inspire me with my own craft and my joy as a reader.

So that's why I think it's so important. We never had that opportunity in high school. At PWK High, I remember sitting there in grade 8, 9, 10, 11, and 12 going, "Why are we reading *The Chrysalids*?" I love *The Outsiders*, don't get me wrong. I never understood *Macbeth*. And here's the crime of *Romeo and Juliet* at PWK High: had one of our instructors said, "Listen! I know you don't want to read it, but this is about—you know how in Fort Smith there's two families that hate each other?"

"Yeah."

"Could you imagine if one of the daughters fell in love with one of the sons—from each of the families?"

"Mr. Bates, that never would happen."

"But what if it did? That's what's happening in this book."

"Oh my God! We've got to read it. We've got to get to the bottom of this."

We never had that conversation.

AH: If you got to retell the story for your own community, or something like that.

RVC: Exactly. And that's the beauty of Indigenous literature: we can tackle those big themes in our own work and in our own languages. What I love about *Three Feathers* is that it is based on a true story that happened in Fort Smith (but I changed the ending), and we're working with our official languages. So, it's in Bush Cree and in English. Next month it'll be in Chipewyan and in English. And in two months it'll be in South Slavey and in English. We're using the translators that we all know and grew up with, so it's locally produced. I think that's really important. We shouldn't discount locally produced books. It's with Portage & Main, which is a recognized, medium-sized Canadian publishing house, but from here on in I'm not afraid to go with a local publisher if it means that our community is reading the stories. They can see themselves in it. They can see our water tower.

The new graphic novel we have with Portage & Main is called *A Blanket of Butterflies*, and it was inspired by the suit of samurai armour that was accidentally mailed to our museum. People are going to see Fort Smith in the graphic novel. That's what I'm so excited about, being able to tell stories from the North, with northern artists, from a northern perspective, with northern editors and northern translators. I think that's what's going to get our community members reading. It's the gossip factor. People want to see who I'm writing about. It's the juicy factor.

AH: I know that you go into schools, and you make sure you talk to teachers about what books are out there, what resources. You share what you know and the books and things that you have. You make a point of going and working with young people. Why do you do all of that? Why is it important to you?

RVC: We never had that chance. We never had people visit us at JBT Elementary. We never had people visit us at PWK High. We didn't have role models who were artists and entrepreneurs, that I was aware of. We never had people who could say, "You can make a great living as a writer; you can make a great living as an entrepreneur; you can make a great living as an artist; here's how I do it," and have those honest conversations with students. Our students are so beautiful! Many of them, they already know what they want: college, university, trades. They want to work with their hands. They want to be caterers. But I think, every once in a while, it's okay to have somebody in and say, "You can make a great living as a writer." I work with thirteen publishers, and they're all looking for northern stories, right now.

I think the world, the international community, is very interested in what's happening in Northern Canada and in what's happening from the Indigenous point of view, walking in two worlds every single day. The other night, we brought caribou meat that was given to me by a friend in Fort Smith to Mini Freeman's house. Out came the ulus, and we now have caribou dry meat in our fridge. Two nights ago, my wife made buffalo hamburgers, and she prepared them in a beautiful way. We got that buffalo meat from the farmers' market. There's going to be a singing on May 9 to determine the next Sundance this summer in Enoch, and we'll be there. I have two drums downstairs that are going to be gifted to two young men in this community. As an Indigenous person, I live in the big city, but at the same time, we're sharing what we have. We're cooking for people. That's ceremony. That's ritual. That's giving. And that's who we are, I think, as northerners. I was told a long time ago, by a great man named Bernie Bergman, a true northerner always leaves each person and each place better than they found them. And I really believe that that's our culture. Share what you have. Cook. Bake. Give. Be there.

AH: "Be there." Like you were saying, it's not all about consuming, but spending the time, listening, sharing the stories.

RVC: Yes, and carrying that forward. Every full moon, all the little ones on the street open all the spirit doors. See, all the little doors, they open up. All the little kids know: full moon, you have to come and open it. Every full moon we feed the birds with all the kids that want to come. We always honour the full moon, because the Tlicho Dene, traditionally, used to follow the full moon religiously. That was their night clock, in a way. That's something that's really important to me to pass on to my son.

AH: And I'm just imagining, the pillow forts and the flashlights come out, and the stack of books, and you can speak to those, like, "I know this person. This person told this story because of this." That's a very different kind of world, if kids can grow up with that.

RVC: At the same time, technology is a great tool for all of us. I've been recording Elders' stories for the past twenty years. I have twenty-four miracle stories. I also have a list of books that matter, kindergarten through grade 12. It's thirty-five pages.

AH: You make great lists.

RVC: Thank you. I break it down. I'm a Virgo, so I break it down. Right now, we've been interviewing nineteen Elders in Fort Smith. Not only have we been recording them, to transcribe them word for word, we've also been recording them in super HDR with video cameras in perfect lighting. We're going to do a book. It's going to be fifteen hundred copies, we're going to give it away for free. It's called *For Our Children: Teachings and Traditions from Fort Smith Elders.* We've gone to the icons of our community, and I'm really grateful. Kyle Napier with the Métis association, and Carla Ulrich, a great director, we just decided that we were going to do it. We were going to do it as a gift.

I think our communities are really hurting. With all the "progress" there's also a lot of drugs, also a lot of addictions. Mental health is at the forefront of many conversations right now. We've had thirteen funerals since New Year's in our little community. So, what we want to do is honour the families. It's pretty rough to be mad at someone if they're always honouring your family, and recording, and finding pictures of your baptism, and your wedding day, and your confirmation, and all that other good stuff. So, that's what I want to do.

You know, I'm forty-three now; I want to honour Fort Smith as much as I can. And by honouring Fort Smith, I think I remind everyone to honour where they're from. Wherever that may be, whether it's Ukrainian or Mennonite or Cree or Sarcee, honour where you're from. Use the technology. I have, on my cell phone, recordings of Mike Beaver singing two beautiful songs, with his permission, because he knew that his niece was about to be born here in Edmonton. He said, "I want you to record these and send them so that when my niece is arriving these are being played." And recording those Elders, saying, "Look, remember that UFO you saw when you guys were harvesting caribou? I want you to tell me that story so that I can share this with your kids in the city." Boom! So, there are no excuses anymore. If you want to honour your Elders, you want to get the answers that you've been looking for, use your phone. Record the videos, the sound waves, the pictures. Get it down.

AH: And share that stuff with the right people.

RVC: Share it, yeah. The greatest joy of my life—as well as just honouring Fort Smith, and being beautifully married and having a healthy son, and living in a beautiful home in a community that I care deeply about, with wonderful people—is I get to meet the great-grandchildren of the Elders that I used to drive around in the HandiBus twenty-five years ago and say, "I knew your great-auntie, and here's a story she told me. I have it as an MP3. I can email it to you. Here it is, word for word, and I'm going to email it to you in a sound wave. You're going to hear your great-auntie's voice. I know she passed when you were a little baby, but you finally get to hear her." That's what I love doing—honouring, and recording, and sharing. That's why it's so important.

I think you've got a good question, because it's open-ended. People can interpret it many ways. I think it's important that people be given a forum to talk about why they do what they do, how they discovered their process. Like Jordan Wheeler said, there are going to be years where you can't write it fast enough. Indigenous literature is so hot, you're selling stories before they're even written. And then there are going to be years when you can't give it away. He's onto something. I think that the international community can only hold on to the attention of certain things for so long. What I love about your question is that it gives you a chance to reflect on your career. This is twenty years I've been doing this, and I love it so much, because even after twenty years you still don't know who's going to come out of left field and knock you on your ass.

"IT STARTS FROM
A PLACE OF KNOWLEDGE AND TRUTH"

A Conversation with David Alexander Robertson

DAVID ALEXANDER ROBERTSON is a member of the Norway House Cree Nation and lives in Winnipeg. He is of Cree, Irish, Scottish, and English ancestry. A busy father of five, Robertson works in the field of Indigenous education with the Manitoba First Nations Education Resource Centre while devoting time to his writing and his family. Robertson also offers speaking engagements and workshops to support teaching and learning through Indigenous literatures and to allow readers to connect further with his books.

Robertson is a prolific writer. He collaborates with artists and illustrators to create his graphic novels, the earliest of which are the four books in the *7 Generations: A Plains Cree Saga* series: *Stone* (2010), *Scars* (2010), *Ends/Begins* (2010), and *The Pact* (2011). A number of Robertson's graphic novels take up residential school histories and the issue of missing and murdered Indigenous women, namely *Sugar Falls: A Residential School Story* (2012), *Betty: The Helen Betty Osborne Story* (2015), and *Will I See?* (2016). With a similar educational mandate, Robertson's *Tales from Big Spirit* series (2014–16) is intended to complement social studies curricula for elementary students: each of these six graphic novels features the story of a prominent historical Indigenous person in Canada, including Shawnadithit, John Ramsay, Gabriel Dumont, Pauline Johnson, Tommy Prince, Mistahimaswka, and Thanadelthur.

Alongside his novel *The Evolution of Alice* (2014), Robertson has recently published *Strangers* (2017) and its sequels *Monsters* (2018) and *Ghosts* (2019), young adult novels in his new *The Reckoner* series. These books are currently being adapted for television. He has also written a children's book, *When We Were Alone* (2016), which features another collaboration with a prominent visual artist and which enables very young children to learn about residential schools, Cree culture, and family.

Robertson's writing has been recognized with numerous honours. He has been awarded the John Hirsch Award for Most Promising Manitoba Writer, the Beatrice Mosionier Aboriginal Writer of the Year Award, and the Aboriginal Circle of Educators award for Research/Curriculum development. His books have won the Manuela Dias Book Design and Illustration Award, the McNally Robinson Best Book for Young People prize, and The Michael Van Rooy Award for Genre Fiction. In 2017, *When We Were Alone* also earned him, along with artist Julie Flett, a Governor General's Award for young people's illustrated literature.

Our conversation took place on July 9, 2015, at his office in Winnipeg. This conversation very much centres on the educational mandates that Robertson takes up with his writing, as he is positioned to focus on education in both his professional role and his creative work. He describes here why it is so important to him to create texts that can teach young people about Indigenous communities and social issues; he wants to encourage readers to learn more.

It is significant that Robertson brings such an explicit focus on learning to the form and content of his creative work. His educational mandate ensures that his texts are crafted for young people and that he connects with teachers and learners through a range of media and talks. In other words, through his work he directly targets readers as learners. In seeking to reach and engage children and teens, Robertson makes intentional use of the graphic novel format, building upon his own enthusiasm for comics. He comments on this strategy in the conversation that follows, suggesting that engaging kids with enticing literature is a highly effective way to lay a foundation of knowledge upon which a better future might be built.

OUR CONVERSATION

Aubrey Hanson (AH): Do you mind saying a bit about your work?

David Robertson (DR): I've done graphic novels and one novel on First Nations history, contemporary issues, and culture. Whatever I work on, I try and have some educational value in it. I try and do (when I can, because I have a full-time job) a lot of school visits and guest lectures at educational institutions in and outside of Manitoba on my writing. For several years in my work, too, I've worked in the communities, and now directly with schools, trying to provide additional resources for students and teachers to learn more about Indigenous history, culture, and languages. That's broadly what I do.

AH: What would you say brought you to writing? How did you end up thinking that writing was important?

DR: There are two things there. One is when did I start wanting to write, and then when did I start wanting to write about Indigenous topics. For me writing was just always natural. I started when I was in grade 3, which was maybe early. My teacher gave us a writing assignment of some kind in grade 3. I think it was for poetry. I didn't want to do the poetry. I felt a little embarrassed about it, because I thought poetry was for girls, and I didn't want to do that. So, I ended up actually hiding in the closet in the back of my classroom. I wrote in the dark, with foolscap pages and those big red pencils. I ended up writing a bunch of poems that day, though. I found that it came pretty easily, and I really enjoyed doing it. My teacher, when I handed the poetry in to her, she made it into this little book. From there I went home and I told my mom, "I want to be a writer, Mom." I think I said, "I want to write a world-famous book." So, I've been writing since grade 3. I still think I'm a bit of a late bloomer, because I don't think I wrote anything good until like five years ago [*laughs*]. I love poetry.

I got into prose writing in junior high, a little bit, then got back into poetry in high school. I was this goofball in high school. I remember in grade 10 I handed in a poem. We had this assignment to do a poem, again. I hadn't written a poem since elementary school. I worked on this poem super hard for a week and handed it in to my teacher. When she was handing the assignments back she didn't give me mine, and she asked to see me after class. I went to see her and she had my poem there and she said, "I don't think you wrote this. I think you copied it." I was devastated, because I'd worked so hard on it. She accused me of plagiarizing it. I went home to tell my mom, because that's what boys do [*laughs*]. My mom flipped—I mean, she flipped in her way, because she's a very proper lady—but she was upset that her son was upset. She went and brought the teacher all my drafts. When you're a writer you have a million drafts of everything. So then my teacher finally believed me, and was like, "Oh, you're the Babe Ruth of poetry" and "I want to put you in all these advanced writing courses" and everything. I said no, because I was so put off by it. I stopped writing for a long time.

I got back into it in university. I wrote a couple of really crappy books that I self-published, which I wish I hadn't done. I won't even mention what they're called, because I don't want anybody to look for them. Eventually I started to think about doing graphic novels. I did that because I grew up really disconnected from culture. My dad is Cree; he's from Norway House.

I was never connected to that when I was growing up. I didn't know anything about my family on that side, really, or my culture, or that side of who I was. That had a really profound effect on me, as I think it does with youth today. I grew up feeling like I wasn't whole, and I had a really negative view, as a kid, of Indigenous Peoples. I bought into all the stereotypes, and there was nothing for me to learn in school about the truth. As an adult, I felt that, if I had had that, then I would have been in a better place, spiritually, mentally, and from an identity standpoint.

I started to think about what I could do to put it into schools, because I was missing that. By that time, I had become more connected to the culture. I worked to learn more about it and finally got to the point where I was proud to be part Cree and call myself an Indigenous person. I wanted that for other youth, because I saw, working in communities, that there was a lot of that same sort of feeling. I started to do graphic novels. I thought, originally, that graphic novels were just cool. I thought if you could put them in a context of Indigenous culture, history, language, that kids would learn a lot. They'd be so pumped to read from the graphic novels, right? That's why I started doing them. That's why I really got into doing the writing that I'm doing now on those topics. I've been going at it now for seven years.

I've done a bunch of graphic novels and I've been really pleased to see that they've done very well in the education system across Canada. They've done well outside of schools, too, which is great, because the conversation needs to happen in schools and outside of schools. Kids need to be learning about these things in class, and they need to be going home and having a dialogue with their parents, or their siblings, or their friends. That's how ignorance gets spread, by dialoguing between each other about things that we don't know about. If we know about them, then we learn more positive things, and I think that's my whole goal in writing the stuff that I do.

AH: You have a personal connection and investment. I identify with that as well. That's a lot of what brought me to the work that I do, too. Growing up, I remember learning a couple things about Inuit people in school but hardly anything else about Indigenous people. It's meant a lot to me to work to change that. I think literature is a great way to do that work. It has a capacity to draw people in.

DR: It's fantastic. And it's way better, to me. I could never stand reading from a textbook in school. Never got excited for it. But if you give kids stuff that they'll engage with, that's half the battle. Then they're learning. If you give them a graphic novel, like on residential schools, what you'll find is the students are way more apt to want to read from the textbook after they've learned from the graphic novel, because they get excited about it. They get curious about the history, and then they want to read more about it—it's just innate in kids. It's a good entryway. I would never say to a teacher, "Just use this graphic novel only." I scratch the surface with them. I think it's an important surface, but there's so much more, and it's the teacher's job to dig deeper into that and provide students with more information.

AH: It sounds like you've thought a lot about the medium, why you've chosen to work with graphic novels.

DR: Originally, there wasn't much of a technical emphasis for me. I didn't really know why they were so great. I just thought—when I was growing up, I only read comic books, graphic novels, and so I thought they would be pretty cool to bring into a classroom. Kids would get excited about them. What I've learned now, after doing them for seven years, is that there are a lot of technical reasons why they're so great. A lot of it has to do with the genre and the existence of storytelling through images and words. The way that images and words connect in the graphic novel format and the comic book format helps students to retain more knowledge. That's important. It provides a deeper context to the storytelling. It gives them visual cues that they can't get just from words.

When you're talking about youth in general that's important, but especially when you're talking about less sophisticated readers—readers that are harder to reach, like boys, struggling readers (who are more often boys), students with learning disabilities or with English as a second language—they're great for all those groups. They're also great for more sophisticated readers. Even though they connect well with struggling readers or less sophisticated readers, they often have more complex plots or story structures that connect with readers who are more sophisticated. They're really a universal tool. I've seen them being used in a grade 4 classroom and I've gone to a university to lecture on the same book. I don't think you can do that with any other form of literature. All that is generally why they work so well in the education context.

There's also this theory on how it connects with a more ancient form of communication. Before we had words, we connected through pictures and images. We put those images together, and those images in sequence told stories. That's all the graphic novel is. It's really one of the most ancient forms of communication. I think that's another reason why they connect so well with our youth.

AH: Before we turned the recorder on, we were talking about the visuals. Your covers, the images, the sequencing, are so strong in the works that I've read. Is there one of your works that you'd like to talk about in terms of the visual elements, or how you've seen it work in education?

DR: I've been to a lot of classrooms. It's interesting, and great, that I don't think I've ever received a negative comment from a student. I've talked to thousands of them on these graphic novels. Which is incredible—

AH: [*Laughs*] That's better than my record!

DR: They learn a lot. They're sophisticated in the knowledge that they've gleaned from the graphic novel, so their attention is there. All great signs. I think a lot about the visual nature of them. I spend a lot of time—maybe more time than on the actual script, in terms of the words you see on the page—on the graphic novels. I've spent probably more time thinking about how the images connect. That's a big challenge in writing them. I work a lot with the illustrator in making sure that they sequence in really interesting ways, in ways that get the best knowledge transfer possible.

In terms of the books that I've done, I'm proud of most of them. I think the ones that are most important to me are the ones on residential schools and missing and murdered Indigenous women. Those are two topics that are really important to me. It's also two topics that, as Canadians, we don't know enough about, or don't appreciate the impacts of. So, *Ends/Begins*, *The Pact*, my *7 Generations* series, *Sugar Falls*, and *Betty*—the new *Betty* that just came out on Helen Betty Osbourne—they all tell stories about either the residential school system or the epidemic of missing and murdered Indigenous women. They do it in ways that are very powerful because of the images. Because of that, people retain that knowledge more effectively than they would in any other way. For example, in *Ends/Begins* there's this sequence where a young boy is brought to a bathing house in one of the residential schools, and the priest is going to rape him. You could read about that in a textbook, and you might read it and think, "Oh, that's horrible," but I don't think it would stick with you as much as it would when you actually see it happen. That's difficult.

I have conversations with teachers who ask, "What's the level of appropriateness in bringing this into my classroom if I'm a junior high teacher, or if I'm an elementary school teacher?" That's a decision that teachers need to make, but always within the context of what's important for the students to learn, as Canadians, and what they're exposed to outside of the schools. The argument I usually make is to have teachers think about it like this: If you're in junior high, your students are at home watching *The Walking Dead*, for example, with gratuitous violence, really grotesque violence (it's a great show; I love it). If they're okay seeing that, then why can't you show them a scene with the sort of abuse that happened to our Indigenous kids in history, and students can be exposed to that in ways that are sensitive but powerful? I feel there is an importance to that that we can't overlook.

AH: I have two kids. Right now, they're almost seven and eight. I've mostly taught older kids, but being with my little ones and their friends, I'm always impressed by their ability to imagine and empathize, to be really strong with the things that they learn. I think that sometimes we don't give kids enough credit for what they can understand and process. I'm more afraid of them learning things too late than too soon, if I don't get there first and prepare them for some of the difficult stuff that is coming in their lives, or that their friends might experience. I want them to have the capacity to be understanding and respectful around the difficult things that other people experience. It's a big question that we have to look at head-on.

DR: I have five kids. I have a daughter who is in grade 6 and a boy who is in grade 4. They've both heard racist comments about Indigenous people in their school. If the kids who are saying these things are exposed to that sort of knowledge at that age, then why can't we expose them to truth at that age? It just makes sense. If my daughter isn't armed with that knowledge, to talk to a kid about something racist that they've said, or to tell the teacher about it, then what's going to happen? It just starts with something small and it gets bigger. That's the way I look at it.

AH: I find that parenting and teaching inform each other in really important ways. With the educational work and writing that you do, you must think a lot about that.

DR: I do. That's why I'm so happy to see these books do well in bookstores, too, because that means people outside of schools are reading them. If people outside of schools are reading them, and they're sharing that, then they're sharing knowledge. Hopefully, if the kids are bringing that to their parents and sharing with them, you have this collision of knowledge, which can only be a good thing in the end.

AH: It goes around in families and in communities, too. How do you think about community when you write? Do you think about issues of representation or of responsibility to communities?

DR: I always think about community, but I think of it in a broader perspective. We're all in the same community. Our successes are tied to each other and our failures are. I always talk about that to students. I get them to look around the room, and I say, "How many cultures do you think we have in this classroom?" There are always ten, fifteen, twenty. And I say, "What do we know about each other?" and I'll point to one kid; I'll say, "Where are you from? What are you interested in?" Then I'll say to everyone else in the class, "Who knew that?" I tell them that that's what we need to be doing. We need to be making the effort to know each other. If we don't, then we're making judgments about each other without knowledge. I relate that back to that historical context of Indigenous Peoples, and I have them think about that. The conversation is always, "How do we function as a community? Are we making the effort to understand each other?" It's a simple act, generating knowledge for each other, but it's also difficult. We just don't do it, right?

I think about community from a larger perspective first, but in working with a lot of the First Nations communities, I do obviously think about what's going on in those communities and how my work will affect them. As much as non-Indigenous kids don't know about Indigenous culture, Indigenous kids don't know about their own culture. I always write my books for Indigenous kids so they understand a bit more about where they've come from, what they've been through as a people, and how it's affected them. Same for non-Indigenous kids. What's happened in this country to Indigenous Peoples? What has been the effect on them? And then, how does it affect us as Canadians? That's really important for me. In terms of First Nations communities, that's my focus. I've been to communities where I've worked with them for over a year, and there've been seven or eight suicides. I'll start a dialogue about it. Why is that happening and what can we do to prevent it?

AH: How do you think about what it takes to build something better in the future? How do you think about the future or about community resilience?

DR: Knowledge. It always starts from a place of knowledge and truth. I think that's actually the only place it can start. From my perspective, I play a small role in building that foundation. If we're going to be anywhere positive in the future, we need to start from a good knowledge base, from a place of truth and acceptance of that truth. When we do that, I think that we can only go to good places. That's the beginning and the end for me.

AH: There's a lot of work to do there.

DR: There's a ton of work!

AH: There's a lot of potential there, too.

DR: I have a small role in that. I do the best that I can with the work that I'm doing, but what people have to recognize is that they all have a role. That's the same thing I tell kids: you all have a role. *Especially* kids. I've always said that, as adults, we're responsible for our youth, and we're responsible for providing that information to our youth, but our youth are responsible for tomorrow. There are two levels of responsibility there. That's the conversation I try to have with these kids, about their responsibilities, my responsibilities, and to take those seriously.

AH: Plus, kids are amazing!

DR: They're incredible.

AH: The way that they can think and ask questions no one else would think to ask. All those little threads of context and history and habit that keep adults moving in certain ways, kids just snip right through those. Sometimes we have to say, "Well, those threads are there for a reason," and sometimes we can say, "What?! You looked at that from that angle and it's amazing what you just came up with!" They have so much energy, and a sense of justice, too.

DR: And they act fully on the knowledge that's been provided to them. I ask kids, "Where do you get knowledge from?" They say, "Oh, my friends, my teammates, my family, my teachers." That's a big group to be getting knowledge from. They only act on the knowledge they have, so we need to be giving them the right knowledge. Kids are awesome. We grow up, we unlearn the things that we knew as a kid. As kids, we look at someone and we don't judge them, really. You accept differences without thinking about them. That's what we need to do. It's very simple. It's true, the things we learned in kindergarten, [*laughs*] they're basic things that we should still be understanding today. We're just people, right? We need to accept that we're kind of the same, but that we have different stories. We need to know those stories.

AH: And have that openness and willingness to engage and learn, and, if we don't know, to ask, which kids are good at [*laughs*].

DR: Exactly.

AH: Do you want to say anything else about why you think Indigenous literatures matter?

DR: I think it's vitally important. That's one of the main conduits of information for our youth, and our adults. It's how we are going to learn about our histories and how our histories affect us. There is a movement now within Indigenous communities and Indigenous artists to share stories through our literatures. We were an oral tradition within our cultures. We're recognizing that we need to shift how we pass down stories, and literature is one of the ways that we're doing that. And it's great that literature is reaching out beyond our communities into our non-Indigenous communities as well.

I think there's a growing movement of reclamation where Indigenous writers are working to reclaim our histories from how they've been told in the past by non-Indigenous peoples. That kind of perspective is very important. A non-Indigenous person was telling stories, a century ago, or even decades ago, from a non-Indigenous perspective. Telling stories from that basis of understanding, we're losing something. If we can have more Indigenous Peoples, talented Indigenous Peoples, making the effort to tell our histories from our perspectives in literature, I think a lot of great change is going to happen. I'm one of those. There's a growing group. I hope it continues to grow. One of the things that we need to be doing as artists is inspiring youth to do that. They'll grow up and they'll be the ones doing it. I think we have a responsibility in that way, too—not just telling the stories but inspiring youth to tell the stories.

AH: That's a big step for thinking about the future and the continuation of stories, but also of people—having good ways to be Indigenous in contemporary times.

DR: For me, it's about making sure that we are generating the right resources—literature or performance art or music—to share knowledge in really engaging ways, and that people know how to utilize that knowledge. A big piece of it is in the education system. My dad and my mom are both educators—that's probably what influenced me to get into it. My dad's a big advocate of this: to ensure that we're making the effort in teacher training programs, whether it's in education or otherwise, incorporating that training on how to facilitate that knowledge transfer to youth from the right perspectives and in the right ways. At a university level, or at an elementary school, junior high, or high school level, I think that's important. You can develop the resources, great, but you also need to have teachers who are able to utilize those resources in efficient ways.

AH: And respectful ways.

DR: Yeah, always from a place of understanding. We need more Indigenous teachers, but the reality is, we need more non-Indigenous teachers who can do it the right way. That's probably the one thing I would add.

AH: You create art that can be used in inspiring and responsible ways in classrooms, but you also do school visits and you work in a number of ways to support that educational work. I'm always inspired by what literature can do. Definitely one of my reasons for enjoying life is enjoying the literary arts and what they can bring us. Working with young people around that inspiration, but also the knowledge that can come with it, is a craft, too, and it's something that is really worth putting time into. I enjoy talking to people who share some of that. So thank you for that.

DR: You're welcome.

"I REALIZED THAT I COULD WRITE WHAT I SEE"
A Conversation with Katherena Vermette

KATHERENA VERMETTE IS A MÉTIS writer living in Winnipeg. She grew up in the city's North End and, with her Red River Métis and Mennonite ancestry, has deep roots in the Winnipeg area. Alongside her growing career as a writer, Vermette worked as an early childhood educator teaching kindergarten, and she carried out a range of educational work related to literacy and the arts. She has an MFA from UBC and has taught creative writing courses and has facilitated writing workshops in a range of spaces, including the University of Manitoba's Centre for Creative Writing and Oral Culture, the University of Toronto, the Banff Centre for Arts and Creativity, and the Winnipeg School Division, among others. As a writer-in-residence, she has worked with UBC, Athabasca University, and, returning to the place where she earned her BA in English, the University of Winnipeg. She is invited to speak, read, teach, and share at engagements across the country. She is also a mother of three.

Vermette's first book of poetry was *North End Love Songs* (2012), and she has recently released a second poetry collection entitled *river woman* (2018). Building on her previous work in early childhood education, she published *The Seven Teachings Stories* (2014–15), a series of children's stories based on the Anishinaabe Seven Sacred Teachings. Her eighth picture book, *The Girl and the Wolf* (2019) is illustrated by award-winning Cree-Métis artist Julie Flett. Vermette is the creator of a short documentary film called *this river* (2015), and, emerging from a commission by CBC Aboriginal, a short video has been created around her poem "Heart" (2015), which is a fierce and loving portrayal of Winnipeg's North End. Vermette is the author of one novel, *The Break* (2016). In addition, she has written a graphic novel series for young adults entitled *A Girl Called Echo*, consisting thus far of two volumes: *Pemmican Wars* (2017) and *Red River Resistance* (2018). Over the years, some of Vermette's shorter writing has been anthologized, for instance in the collection *Manitowapow: Aboriginal Writings from the Land of Water* (2012). Her work is featured in a graphic novel anthology called *This Place: 150 Years Retold* (2019), and has appeared extensively in literary journals and magazines, from *Red Rising Magazine* in Manitoba to the *Cordite Poetry Review* in Australia.

Highlighting the work of other Indigenous authors through her editorial work as well, Vermette has edited a collection of erotic Indigenous writing called *xxx ndn* (2011) and worked collaboratively to edit the book *Impact: Colonialism in Canada* (2017). She also co-edited (with Warren Cariou) two robust special joint issues of the literary journals *Prairie Fire* and *CV2*, entitled *ndncity* (2017) and *ndncountry* (2018); these feature Indigenous writing from Winnipeg and from across Canada, respectively. *An Anthology of Indigenous Literatures in English: Voices from Canada*, co-edited with Armand Garnet Ruffo, was released in early 2020.

Vermette and her writing have been recognized with a number of awards, most prominently the Governor General's Literary Award for Poetry for *North End Love Songs*. That first collection also won the Lina Chartrand Award for activist-inspired poetry. Her novel *The Break* has also been widely celebrated: it won the Amazon.ca First Novel Award, the Canada Council for the Arts Burt Award, three Manitoba Book Awards, and was a finalist on CBC's Canada Reads contest. Notably, the novel's French translation, *Ligne brisée*, won the Radio-Canada Combat des livres contest. *The Break* was also a finalist for the Rogers' Writers' Trust Fiction Prize and the Governor General's Award for English-Language Fiction in 2016. Vermette's collaborative film *this river* (2016) won a Canadian Screen Award for Best Short and the Coup de coeur du jury award from the Montréal First Peoples Festival in the same year.

Katherena Vermette and I met at her office in downtown Winnipeg on July 10, 2015. In sharing her path to writing and her early writing experiences, Vermette offers insights into her education and exposure to literature, particularly poetry. She describes the impact on her emerging poetic practice of the distinct poetic traditions that she learned about in literature and writing classes. She describes how she was able to grapple with Eurocentric poetic traditions and forms, navigating these in relation to her own experience. Exposure to other Indigenous writers—especially Métis writers—encouraged Vermette increasingly to manifest her own voice and experience in her writing. She describes a significant shift: from composing poetry according to Eurocentric conventions to a poetry rooted in Indigenous place, voice, and experience.

Vermette also raises the question of appropriation of voice, or of who has the right to tell stories about Indigenous experience. It is worth noting that our conversation took place well in advance of the 2017 controversy around cultural appropriation that emerged in response to the provocative editorial in *Write* magazine (discussed in the introduction to this volume): the concern over non-Indigenous appropriation of Indigenous stories and perspectives has a long history in Indigenous communities. What Vermette offers in this chapter is a thoughtful reflection on her own positionality and voice, as well as an insistence that Indigenous stories are best voiced by Indigenous people, in relation to their own experience. Questions of responsibility, voice, and permission inform her thinking on what she can write about.

Another significant strand in this conversation is the notion of empathy as it shapes learning. Vermette considers why stories can be effective in bringing others to learn more about Indigenous perspectives, and in particular how readers can relate to stories or empathize with people's experiences when those experiences are portrayed through story. In this way, she suggests, stories can be a way to open up learning. Bringing readers into stories and into learning is a powerful way to bridge the distance between Indigenous Peoples and settler Canadians. Vermette explores these notions through literary and educational perspectives. Her thinking in this chapter highlights the complexity of relationship-building processes, while foregrounding the role that stories can play in precipitating social change. Indigenous literatures are a way of calling people into deeper mutual understanding and thus into more respectful relationships.

OUR CONVERSATION

Aubrey Hanson (AH): To start off, do you mind telling me a bit about your work?

Katherena Vermette (KV): My perspective on writing really centres around Indigenous experience, particularly my own story. I find that I'm often obsessed with the idea of permission and whose story I have permission to tell, and whose stories certain people have permission to tell. I'm still trying to figure out how to tell my own story, so I'm very much concentrating on this one space. I write a lot about this place, about Winnipeg and about the North End, and about inner-city children and those kinds of experiences. I'm very much concentrated on figuring that part out. I know that at some point I'm going to move outward from that focus, but I feel like I'm still there.

AH: What do you think brought you to writing? What about teaching? What about school? What about your educational experience? Did that support you, or was it something totally different?

KV: Well, I started writing when I was young, and I don't remember why. I remember very specifically that it was the summer that I moved to the North End, actually, and we had extra school supplies. We had an extra Hilroy notebook that my mother gave me and said I could do whatever I wanted with it. For whatever reason, I chose to write a poem. I have no memory of learning what a poem was, or learning anything about that. But, given the opportunity to do whatever I wanted, I chose to write a poem. At some point some teacher somewhere taught me what a poem was, because I wrote very poorly rhymed, bad-metred poems for way too many years.

AH: [*Laughs*] I think we can probably all dig up a lot of those.

KV: From an education perspective, that was the avenue that I was attracted to, and so someone taught me that. I did not have a literary household. My parents always read, but they have their own unique reading tastes. It was not poetry. Poetry was nowhere. So I don't really know where this connection with poetry came from—and it was very much European poetry, at that time.

Then, actually, when I was about twelve, fourteen maybe, I read *In Search of April Raintree*. This is a seminal work and Beatrice is the most amazing person in the world.[4] That was a work that not only spoke about this place, but spoke in a voice that was so close to my own experience. I wasn't in the foster-care system, but there are a lot of similarities. She's a Métis person, and she was speaking in this voice that was so close and so familiar to me. That's really where I opened my eyes to the idea that I could write, and that I could write about this place. I didn't have to try some silly iambic pentameter that wasn't co-operating. Her writing really opened that possibility for me in an incredible way. I wanted to be a writer. I wanted to be an artist in the way that kids want to be movie stars. But I didn't know that I *could* be. It was that "ah-ha" moment, that eye-opening moment where I saw, through Indigenous literature, what ended up being what I wanted to do with my life.

That was also something that happened in the classroom. I went to a very small inner-city—well, North End—school, and it was very under-resourced in a lot of ways. We had a really nice group of dedicated, non-Indigenous teachers who, although they were very Eurocentric in their methodology and everything like that, were also very genuine people. I was very lucky to have them. That's where I got that book, and where I started writing.

I started writing very journal-based, cathartic, emotive writing for really a long time, all through my teenage years. That's all you do when you're a teenager, right? You're so self-obsessed. I'm still self-obsessed. I'm an artist; we're all self-obsessed. You're just like, "My brain is so fascinating" [*laughs*].

AH: [*Laughs*] There's a lot to process when you're a teenager.

KV: [*Laughs*] There's a lot. My girls are teenagers and I watch them go through that. You just can't get away from your head, and your brain, and what's going on, and everything. Everything is just exaggerated so much. For me, writing was an outlet; it was a huge coping mechanism for me. I know that I wouldn't have survived if I hadn't had that outlet and I hadn't had that space. Just that thing that I started doing, which was scribbling in journals, trying to articulate my experience, my emotional map, fascinated me and almost distracted me from everything else that was going on. It was a survival mechanism.

AH: From there, was it just a matter of sticking with it? Or did anybody else support you along the way? Or did you read more?

KV: When I was sixteen I walked into a creative writing class. It's neat, because through this process, after I won the award,[5] I went on the radio and I said, "I owe it all to Ms. Darling." Then we found each other, and she brought me back to my old high school, and I did this whole "Kate, this is your life!" kind of afternoon. It was fabulous.

AH: That's cool.

KV: [*Laughs*] It was so cool! I've been very blessed with many great teachers along the way. It was a creative writing class in high school, and I walked in there as a sixteen-year-old, just knowing that I wanted to write. I thought writing was cool. I think I was probably still trying to rhyme. She provided me with poetry—again, very Eurocentric poetry—but that's where I learned about T. S. Eliot and e. e. cummings, and I became quite well read in all of that poetry. Any writing that provided me with something different. Any different way to express a feeling. I was still self-obsessed, sixteen—so totally living in my own brain, and really looking for interesting ways to talk about my own experience. My writing was very emotion-centric for a really long time.

I also got into the idea of Imagist writing—the idea of writing about what you see, like the Romantics and the Imagists. That's when I really started noticing that what I was seeing wasn't what these poets were seeing. For a while I wrote what I thought I was supposed to write. I think until I was in my twenties, I wrote what I thought I was supposed to write. I wrote about emotions, and I wrote about trees (well, I still write about trees), but, at some point—and it was through Indigenous poetry, reading and being exposed to

Indigenous poetry—that I found a cadence and an approach and perspective that isn't in European poetry. Again, it was that moment of familiarity, that moment of light shining on something. I realized that I could write what I see. Just like all the poets do, but I could write it from this perspective, and write about what I actually see—that it's just as poetic as all of those other things.

AH: That's a powerful thing to realize.

KV: It was a slow release. That's when I started writing about the inner city. That's when I started writing about people. I started really digging. I didn't want to write about myself. I went through this big switch. I was totally obsessed with my own emotions, but then I grew tired of that and I wanted to write about what I was seeing.

The Imagist perspective is not emotive, and is very sterile—painting pictures, not imposing emotions. I approached my world with that lens, searching for beauty. Searching in these pictures of Indigenous people, who are represented very negatively out there in the world, and looking further—trying to show where they're beautiful. That's where a lot of the bird poems in the book come from.[6] I'm making these character sketches, almost, of these women and these girls, really trying to show how they're beautiful. Perhaps that's the thesis: how are they beautiful? What is beautiful about them, even though so much about them is not necessarily perceived as beautiful?

I think that is what I try to do with poetry, most of all, is to blend those two worlds as much as possible, and use both. Indigenous poetry is so rooted in storytelling and so rooted in voice, a very specific voice and a very powerful voice. European poetry is so aesthetic and lyrical and almost tries to be distant, not intimate—whereas I want to be very intimate. I want to tell a story.

AH: You've thought a lot about education and what happens in schools. Do you think about how literature can make differences for young people in their schooling or in their education? Do you think about the role of literature in that?

KV: That's a big question. I'm going to see where I go.

AH: Yes! You can go sideways with it.

KV: Okay. I'm going to go sideways. I remember when I took an honours degree in English, because I thought I was going to be smart. I realized I wasn't an academic at all, but I remember I had this wonderful teacher—again, I had great teachers. We were doing fundamentals in literary study, and she introduced me to the idea of literature as cultural products and to the idea that literature is representative of experience. I remember that she had this big question: "Is it still valuable even if it's not considered good?" And that just blew my mind!

As a writer you're constantly trying to be "good," and then you go into this publishing world—particularly as an Indigenous artist coming from an Indigenous perspective—and you immediately are met with this wall of disinterest because of what you're writing about. It also happens the other way around. I look at Canadian literature and much of it doesn't necessarily interest me, because it's a perspective that I'm not interested in. Interest is completely subjective. When you're writing from an Indigenous perspective, with those aspects of Indigenous poetry—the voice, and the story, and the cadence, and coming from this oral tradition that is very different from the European aesthetic—some people don't relate to it. Some people don't think of that writing as "poetry." So, for so long I was in this category of not being considered "good" because I was writing something different. Many of my friends have had similar experiences writing as Indigenous people within the context of Canadian literature. The idea of "good" is so incredibly subjective.

So yes, literature is valuable whether or not it's considered "good," because that "good" is completely in the eye and the ear of the reader. No matter what their education. I'm a big believer in the fact that value is completely subjective, particularly when it comes to poetry. No one person, no matter what their education, has the same opinion of certain poems. I can read a bunch of poems that someone with my same education level might think are wonderful, but I'm not relating to them. So absolutely, something can be valuable even if it's not considered "good." From the perspective of Indigenous literature, for so long it's been looked on through a European lens and then it's been considered "bad" because of where it's coming from.

For instance, *In Search of April Raintree* has what I consider a non-style style, because it's very conversational. She's not playing into any aesthetic. She's not playing with metaphors. She's telling a story. It's life story. So much Indigenous story is telling life story. My friend Duncan said that—Duncan Mercredi, another person who works a lot in schools. When I was putting together my first book, he said, traditionally, in Indigenous circles, you introduce yourself. This is how we introduce ourselves when we start, particularly when we go to different places. You introduce yourself by where you come from. You thank people for welcoming you in their territory. This is a universal practice on the continent. I think on all continents, actually.

So, when I was putting my first book together, Duncan said that my book has to do this. It has to introduce me to the world. That idea really centred the book on talking about where I come from. You understand a person based on where they come from. You understand me based on understanding how

I grew up. If you don't know how I grew up, and where I grew up, and my place in the world, you understand much less about me. So that's what I did. I think that's what many Indigenous artists do. Many artists of all cultures do that in some way or another. It's the idea of defining yourself and doing that form of introducing.

I think that's incredibly important for Indigenous students. And for non-Indigenous students, but it's different. Indigenous students need to see those voices that they know and that are familiar to them. They need to see those reflected in what they read and what they're exposed to in their school. Non-Indigenous students need that, too, particularly if they have no concept of Indigenous culture at all, which happens in so many communities in this country. It's kind of amazing.

Particularly for newcomer Canadians. Newcomer Canadians get absolutely no education about the Indigenous Peoples, so they are relying completely on oral stories within their own circles—and, as a result, stereotypes and prejudices that already exist can be perpetuated over and over again. They aren't given any concept of who Indigenous people are. The only way you can get to know any person is through them introducing themselves and telling you a bit about themselves. A very easy way to do this is to use the resources that are already there, which are these stories that people took the time to write.

AH: We're talking about the importance of literature for learners, and again, I'm going to go a little sideways. Where I work in Calgary, in our school of education, there's a very strong impetus to build teachers' capacity. We're educating teachers who are going out into teaching, and educating continuing teachers. There's a strong impetus to support and educate those teachers in teaching Indigenous content and in meeting the needs of Indigenous students, and doing all that work that all falls under that umbrella of "Indigenous education." There are a lot of people who are super keen and who are prepared to do the work, and who are ready to take it up, and ready to go. Then there are folks who need more support, those who don't have the context or the background, or who need support, even in just saying, "What is my relationship to this work? Where do I find accurate information? What do I need to unlearn in order to learn?" Then of course there are folks who are resistant, and racism comes up, and colonial attitudes are of course there, and that stuff has to be dealt with.

So, I think of that big umbrella of "Indigenous education" when it comes to thinking about educators' perspectives. One golden strand in all of that is that literature can make some of those challenges in the classroom just a little less challenging. Say you want to teach a student about a concept, such as residential schooling, but you just explain it by going over the facts. Introducing that history through a story that tells somebody's experience is often more accessible and successful, because there's empathy involved. Some people prefer just the facts, but I think that stories can open more doors for people.

KV: I think there's value with both, but I think the stories are always the way in. They are the accessible way. Particularly when they're conversational. Particularly when people can read them and they're at their level, whatever that level is. Stories are the way that people relate to that experience. You learn emotions through talking about people's experiences in stories. If someone is portraying their experience in residential school, you know that they were a kid at the time. You know that they were vulnerable. You know exactly how they were small and what that experience is like. You can imagine, because this is what we do when we read things. We imagine what it would be like if it were us. Where was I when I was seven years old and what was I doing?

But then when we read statistics, they're cold. I can read statistics all day long and I'm not necessarily tying them to one person, but if I can tie an idea to one person, who I can relate to, who I have a commonality with, then suddenly it's like I've made a friend. We can talk about any kind of experience, but if you have a friend with that experience, you're more connected to them, because you have different commonalities and you realize how close it is. Where settler Canadians I think don't relate to the residential school question is because they don't have a medium. They don't have something similar—unless they read a story about it that they connect to emotionally.

Is it Maya Angelou who was saying how you forget what people say, you forget what people do, but you'll never forget how people make you feel? We carry memory with us in so many different parts of our body, and most of it is kept through feeling. We remember things about feeling. We remember the book we read based on how it made us feel. We remember the poem or the song. We know those songs so intimately. That's what art does. Art is there to make you feel emotion. Art is there to make you understand emotion in some way that you might not have understood before. Poetry does that, because it's trying to paint a picture using different words than you would normally use to describe it, and therefore you see it in a different way.

That's what stories do, too. We need that empathy. That's what I think is lacking, and that's where settlers might hold on to their prejudices, because they don't have a way to develop empathy. They've never been taught to be empathetic toward Indigenous people, and so they don't understand.

I know through working with a school division here, recently they passed an Aboriginal education policy where it was mandated: they needed to have more Indigenous education in every single grade level. Every single core subject had to have an Indigenous component. Then you had all these teachers who had been around for about ten years and have absolutely no training in Indigenous education. They're teachers: teachers are tired; teachers are overworked. They're suddenly told they have to do something, but they have no inroads because it's something they've probably always avoided throughout their career, because they've had no means. So then they get resentful, because they don't feel trained, because they don't feel supported, because they don't understand how to connect with this work.

I think you have to get the teachers on side with how they can connect. What really caused them to feel that moment of empathy? What do they relate to—whether it's a child in residential school, lack of clean drinking water, poverty—whatever issue it is, you have to go to it through empathy. Otherwise you don't care and you're just going to be throwing out statistics to your classroom. They might have all the facts right, but they still don't have a connection to the experience. They still haven't changed anything, and they still don't see how it relates to them. Empathy allows you to understand how it's related to you, whether it's because we're all human, or whether it's because we live in this place called Canada—whatever connection we have.

AH: It's not just about them having access to resources or information—because there's information out there and there are more and more resources—but a matter of building that relationship to the experience and to the facts. But, more than that, it's about having a connection to people's stories and people's histories. And the community piece, having a sense of what it means to connect with community. I mean that in a couple of ways, like communities of support among educators, but around Indigenous communities, too. What it actually means to get to know the groups around you and the place that you're teaching in.

KV: Yes. And knowing those Indigenous students, and trying to understand what their perspective is, as much as you can. Because as much as we want to empathize with everybody, we can't fully understand everyone else's experience. We have to always strive to empathize with one another. That's humanity. You want to do it for those Indigenous students. You want to figure out ways to empower them.

My partner works in a high school where 52 per cent of the students are newcomers. There's a small component of Indigenous students. There's a small component of European students. The Indigenous students are consistently doing less well. They're less successful than their counterparts. His job is to empower them. His job is to figure out why they're not connecting, what they're not connecting to, and help them succeed. That is incredibly important. Part of this work is what I call "ambassador work," because we're still trying to share this experience of what it means to be Indigenous with other people. The non-Indigenous students have to understand what happened here.

I think a lack of understanding of our history is not helping anyone. I think settler Canadians need to understand it. I think newcomers definitely need to understand it, because they're walking into the history of this place. We're not serving anyone by pretending it didn't happen. We pretend it didn't happen, and then we don't understand why certain social situations are the way they are.

AH: Do you think about creating social change explicitly? Do you think about responsibility or community connections?

KV: I remember in the process of writing my poetry book—and writing a poetry book is very different than writing poetry; you can write poetry and it's just one-offs—that at some point my editor told me I had to decide where the activism paused and the poetry started. What I write about is socially charged. It's culturally charged. I don't know why, other than that's just part of the experience that I live.

There was one writer who said that just to be born Indigenous in this country is a political act. Indigenous people were not supposed to be here in 2015. They were supposed to be eradicated. They were supposed to be assimilated. So just to have any sort of cultural pride, cultural experience, in and of itself is a political act.

That's something that I've really taken with me, and it comes through in my writing. There is a lot of social awareness, and maybe it aspires to be activism in the work, but there's also poetry there. There's also writing there. When you get down to writing a story, you can't write about a big social issue. You have to write a story. It can include parts, or examples, but you have to write a story. You have to write about people. You have to write about people having a human experience. When I write stories, I write primarily about Indigenous women, Métis women, who are inner-city residents, who have all of these things that are familiar to me, that might not be familiar to other people. You can look at it, as a critic and as an academic—you can look at it like, "Oh, this is representative of this and, oh, this is representative of that"—but as a writer my only activity and my only job is to write a story.

I have to really let that social part go when I write a story. I have to just trust that it's going to come in there. I don't put that in there. I can't write a novel and start it with, "There are thirteen hundred murdered and missing women in this country, and no one seems to … " I can rant about that all I want (and I do), but when I write a story, it has to be a story. I can include those parts if I choose to, if my character is going through those experiences, but I can't be didactic with it. I can't be preachy with it. That's not the job of a story. Again, if empathy is the goal, then people are only going to be empathetic if you're telling the story about a person with a problem, and they have a situation, and they try to solve it, and then they go through this character development—that's a story. That's the only thing it's supposed to do.

I think we're still at the point where having those characters—just the fact that they are Indigenous—that's still revolutionary. We're still having a humungous lack of characters of any colour other than Caucasian anywhere—in our movies, in our theatres. We're still searching for these voices. We're still trying to be representative of the society that we live in, which is still predominantly portrayed as so Western, and so European, and so Caucasian. We're still having to do that part of the work. So just by being Indigenous, my characters are political, even if I'm telling a mundane story.

I remember I was workshopping a story one time, and it involved these two characters. One of them had a husband who was cheating on her and he left, and she was just ranting with her girlfriend about it. It was a funny story. The writer who was leading the workshop was non-Indigenous, and he said, "It really surprised me, and I didn't figure out until three pages in, that this person was really Indigenous." Because I didn't come out and identify their culture. But it was very clear to me, hearing those voices, and very clear to my friends, hearing those voices. I used a lot of references like, "Oh, he went back home" and "he's living on the rez." But because I didn't say, "So-and-so, an Indigenous woman" when I started, everyone assumed that these characters were white. If you don't put those disclaimers on them, people assume they're white. We do this, too, because we're so trained to write, to read with this white lens. All the characters who are non-Caucasian have some sort of identifier, and all the characters who are Caucasian don't have the identifier. It's amazing.

I'd never noticed that before. I was just writing a story about two people, and they were ranting, and it wasn't cultural at all. Well, it was cultural in the way it was: it was women, ranting women. It was representative more of that culture. But it was striking to me how people make that assumption of whiteness all the time. That completely non-political story (though it really was political, because it was incredibly feminist) was political. I think you have to own it a little bit, because that ambassador role comes at you really automatically and very naturally. You have to own it and take pride in it, and try to be as responsible with it as possible.

AH: If you think about that ambassador role, and the representation, and the story work that literature does, where would you like to see it go? If all of this stuff is powerful and successful, and if it goes forward in a good way, what would you see as the ideal? If you could make your writing do one amazing thing, what would you have it be?

KV: One amazing thing? My only job is to tell my story. And if anyone can relate to that, like one person, then that's all I can do. That's all I can do. And you hope for more than one person to read it, but it's poetry in Canada, so you're really lucking out if there's more than one person reading it.

What I find amazing is when people tell me that they look at something in a new way through something that I wrote. I think that's amazing. I think that's magic. I think it's amazing that I can do that, because I know other people do that to me all the time. Richard Van Camp is a beautiful example of looking at something in a completely different way. Warren Cariou writes some amazingly politically charged poems that I did not expect from him at all. But that's what you do, and that's what writing's supposed to do. So anytime that happens, it's wonderful.

I don't feel comfortable being a representative of anything beyond myself. But you are. You are. I identify myself as a Métis person. I am a representative of the Métis Nation no matter what. I'm a person. I'm a mom. I'm a Winnipegger. I'm a woman. You end up being a representative of who you are all the time, and you want to be as good an example as possible, because that's your job. I'm not necessarily comfortable speaking for other people, because everyone has different opinions, but I'm also recognizing that people are thinking those things when I am talking. I end up being this representative.

So that's when I always go back to the idea that this is my story. I was talking to you before about how I'm obsessed with the idea of permission. I'm obsessed with the idea of what we're allowed to say and whose stories we're allowed to share. We don't talk about this enough in Canadian literature, and in mainstream art culture in general, where cultural appropriation abounds. This idea that as writers we can tell absolutely any story we want, from any perspective, is wrong. I feel bad saying that, but it is wrong.

I just finished my MFA at UBC last year, and nowhere in any of those classes did we talk about cultural appropriation and the idea of what stories we can represent authentically. I saw many people who were writing from outside of their cultural base, outside of their gender, outside of their place. I had one classmate who wanted to write something from a city they had never even visited. As much as we're artists and we can do whatever the heck we want, I think there's also a responsibility of being able to write something with permission. If you're writing from a culture that's not your own, or from a people that's not your own, you need to get permission. You need to make sure that you're including the community in doing that.

We are long past the time where non-Indigenous people need to tell Indigenous stories. I don't think we ever had that time, but for some reason people got really obsessed for a really long time about telling Indigenous stories, either from an archaeology perspective, or an anthropology perspective, or ethno-whatever. We don't need to do that. At this point it's become a very politically charged idea for a non-Indigenous person to tell an Indigenous story, because there is an Indigenous person who can tell that story better. I think we have to be really careful to make sure that we tell our own stories.

I recently made a children's story series based on the Seven Teachings of the Anishinaabe people. I'm not Anishinaabe. It was something that I taught as an early childhood educator; I was teaching the Seven Teachings. So, when I went in and wrote those stories, I wrote them as a Métis person, as a storyteller, speaking to children in a very universal way. I didn't bring up the tradition, and during every step of that process I engaged my friends and my co-workers and my Elders to make sure that I was doing this the way I was supposed to.

I'm still very conscious of that idea. We can only tell the stories that we can tell. We can't tell someone else's stories. We have to be very careful whose stories we are telling. People have talked about this recently with the things that are happening in the US, and also the things that are happening through the TRC *Final Report*, and the murdered and missing women. A lot of non-Indigenous people, and non-African-American people in the States, are talking about their response, but we have to be careful that those people are not taking up space that might otherwise be shared with someone else. There's been a big history of people talking over other people.

I think this is something that is incredibly timely in Indigenous literature, because we have so many powerful voices coming up. I'm very reluctant anytime a non-Indigenous person is telling an Indigenous story, because I know a dozen Indigenous people who can tell that story. So why aren't they telling it? And why aren't we letting them tell that? Saving that space for them?

AH: Thinking about the experiences you have, and the work that you do, and the investments that you have, and based on where you're speaking from, why do you think Indigenous literatures matter? Do you think they matter?

KV: Do they matter? Yes, they do. I think they do, because as much as some experiences are universal, no one can tell that story like the person who lived it. I think that those are incredibly valuable. It is important, not only to validate the voices of those who have had those experiences—and not only because if we don't listen to them we'll lose them. In many cases our Elders are now speaking and sharing these stories, and there's an immediacy to having them share their stories, because otherwise they'll be lost. Indigenous literature provides the space for that to happen. There are so many open spaces for Indigenous literature. And when I say Indigenous literature, I think about the literature made by Indigenous people, whether those stories feel Indigenous or not.

I think that that Indigenous perspective is one that is lacking in the world, and I think that we're just hitting our stride. Those voices are still absent in so many places. I think we're still working at getting to that point of representation, which I think is incredibly important for everyone. I think our literatures need to reflect our population and our society. In Canada, we still have a literature where it's still 70 per cent white male and 50 per cent of those white males are white men over fifty. I'm not invalidating their ability to tell a story or to share their perspective, but I feel like we've heard those stories. We need to hear other stories. The stories that I'm interested in reading—and the stories that I know students who I work with are interested in reading, and people who I work with are interested in reading—are the ones that haven't been told yet. There are so many stories that haven't been told. There are so many people who are just coming into their power to tell stories.

I'm so interested in what our young people are talking about, because young people coming up behind me—I think it's Indigenous people fifteen to twenty-four—are the fastest-growing demographic in this country. There's a huge number of people who have a completely new perspective, and completely fresh ideas, and fresh ways of looking at things, more than any of us do. I really think that that's what we're doing: we're making space for them. I think there's so much that we can learn from them. Just as there's so much we've learned from the people who have come before us, we learn from the people who come after us. And I think we're just starting. We're just starting to understand this idea of hearing other people's stories.

I remember when I was a kid growing up—this is my last story—my dad loved John Wayne. He loved John Wayne movies. I remember movies like *Dances with Wolves* and *The Last of the Mohicans* were really big in our house, just because they had Indians in them. Just the sheer presence of Indians. Even if they were the bad guys. Even if they were completely unintelligible, it was a big deal in my house. And that's kind of sad, thinking about it, that those were my role models.

I just think it's amazing. Now my girls have grown up with my life and all these role models and a completely different perspective. My dad's always been fiercely prideful of our culture, and I'm very lucky and fortunate to have had that my entire life. But I still had this other world that showed me a very different side of it. And my girls are just further down that line of knowing.

They come in and they have a completely different perspective. They have never seen a John Wayne movie, that I know of. So, it's something different. I'm really curious as to the things they're going to come up with. And then their children, and then their children. We're all along a line, but we're really just getting started.

"IT COMES BACK TO RELATIONSHIP"
A Conversation with Warren Cariou

WARREN CARIOU WAS BORN into a family of Métis and European ancestry in Meadow Lake, Saskatchewan. His memoir *Lake of the Prairies* is a rich narrative sharing his personal stories of growing up in Meadow Lake and developing his identity in relation to the communities around him. He also shares some of these experiences in our conversation here. Although he moved away from Meadow Lake for his education and career, Cariou has strong roots in that place. It continually shapes his creative and scholarly work, for instance through the cultural and environmental topics that he considers in writing, films, and research. One of these is his interest in petroleum culture: communities around Meadow Lake have been affected by industrial development because of the nearby bitumen sources, and his explorations of those impacts show up in his writing, filmmaking, and photography work. He has developed a technique for creating petrographs—photographs actually made using bitumen scooped from the Athabasca River near his home—and uses them to portray strip mines, tailings ponds, and other symptoms of petroleum operations as they appear on the land. This painstaking process speaks to Cariou's meticulous and responsive approaches to his work and his ongoing commitments to land, community, creativity, and storytelling.

While Cariou has held a range of occupations over the years, from construction labourer to political advisor, his educational journey has led him to an academic role. During his studies, he moved from the University of Saskatchewan, where he earned an honours BA, to the University of Toronto, where he earned his MA and PhD in English. Cariou has now been a professor in the Department of English, Theatre, Film, and Media at the University of Manitoba for more than fifteen years. In 2008 he took some time for research at Arizona State University after he was awarded a Fulbright Visiting Research Chair. He held a Canada Research Chair in Narrative, Community, and Indigenous Cultures for ten years at the University of Manitoba, and is presently director of that school's Centre for Creative Writing and Oral Culture (CCWOC). The CCWOC makes space for research on oral cultures and is a site for creative and scholarly work on stories, hosting resources, events, and community connections. Cariou has worked with several of Canada's most accomplished Indigenous storytellers to promote cultural sovereignty through the performance of traditional narratives. In his faculty position, Cariou teaches courses in English, particularly in Indigenous literatures. He is recognized throughout the Indigenous literary arts community for his attentive work and prodigious creativity; for instance, he was elected president of the Indigenous Literary Studies Association for the year of its inaugural community gathering in 2015. As a scholar, Cariou carries out and publishes research on Indigenous literatures and storytelling, Métis culture, and the cultural politics of petroleum development.

Cariou's first creative book was *The Exalted Company of Roadside Martyrs* (1999), a pair of novellas. His memoir *Lake of the Prairies: A Story of Belonging* (2003) followed a few years later. That book has been awarded the Drainie-Taylor Prize for Biography and a spot on the shortlist for the Charles Taylor Prize. Cariou has also published short stories in various collections, including *Stag Line: Stories by Men* (1995) and *Due West: 30 Great Stories from Alberta, Saskatchewan, and Manitoba* (1998). As a filmmaker, he has collaborated on two film projects about the petroleum industry and its impact on Indigenous communities and the land: *Overburden* and *Land of Oil and Water* (both 2009).

Alongside his own creative practice, Cariou works persistently to bring other authors' writing to light through his editorial work. He edited a collection of Indigenous writing called *W'daub Awae: Speaking True* (2010) and co-edited a volume of Indigenous writing from Manitoba called *Manitowapow: Aboriginal Writings from the Land of Water* (2011). This latter volume garnered a great deal of public attention: for instance, it won the On the Same Page contest in 2013, in which it was voted the book all Manitobans should read that year, and it was included in CBC's Great Canadian Reading List: 150 Books to Read for Canada 150. Cariou serves as the general editor of the *First Voices, First Texts* series, which brings forward Indigenous works deserving of greater attention and republishes them in new, critical editions. For twelve years he was the fiction editor for the Canadian literary magazine *Prairie Fire*, and he has co-edited (with Katherena Vermette) two special issues of that journal featuring Indigenous writing. Cariou has also supported the literary community by serving on prize juries for literary awards, including the Giller Prize.

Warren Cariou and I met on July 11, 2015, at his home in Winnipeg. It was a beautiful, sunny Manitoba afternoon, and our conversation stretched out at a leisurely Saturday pace as we sipped tea on his front porch. In sharing his background and his personal journey into the literary world, Cariou focuses on his home in Meadow Lake, his family, and the stories that surrounded him growing up. He offers a careful consideration of his own Métis ancestry and of the relationships that shape his understandings of community. Cariou's narratives here add depth and complexity to the notion that Indigenous writers are held up as representatives of their communities: he highlights the responsibility that this dynamic entails for writers and publishers, but also challenges any overly simplistic conflations of ancestry, identity, and community. Instead, he asks good questions about how community connections might be enacted.

With his creative and professional focus on storytelling, Cariou shares his perspectives on the particular significance of oral stories and storytelling performance. He interrogates the valorization of written literature, and especially of the book as a commodity, over oral forms that offer more immediate, relational ways of sharing stories. He also dialogues with the converse side of this argument, recognizing that print books offer a form of validation to Indigenous communities, in that the book, as a valued object, demonstrates for people that Indigenous stories are valuable. With his descriptions of literary events across Manitoba and beyond, Cariou offers a glimpse into community engagement with Indigenous literary arts that conveys a sense of momentum and significance in the present. Speaking also as an educator, he makes a connection between the growing popularity of Indigenous writing among mainstream audiences in Canada and Canadians' desire to learn about Indigenous histories and perspectives. Pedagogically, Cariou pinpoints how stories have the capacity to foster empathy and to help listeners connect with the narratives they are hearing, thereby opening up an opportunity for deeper learning than can be enabled by mere facts and figures. As we were speaking soon after the release of the TRC's *Final Report*, Cariou characterizes the rawness of that moment in Canada, suggesting also that it has revealed an openness to learning. Through his reflections on the power of stories to reach people, Cariou shares his careful optimism that such learning might help people move toward some kind of response to Canada's difficult histories.

OUR CONVERSATION

Warren Cariou (WC): I come from a community called Meadow Lake in northern Saskatchewan, which is a community with a troubled history in some ways. It's a place where the difficulties of the colonial relationship are very visible. They were very visible when I was growing up, and probably in the fifty years before I was born. There are a lot of First Nations people there (ten First Nations in the general area), a lot of Métis people, and a fair number of European settlers as well.

My family was right in the middle of those communities, though I didn't fully understand that when I was growing up. My dad was Métis and his mom, my grandma, spoke Cree and sold Avon on the reserve and things like that, but somehow I didn't really figure out what that meant. I write about this in my book *Lake of the Prairies*, growing up in this family. My dad had fifteen siblings, so a gigantic family, and incredibly talkative, argumentative. Now I know—they're Métis. When I go to other gatherings of Métis people, this is exactly what they're like: very boisterous, love to dance, love to have fun, and storytellers. My dad was an amazing storyteller. A number of his siblings, my aunts and uncles, also were. I grew up in this milieu of storytelling and of being larger than life. On my mom's side of the family, my grandma is of Norwegian ancestry and my grandpa was of German ancestry. Their family was close to us as well. They're very different. They were very silent, Lutheran, hard workers. They had their times when they would have fun as well, but it was not quite the same. So, I grew up between those two poles of very different communities.

It was really only as an adult that I came to understand what it meant that my dad actually was Métis. Looking back, I can see that he had given hints, but he had never gone out and said it until quite late in his life. My own position in the community, or my own idea of myself in the community, was revised when I learned that. Growing up thinking I was a white kid basically, given that the community was so racially divided—and there was a lot of tension between the Native people and the white people—we just thought that was the divide. In fact, it's much more complicated than that. My adulthood basically has been trying to reclaim that part of my identity and understand my connection to Métis communities. Also, being sure that I'm not forgetting the other side of my identity. I think part of Métis identity is that it's always a negotiation. Maybe for some Métis people it's not, but for many it is. Riel says we want to honour our fathers and our mothers, not just one side or the other. So that's been something that I've been working through and trying to understand in my writing.

A lot of work I have done is about Meadow Lake, about the tensions there, and also some of the improvements that have happened over the years, now that we recognize that so many of the people we thought were white people in Meadow Lake are actually Métis. It's not that they were necessarily passing, but they were not advertising their Métis identity either. But now there's a pride there that was not there when I was growing up. That's been a really good thing. And now that First Nations in the community are one of the major employers in the area. They collectively own the saw mill. Things have changed so dramatically in the economy of the area. I think it is a place where kids can be proud of who they are now—who are Aboriginal or who have Métis ancestry. That was not the case when I was growing up. There are still lots of problems, tensions, hierarchies, and economic disadvantage, but things are definitely getting better.

Anyway, that's where I'm from, and a lot of my writing is about the area. Especially now in the last ten or fifteen years, when oil development has really moved in. That's sparked a lot of my work on petroleum. Even more broadly now, my work is on energy and Indigeneity, and on the fractured relationships between those two communities. Or the ways in which energy development imposes certain—usually negative—structures and experiences upon Indigenous people. In my current work, I have that strand, which is a lot of work I'm doing, on Indigeneity and oil and energy. The other strand is on oral culture, storytelling, and relates to my work at the Centre for Creative Writing and Oral Culture.

Aubrey Hanson (AH): What brought you to writing? I think a lot about being Métis and what it means to inhabit that Métis-ness and to take it up in a responsible way, so I know that that's what I'm going to pick up on, but I want to ask you if that's what you're saying. What would you say brought you to writing?

WC: Right from the very beginnings of my earliest memories, there is storytelling in my family. There's a picture of me, which I actually have in *Lake of the Prairies*, where I'm sitting on a child's potty [*laughs*], and I'm writing, and I have these big glasses on. I'm writing. I clearly can't write yet; it's when I was, like, two years old. I had this idea that I was going to record the things around me. I have very strong memories of having those old Hilroy writing tablets. My dad would tell a story and I would write it down, but I couldn't write. I was just writing curlicues. For me, it always comes from storytelling. My desire to be a writer, in the community I grew up in, was outlandish, but it was always because I wanted to write down the stories. Maybe partly because of my mom's side of the family and their shyness; I have that as well. All these amazing larger-than-life aunts and uncles and my dad—I felt like

I couldn't quite do that, but I could write it down. I could at least partake in this other way. That's where it really all starts, and for me it always comes back to that.

The storytelling informs the writing that I do, and then that's also why I ended up working in film. It's a desire to create a story out of other people's stories. In *Land of Oil and Water*, it's mostly not my voice; it's the voices of these wonderful, amazing people we interviewed, and the film is just putting those together into a larger narrative. I really like that. A lot of the work I do at the Centre for Creative Writing and Oral Culture is working with story-tellers to help them create a recorded version of their work, if they want to. Learning about the stories definitely influences my writing.

From early on, I wanted to be a writer, even when that didn't seem to be a realistic option. When I was sixteen, I went to this writing workshop, or school, in southern Saskatchewan, which at the time was very unusual. Saskatchewan was only the second place in Canada, as far as I know, to do that (Banff being the first). I went there at age sixteen and I met Jack Hodgins, and David Carpenter, and some other writers, and that really reinforced my desire to do that. I think if I hadn't grown up in Saskatchewan and had that opportunity, I may not have taken that step to write. I was really wanting to be a writer, more than I was wanting to be a professor. The professor part just sort of came. It wasn't that I was resistant to it, but it just worked out that way. I never had a dream to be that [*laughs*].

Within my academic work, the creative writing element or the storytell-ing element is very often present as well. Academic writing that I do tends to not be straightforward academic prose. The storytelling thing gets in there somehow. It's worked fine, and I'd rather do it that way. If I had to shoehorn it into a different discourse, I guess I would, but I feel like it can work without having to do that.

AH: Along the way, did your formal schooling encourage you?

WC: I had a couple of English teachers in high school who were pretty supportive. Looking back now, one was Mrs. James, who was my grade 12 English teacher. She encouraged us to think big, to dream big. She had moved to Meadow Lake from England and so she knew about the wider world. She loved the rural area where we were, but she wanted us to think about other things beyond the borders of Meadow Lake. That was a real inspiration for me. I remember when I first started writing. I had done cre-ative writing assignments sometimes in class, and she was very helpful, but, also, she wouldn't just say, "You're doing well"; she would challenge us. She would say, "Okay, this is good, but I expect that you can do better."

I feel that sometimes our Aboriginal writers now lack that. People are just so happy, like, "Here's an Aboriginal kid who's written something. Let's congratulate them." I actually feel that that's patronizing, and it's not that good for the person if they think they're already at a good level when they're not necessarily there. Even some published writers are at that point where they could go to another level, but they're already getting accolades for what they're doing. In my work as an editor, I work with some Aboriginal writers who are already really good, and still they try to raise that bar. It's great to have a receptive audience, but if the audience is being receptive just because they think, "Oh, isn't it good that a Native person wrote this," that's very patronizing.

AH: It's exciting that there's all this growth in Indigenous literary arts. There's a lot of momentum. I don't spend as much time around writing and publishing, but it feels like there's space for people to speak up and to share their stories. And you want it to be good. You don't just want it to be there.

WC: Exactly. We just came from a workshop in Saskatoon on Indigenous editing, with Greg Scofield, Greg Younging, and Deanna Reder.[7] Working with these very accomplished editors (who were not really the students; they were equal participants in the workshop), that was something we were thinking about. There's a real demand now among publishers for Indigenous stories, and that's great, but a lot of times the publishers don't understand what they're actually looking for. They just think, "This is hot." It's different, and sometimes they don't understand that. We had really interesting discussions about that.

It's so interesting to see that Aboriginal writing has reached a point where it really is one of the hottest areas within Canadian literature. When I started my PhD—that was in 1993—I had a vague idea that I would like to do it on Aboriginal writing. That was at University of Toronto, and I was told, "That's not a field. Don't do that" [*laughs*]. In a sense, that actually was true at the time. Now, it's gotten to this stage in Canadian literature where Canadian literature scholars can't do that work without having a fairly good understanding of Indigenous literatures. It's a pretty significant part of Canadian literature now. Things have changed a lot for the positive, and a lot of voices are being heard now, which is fantastic. I think we still need to have those standards be high—and also to be sure that the reasons that these writers are being published and promoted are good ones.

AH: Do you think about community when you think about why we need to have high standards?

WC: Community is a nebulous concept. Often that takes the form of family or takes the form of particular individuals that you have a relationship with. I think that's something that non-Indigenous writers or scholars don't necessarily think about in their work. They may, but I think it's much more common for Indigenous writers and scholars to be thinking about. "How does my work represent my community in the larger world?" for one thing. Also, "What will my community think about this? And am I being ethical in my representations?" Again, I think this is something that non-Indigenous publishers don't really think much about. They say, "Okay, if we just follow the general rules of publishing, that's fine." But what happens is, if something is inaccurate, or something really shouldn't be brought into the public domain, and it's published, the person who is going to get flak from that is the Indigenous person who's involved in it. It may not be a legal issue, but it will be another kind of issue, a much more important one.

The notion of who you're writing for is an interesting one. By "writing for" I don't just mean your audience, but what community you're representing. As an Indigenous writer, or Indigenous scholar, I think your work does always represent more than your own perspective, whether you want it that way or not. I think for most artists and scholars in that position, it's not like they wouldn't want to be associated with their community; that is who they are. I think that developing and fostering that relationship is part of their work, usually.

AH: How do you articulate that, for yourself?

WC: That's complicated. I think in the case of Métis people, very often it's complicated—just the definitions of what is Métis, and how do you connect to the community. For me, not really understanding or identifying myself as Métis when I was growing up, that's still an ongoing negotiation. Maybe it will always be. I've been really welcomed by people in various Métis communities. I don't think there is one singular Métis community. I've been encouraged to explore the complexities of my perspective on Métis identity. I've felt blessed by that. Some of the Elders who have spoken to me and have gone out of their way to help me and to give me advice, they've been really important for me.

I think it's a little different when you see a writer who comes from a very specific community, especially if it's smaller—maybe because it's a reserve or something like that. They speak for that community, in a sense, whether they want to or not. Maybe there are problems with being seen from the outside to be speaking for your people in a tokenistic sort of way. I think with Métis it's a little different, because there is such a broad panoply of different Métis communities.

For me, now, it's more about specific relationships with specific people and with my family, although my family is also conflicted about it. I don't think there is anyone outright saying, "No, we're not Métis," but there are people who think, "Who cares? Doesn't make any difference to me." And others who feel it does make a difference. I don't want to say that either is right or wrong. I think people's ideas of themselves are very fluid, actually, and very subject to revision.

AH: Just to reciprocate a little with your sharing, I feel I have a lot in common with that position. I have Métis and German on my mom's side, and then on my dad's side we have mixed ancestry. I'm doing some digging this year into my grandma's side. Her stories are not the stories that get told. My dad's dad was Icelandic and that history is very strong—Gimli, Manitoba, all that Icelandic heritage got passed down in interesting ways. In my bigger family there are folks who are like, "We're part Native," or, "Absolutely, we're Métis, we're Red River Métis," and then there are folks who deny or erase it in various ways. It's a big spectrum. A lot of the family is not identifiable; nobody would look at us and say, "Oh, are you Native?" So, I identify with that complicated positioning and navigating.

Some of my mentors and teachers have shown me that it's not really about your own identity questions; it's about your responsibility questions. That makes me feel better. I can do my work. If it's good work, I should do it, and really who cares about my questions or insecurities? Do it well and do it accountably, and then the rest falls into place a bit more.

WC: That's true. It really is about how you are in relation to people, not who you are, per se. How you're relating to the community.

AH: Those questions mean a lot to me, and the ways I shape my work are often about stitching together some of those ruptures. It's a possible thing to do in writing and in academic work.

WC: I have thought about this and read about this for a few years now, maybe twenty years. I still haven't got a final easy definition of who I am, and I don't think I ever will. But I do feel like I have allegiances and connections, really close connections to particular people and particular family members, but also others who have given me the gift of showing me what my role could be, to help me with that. It comes back to relationship and how you act, rather than just who you are.

Or claim you are. There are still ongoing questions circulating—does that mean that Indigenous identity is purely performance based? We have the Andrea Smith controversy that's going on right now, and going right back to the Grey Owl controversy, et cetera, and various other hoaxes. That is still a question for me. I do think someone who knows that they are not Indigenous and pretends to be that—obviously there's a problem there. But, especially within Métis contexts, there was a lot of shame for a long time and a lot of people didn't want to talk about things. So, trying to come out from under that, there are a lot of people who are uncertain where they really come from.

AH: It's a fuzzy area—not just, "Well, you are or you aren't Indigenous."

WC: I think the general public, the non-Native public especially, just want to know: "Are you, or aren't you?" That goes right back to John A. Macdonald. That's what he wanted. In fact, the Métis—he was okay with Indians being Indians, and he was okay with the settlers being settlers, but Métis—that was not an option, as far as he was concerned. And he enforced that, with guns. People just want to know, and everyone wants to pin down everyone else, and never want to be pinned down themselves. I think that's very noticeable in the history of the Métis. But the amazing historical fact that the Métis continue to exist and are flourishing now is a pretty incredible thing in the face of all of that. There are so many people that say, "We are still here. We are not going to be erased by your need to draw a boundary." I find that fascinating and inspiring.

AH: Do you see a role for the literary arts in that flourishing?

WC: Absolutely. That's been crucial. You were asking me about models and mentors when I was growing up, and I told you about my teacher Mrs. James, who was from England. One of the other people, whom I didn't meet at the time, but whom I was very influenced by nonetheless, was Maria Campbell. Her nephew, Stan Morin, was in my class. I remember hearing about this book. He came to class, and he was all proud. He's like, "This is my aunt! She wrote this book! My auntie wrote this!" I was like, "No way! Really?"

I didn't meet Maria Campbell for years, but she was the first writer that I thought was a real person, who's still alive, and I'm connected to in some way through my friend. So, reading *Halfbreed*, even then—that was very early, and I didn't really grasp the depths of it—that was a big thing: for me to know that somebody, not only someone from near where I am, but someone who is Métis, who is Aboriginal, could write a book. And my friend was related to her—

AH: Which makes it all that much more real.

WC: Yeah. So that was a big inspiration. Obviously *Halfbreed* had a big impact on the national consciousness. She's very much attempting to say, "Look, we are here—we are still here." That is, in a sense, the message of the book, when addressed to non-Indigenous Canada. That had a huge impact.

A number of other texts in that seventies-and-earlier era, for flashes of time, would have a real impact and bring the national attention to the fact that Indigenous people hadn't disappeared as they were predicted to do. But at the same time, those writers also—as Maria Campbell did for me when I was a kid—provided a role model for others all across the country, who may not have written anything for another ten or fifteen or twenty years after that, but still, they provided that inspiration that led others to tell their stories.

I think writing has had an outsized impact, actually, on people's ability to understand or to picture the validity of their culture—partly for unfortunate reasons. Within our Western system of education, we're educated to think that a book is the ultimate form of an idea. When it becomes a book, then there is a sense of accomplishment and pride. It can be a commodity. It has a circulation in a capitalist system, but it's not just a commodity; it's a commodity that has an intellectual cachet to it. I'm conflicted about that, because a lot of the work I do on storytelling—I work with storytellers and learn from storytellers—some of them don't have books, and most of them are largely unknown. They don't get anywhere near the cultural attention that they should.

Our stories generally—traditional stories of Indigenous communities, but also everyday stories that are told—are almost invisible in a lot of contemporary culture, mass culture. I find it interesting that it's when those stories are turned into a commodity and placed into this system of literary value that they can be celebrated. Whereas the oral stories are not. I am disturbed by that, in a way. I think there is still a very strong colonial bias toward text. One of the reasons I'm so interested in stories as *performed* stories is because they are very resistant to commodification.

AH: That's one of the tensions we're always dancing with, doing anything in writing and working in English. We're walking hand in hand with the acknowledgement that every choice you make in print is not an oral conveyance and doesn't carry—people of course talk about putting oral into the written, but—I was going to ask you to say a bit more about why storytelling is important and what it carries. I think it needs to be said again.

WC: That's one of the major things that I'm trying to grapple with right now. I have written quite a few shorter pieces about orality in general and specific oral stories. I'm trying to figure out, what is the value of oral storytelling as oral storytelling? Not as an occasion for a text. Not as something to be recorded, even. Just that relationship that happens when a storyteller is telling a story, whether it's a traditional one or an everyday story.

For all our rhetoric about orality, I think—in the academic world, in the larger non-Indigenous community, and also for a lot of Aboriginal people as well—we have been colonized to think that it needs to be commodified to be valued. That it needs to be turned into a book or it needs to be recorded, to be "saved." That salvage anthropology thing goes on with storytelling. I do it, too, but I'm very conflicted about that. When you record it, you think you own it, but you don't. To me, the story actually doesn't exist in that thing anymore. There's a lot more to the story than just that individual telling that gets recorded, or than that commodity that circulates as a thing. To me, the story isn't really a thing, at least in that capitalist way. It's a gift. It's a spirit. It's something that permeates our being in a different way.

I'm trying to understand what place oral stories have in the contemporary world. So much of what I see is this real mania for recording them. Again, I understand that, because a lot of our storytellers are in their seventies and eighties. But it can't be just, "Record it, put it away, and you're done." If a story is just recorded and then archived somewhere, then it is dead. It's just a thing just like everything else in the capitalist world. If you take the time to actually learn it and remember it in your body and share it in some other way, where and when it's appropriate, with the protocols that are attached to it, then I think it has a different life.

That's not to say that there's a total separation between the two. Louis Bird, who I work with quite a bit, is a great example of this. He is an amazing storyteller, and he has an incredible memory for the stories. One time, he was here teaching a Cree stories course I was a part of. I introduced him to the class: I said, "Here's the text" [laughs]. They were freaked out, because we had no book. They would write down everything he said, to try to follow him. Eventually they realized, when you do that, you're not actually paying attention. We finally had them put the pencils down. We've lost our ability to remember in that way, or even to pay attention in that way. It's a very hard task. It's not easy. Louis himself, in his own career as a storyteller, began by recording his Elders. The recording machine that he had was so big at first, he says, that he couldn't move it around. He had to bring the Elders to where he was. He recorded many stories, but he didn't just put those away. He didn't just write them down and say, "Okay, I'm done." That's just the very beginning. He then learned them, either by listening to the recordings, or by going back to the Elders and hearing them again and again, until now they are part of him. There are so few people who have done that. Probably he would say that the recording was crucial, because he could then remember, and he'd go back to the stories again and again. But he needed to actually make them part of who he is, not just make a commodity, separate himself, and go on to do something else. That's something that I think is really missing in our world.

There's this sense of the story as a fragile thing, and orality as a fragile thing. We can see the state trying to interrupt Indigenous cultures by recognizing orality as having a certain weakness. Basil Johnston talks about one generation from extinction.[8] If you can just stop the transmission of all that cultural information from one generation to another, they're done. A particular Indigenous community and their culture is disappeared. It becomes a museum piece. It's not alive.

I think orality is stronger, though, than that might make us believe. I'm still struck sometimes—I listened to that story, I can't fully remember it. What's happened? Where's the story gone? This idea of always thinking about stories in relation to loss is a problem, because stories are about plenitude, and about relationships that are personal and present.

AH: I've been thinking a lot about relationships. There's this proliferation of knowledge and things can just be posted out there into the world and everyone can access it. But, if you don't have a way in, or a relationship to it, and motivation, and an ethical sense ... For instance, if you hear a story in the room with someone, you have a shared experience. There's tea and bannock, or whatever, and that story is being told for a reason that fits with your life experiences at the time, and there's a place, and there's a whole thing that happens around that. The stories I've experienced are mostly kitchen table stories from women in my family. They're about what somebody's going through at a particular time, and the thing that you hear out of that story is something you need to hear then, and then later, too, the layers come and you remember. It keeps teaching you throughout your life. That teaching might just be the simplest thing about how to navigate a friendship or whatever it might be. Those resonances, I think that if you actually hear those, it's because of that relationship. All of those complex factors that made the story what it was then.

Then contrast that with how you can find anything on the Internet. Maybe, sure, there's still a need to find something. But when I bring it back to teaching, there's this pressure or impetus put on teachers now, that there needs to be learning about Indigenous Peoples and histories and contexts. It's a positive thing, but teachers are being asked to do this work, and some of them have context and experience and some of them don't. Some of them feel really uncomfortable with that. Like, "Well, I'm not trained. It's not my history," and all that. It's a difficult thing to overcome.

In some ways, that piece around having a relationship with the person, and the knowledge, and being in a particular place together, is more—I'm at the very beginning of thinking about this. People come to me, and say, "Oh, you do education and Indigenous literatures? Awesome! Can you give me your resources?" Basically, they are asking me, "How do I teach this? What can you give me?" And I'm starting to ask myself what I should be providing.

Before, I was like, "Oh, here are these books, and here's a list of authors," et cetera. Now, I think actually what people need is that way of thinking about those relationships instead—instead of, "Here's a list of information." The information is already out there. If you just google "Indigenous literatures for kids," there's tons. Some of those questions about relationship I've learned from learning a little bit more about storytelling.

What you've said really speaks to some of the questions I've been thinking about in that way. How you make all this magic happen in schools is something I really care about. How do I support teachers in teaching Indigenous literatures well? It's not easy.

WC: That's for sure. One of the things that would be ideal—and I realize there will be practical limitations in terms of funding and things like that, but—something that I do in my university classes is I'm able to access enough funding to bring a storyteller or two into my class. It's not just playing a recording of a storyteller. That's good if you can't bring a person in, but it's really not the same thing at all. Within the school system, hopefully there's still some openness to that.

One of the factors in the devaluing of storytelling is that sometimes it's thought, "Oh, that's for kids," which is really unfortunate in the adult world. These stories are not simple. Often elements of them are meant for kids, but then there are all kinds of layers. Louis Bird says there are five ages that he tells stories for. I think there may be some possibility within the school system for making that a part of the learning process around Indigenous literatures. It doesn't necessarily have to come first, but it could.

Often in my Indigenous literature courses, I'll try to have a storyteller come in within the first week or two. That—rather than what tended to happen, and probably still does happen quite a lot in Indigenous literature classes at university—is to just start off with a couple things on the oral tradition. You have a few written texts on the oral tradition saying okay, "That's what it used to be, and here's what we do now." But actually, these stories are still being told. It happens a lot in other representations of Indigenous cultures, that the old ways are fetishized, but also that they're gone. That's just not at all true. So something about the contemporaneity of Indigenous oral cultures, trying to foster that, would be ideal.

It may not always be possible to have a storyteller come into the class, but at least if you have a video—there are many wonderful resources online of great storytellers who have posted their own stories. You can have a video or two that the students can interact with. Since some students are digitally savvy, they can follow that up and do some more learning that way. That's one thing that digital technologies have been enabling: thinking more about performance as something that is shareable in a broader way than it used to be.

Very often Indigenous literatures are attempting to apply techniques from oral storytelling and to mimic some of the things that storytelling can do. That can be transformative for readers. Thomas King is one of the writers who comes to mind. He's writing this high postmodern kind of writing—it's very complicated, sophisticated, very aesthetic work that he's doing—yet it is also in this conversational idiom. That's very interesting for readers who are not familiar with Indigenous cultures. This can be really complicated yet seem extremely simple at first—which is what stories at their best always are.

We've also seen it in in academic culture: we've seen a move away from high theory. When I was in grad school, we had to have impenetrable prose to be taken seriously, and now that's really been cast aside. We realize it's much more difficult as a writer to write in a simple way and still get your complex ideas in there. That's much better, because a lot more people can benefit from it.

AH: If you can't actually explain it without drawing on particular discursive patterns or terminology, then do you really know what you're saying? [*Laughs*]

WC: Or is it just this exercise in self-aggrandizement? We're moving more toward thinking that the apparent simplicity of an oral story can hold all the complexity that any kind of discourse can hold. That is also great in terms of Indigenous literatures in the classroom, for younger readers as well, because there isn't that barrier, necessarily, that high levels of diction are going to pose for the kids. And yet the work can be as complex as any. It brings a better awareness of the multiple levels of meaning that language can hold. Something can seem really straightforward, but then when you step back and think about it, it's not at all—which is a powerful thing for young people to learn.

AH: For me that mirrors with questions on all of the social issues and histories that young people need to learn. I'm thinking about the role of stories and literature in supporting that work, but also in calling for that truth.

WC: Shirley Sterling's *My Name is Seepeetza* is an amazing book in its simplicity, and yet it contains so much. There are many other examples, but there's a book that has been taught in classrooms a lot, and should be. It is getting at our very difficult history, but it is doing it in a way that is opening the discussion. I think that the standard historical, chronological timeline approach doesn't really give people an opening to understand the personal impact. Statistics and all that are important, but stories make it so much more personal.

That question of issues and how we teach all of the horrible things that have happened here in the history of the colonial project—to me, the stories are a really good way of doing that. One thing is that they make it more personal, which can make it more traumatizing. That has to be kept in mind, especially for students who may be affected by this in different ways. Literature is very good for imagining oneself into a situation. More standard, straightforward history is not necessarily so good at that.

AH: I've seen a lot of high school English teaching where English is this space where we read these really dark texts, and there are traumatizing experiences. We put teenagers through this stuff repeatedly. Meanwhile, in social studies, they're learning about imperialism and then the slave trade and so on. They're being given all of this emotional stuff and are not really supported in working through it, depending on the teacher. It might just be, "What happened in chapter 10? What's the theme of this?" As opposed to, "This girl just went through this violent experience. How do we talk about that?" I hope that including more Indigenous content in schools will help people to think, "Hey, maybe we should be working on the emotional intelligence and the empathy and the respect for people's experiences instead of just leaving kids to deal with the difficult stuff we're teaching them." How do we create humane relationships and listen to each other's perspectives—and not just go away and feel bad about it after, but turn it into something beautiful in some way? We need to have a way of doing that.

WC: Absolutely. When I teach first year, in my class—which is not focused specifically on Indigenous literature—I like to have a unit on empathy. Again, one of the things literature is really good at is creating or fostering empathy. That makes a way for the students to think about things, not just in very technical terms: "Here's colonialism. We need to know about that. We need to know the apparatus of how that was deployed. We need to know the psychology of the colonial imagination and how what it's really all about is theft of land and resources and trying to ignore the existence of Indigenous people." I think if you see it in a specific way that a story can present to you, it can foster a kind of empathy that all the technical knowledge is never going to provide to you. That, to me, is a potential building ground for movement toward reconciliation. Maybe *reconciliation* is too grandiose a term, but movement toward some kind of working through.

I think what we tend to forget, when it comes to the level of curriculum where we're talking about slavery, or colonialism of the Americas, or imperialism, is that it it becomes too much about facts and figures. Of course, those are crucial to bolster the stories, to recognize the truth of what has happened, but it's such an emotional thing. That's what we need, and probably more so with young readers—to try and give them the opportunity and the tools to deal with this emotionally.

We see this in the public discourse as well: there are a lot of people who just don't want to think about it—about what's happened and how they're complicit, even complicit at a distant remove. They're benefiting even if they weren't active in some way. All the comments that happen underneath the news stories—I don't really let myself read those anymore—usually that is a knee-jerk reaction. I think there's a psychology of guilt there, and people just respond by shutting that out completely and othering everyone who wants to say, "Hey, we need to deal with this." It's an emotional thing. I think people need to go through a whole emotional process.

I've certainly seen that in relation to taking groups of students into Native communities. I took some very bright students up to northern Manitoba a while ago. Some of them were Indigenous, but a lot of them weren't. We were talking about living conditions in some of the communities up there, so a lot of the community members were talking about how they don't have running water. They don't have what we think of as basic necessities of life. Watching the non-Indigenous students, some of them—just the traumatization that they went through: they suddenly recognized the reality of this. This is not just a technical thing that they learned about in school. This is real. They were shocked. I think they themselves were surprised. They thought they knew it, but they actually didn't know it at all, because they hadn't had a relationship with somebody who was experiencing that. I think literature can help us that way. We can't necessarily have community members from northern Manitoba come to every classroom and say, "This is what my life is like," but I think a story can help to do something similar.

I should say also when I was talking about that situation, a lot of the Indigenous people were shocked as well by these students reacting in such an emotional way. They were like, "What have they got to worry about? We're living through this." Actually, many of the Aboriginal people, they've lived with it for generations. They're like, "Okay, we're living, it's fine." They were actually comforting some of my non-Indigenous students.

So, I don't know that literature can do that whole function, but I think if students can have a way of getting a sense of what someone's life is like, someone who has been on the receiving end of this colonial project for however long, then that can go some way toward them thinking about and working through the emotions of that.

I think, as a nation, we're at the very beginning of trying to work through the emotions that will have to lead to some kind of action later. After the

TRC, we're in this very raw moment right now. A lot of Canadians don't want to think about it at all. There are a lot who do, but I don't think they have really figured out yet how they're going to approach that. How they're going to process their complicity in what is still happening—not just what has happened in the past, but what is still happening. That is an emotional process. It's one that involves the unconscious a lot. Again, this is the kind of thing where facts and figures don't really work very well. I think that's where stories and literature can really help us. It can take us into that space where it's about a relationship, or we're starting to get a sense of the real impact on real people's lives. That's what I'm hoping.

I do think that one of the reasons that Indigenous literatures are so popular right now is that there are a lot of Canadians who are not Native but who want to learn more and want to get a sense of what it must have been like, or what it still is like. Of course, things are not solved in any way, but we see this popularity, for lack of a better term, of some residential school memoirs in the last little while. A lot of Canadians really want to understand, not only how this could have happened, but what was it like for someone who actually was in it. That can make a big difference, over time.

AH: People are listening now. That puts more pressure on scholars and writers. It changes the nature of the responsibility. As someone I recently spoke with put it, "People are listening now. So, what are you going to say?"

WC: That's a really interesting point. For so long, Indigenous writers were writing and just trying to say, "Hey, you need to listen!" With *Halfbreed*, you certainly see it, but earlier as well. In many cases, literally no one was listening, or almost no one. Now that's changed. For me, being here in Winnipeg, it's very interesting because we have such a large and vibrant Indigenous community here. At my centre we often have Aboriginal writers, or storytellers, and have events, and we usually have them downtown or in the North End. We get huge turnouts all the time. Lots of Aboriginal people coming to the events at bookstores, as well. It's not just the non-Native audience out there, but there's such a support and pride that people in our communities feel when they see, "Hey, there's somebody, who's one of us, who's telling a story that's important." They really support that, and they really enjoy coming out. I think that's true, probably to a lesser extent, in other communities, too: just the fact of so many Aboriginal people here in Winnipeg makes it very noticeable. It's a fantastic thing to do the work that I do, to be in this place.

That's something that I hadn't really talked about as much in relation to the effect of Indigenous literature. I'd been saying there are some problems with the effect of it, in the sense that it makes us maybe ignore our storytellers and just look at our writers, but I think I have to give a lot of credit, also, to the writers who have taken some of the teachings that are there in the stories, or some of the ways in which the stories approach narrative, and tried to bring those into a literary realm. The effect that has had, in terms of making people feel proud of who they are. It's very basic, but I think that is crucial. Niigaan Sinclair and I edited this anthology called *Manitowapow: Aboriginal Writings from the Land of Water*. We just looked at Indigenous writers from Manitoba. The boundaries are incredibly colonial. Manitoba's boundaries are not really even connected to geography, but we decided to do that as a kind of experiment. So we gathered many writings from different communities and different cultures that have a presence here in Manitoba. We thought we were the experts, and we live here, but there are so many writers that we didn't know existed, that we discovered in that process.

AH: Which is great, really.

WC: That's fantastic. There's way more work to be done. We've challenged other scholars in other provinces to do something similar. I know that Jesse [Archibald-Barber] is doing one in Saskatchewan and hopefully others will do it in other places.[9] One of the things that has been so amazing about that project to me is, first of all, the discoveries we made. We thought it all started with *Halfbreed* and *In Search of April Raintree*—of course crucial, crucial books—but no, there's so much more before that. There are a lot of other texts in between then and now, also, that didn't get the attention that they deserved. And writers.

But going to our book launches for that book—and between Niigaan and I, we did at least fifty, I would say, around the province and on a northern tour—and every place that we had a launch or an event for the book, just to see all the Aboriginal people who came out to that launch, and to see the pride in their faces, was incredible. Often our excerpts of someone's work in our book are three pages or five pages long. I think the authors felt happy to be included, but just to see the audience members who were not writers, and that the general public was interested in it as well. There's something interesting about that, for Indigenous people. There's a great sense that our stories can be shared, and we can now have access to them again, if they've been lost or ignored. That's fantastic. Look at the richness of what's been accomplished in our communities. *Manitowapow* became a bestseller. It was the bestselling book by Manitoba publishers in all of 2014. That was a surprise to me. I knew that in the communities people would really appreciate it, but I didn't know that there would be so much interest in the broader picture.

This is a really great way to see how literature can remind people of the value of their stories. And can build pride and build a sense that we do have something really valuable to contribute. That, I think, is absolutely crucial. That can be on the level of *Manitowapow*, where there's a huge event, with lots of writers and lots of community members who come, and such an amazing sense of community well-being. But it could be also an individual young writer or young student who just reads that and says, "Hey, you know, I might be able to do that," or, "These are stories that people value." This is new, at least for several hundred years on this continent, for Indigenous people to feel that their contributions and their culture are not just valuable within the communities, but are also seen to have a value outside of the communities. That is a really important thing.

So much of what I see in my own hometown is how shame becomes internalized—a sense that you're not good enough. I've seen that play out in people's lives in really tragic ways, from early on. Some of my friends that I went to school with—wonderful, amazing, intelligent people—ended up on tragic paths. I don't know that it could have saved them all, or even any, necessarily, but I think having a sense of pride and a belief that your contribution can be valued has an incalculable effect on your future. I think really seeing the stories being celebrated and seeing that they're valued, in a book form, can build that. So I've been criticizing the book as a capitalist commodity, and I think that it *is* that—partly because of that cachet that the book has, within the capitalist system, that we feel it is the ultimate validating object. But that can be used for good, too. Really, in a lot of cases, various editors, artists, writers have been able to do that—to help build the pride a community can have, by bringing these stories into a book form.

That is something that definitely keeps me going. Greg Scofield and I right now are working on an anthology of Métis literature. That will be lots of fun. We've got lots of material gathered, and we just need to figure out our structuring principles and things like that. There's lots of room for more of this kind of thing within other Indigenous communities. There isn't an anthology of Cree literature—that I know of—for example. Each community could have their writers gather together. There is a lot of potential there. That's one of the next tasks for various scholars.

The importance of fostering a sense of pride in the people is really crucial. Going up to various northern communities, as well, and seeing when we can have a writer come from that community and give a reading, and what effect that has on the students—that's amazing. My other ongoing commitment is to try to find a way to give storytelling and storytellers more of a prominence: within Indigenous communities first, where they have a prominence, but we also need to do the same kind of thing that's been done for literature, to show the world: look how incredibly important and engaging this is! Lots of people in various parts of the Americas are doing that, but I think it's at an earlier stage. That's something that hopefully our educators can be a part of as well, by trying to incorporate storytelling into the classroom as much as they can.

"THAT'S THE PURPOSE OF STORY"
A Conversation with Lee Maracle

LEE MARACLE IS STÓ:LŌ and was born in North Vancouver. With decades of experience as a writer, critic, mentor, and educator, Maracle has a formidable presence within the Indigenous literary world. Maracle is a grandmother and mother, and currently holds mentorship and teaching roles at various post-secondary institutions in Toronto, including at the University of Toronto's First Nations House and its Indigenous Studies Program. She has worked to support the Indigenous literary arts through creative writing instruction and mentorship work across Canada, for instance through programming at the Banff Centre. Early in her career, Maracle helped to establish the En'owkin Centre, a multidisciplinary centre for Indigenous arts and higher learning. En'owkin is widely recognized for its support of Indigenous artistic practice and its work with the Okanagan language. These disparate roles are evidence of Maracle's enactment of Indigenous knowledges and traditions through the arts.

Maracle's education includes real-world experiences and activism—some of which are portrayed in her autobiographical book *Bobbi Lee, Indian Rebel*—as well as formal education at Simon Fraser University and a significant career in writing and teaching. As a prominent figure in the Indigenous literary scene, Maracle has served as a visiting scholar or writer-in-residence at a number of institutions, including the University of Waterloo, the University of Guelph, and Western Washington University. She was awarded an honorary doctor of letters from St. Thomas University in 2009, and in 2018 she was named an officer of the Order of Canada for her contributions to Indigenous writing.

Appearing in 1975, *Bobbi Lee, Indian Rebel* was among the first Indigenous works published in Canada. Maracle has published multiple novels since that first book, including *Sojourner's Truth* (1990), *Sundogs* (1992),

Ravensong (1995), *Daughters are Forever* (2002), *First Wives Club, Coast Salish Style* (2010), *Celia's Song* (2014), and the young adult novel *Will's Garden* (2002). Also a respected poet, Maracle has published two collections of verse: *Bent Box* (2000) and *Talking to the Diaspora* (2015). Well known as well for her critical writing alongside her creative practice—indeed, many would challenge any strict division between these two categories in her work— Maracle has published several books of criticism and collections of essays and speeches, including *I am Woman: A Native Perspective on Sociology and Feminism* (1988), *Memory Serves: Oratories* (2015), and *My Conversations with Canadians* (2017). Gathering writings by Indigenous women, Maracle also co-edited the collection *My Home as I Remember* (2000). Short works, both critical and creative, have been anthologized widely during her career.

Maracle's writing has earned her a spread of awards and recognitions. She won a J. T. Stewart Voices of Change Award in 2000, an American Book Award from the Before Columbus Foundation, also in 2000, and the 2009 Queen's Diamond Jubilee Medal for her work in support of Indigenous youth. She was awarded the Ontario Premier's Award for Excellence in the Arts in 2014, the Anne Green Award from the Calgary Writers Festival in 2016, and an Alberta Book Publishing Award in 2017 for *Memory Serves*. She was awarded a 2017 Mark Bonham Centre Award for the advancement of sexual diversity from the University of Toronto. In Montreal in 2018, she won a First Peoples Literary Prize at the Blue Metropolis Festival. Also in 2018, she won the Toronto International Festival of Authors Award and *My Conversations with Canadians* was shortlisted for the Toronto Book Award. In 2020 she was a finalist for the prestigious Neustadt International Prize for Literature, an award often called the American Nobel. Through her writing and her public presence, Maracle earns respect for her commitment to Indigenous sovereignty and to the strength and agency of Indigenous women.

Maracle and I met on August 7, 2015, in her office at First Nations House at the University of Toronto. With her understanding of my project and questions, Maracle immediately began to explore the deeply intertwined questions of reading and teaching in relation to Indigenous literatures. She shared with me her insistence that reading and teaching Indigenous literatures cannot be done through Eurocentric methods and measures. Western thought, she explained, has its own history and is loaded with presumptions that do not fit Indigenous literatures. Teaching from that perspective means that the learning is going to go a certain way—and not one that fits with Indigenous understandings of learning and story.

In the first part of our conversation, Maracle showed me a circular Anishinaabe curriculum model—one she had recently been working with at First Nations House in Toronto—and explained how learners can enter the circle and pursue an infinite number of spokes within it in order to work for transformation. She pointed out the sophisticated structure of that model and the way it foregrounds the individual's agency in learning. By comparison, she described how Western models hold the teacher up as someone who has mastered knowledge and seeks to transfer it to students, who supposedly do not have it. A better way of looking at learning, Maracle argued, is to see yourself (as the learner) at the centre, pursuing whatever it is that strikes you about the topic being studied.

This point is significant because of Maracle's ability to describe—and enact—traditional Indigenous knowledge systems in relation to literary pedagogies and critical processes. In our conversation, she articulates a crucial insistence that, from within Indigenous frameworks, stories cannot be understood apart from their impact on living beings. Stories are about people, about carrying forward relationships and understandings. If the purpose of story is to have an impact on people's lives, then the purpose of teaching literature must be to enable learners to build understandings based on what strikes them through the story. The teacher, in this model, is not an elevated figure who passes mastery down to the students. Throughout our conversation, Maracle circles back to this understanding of teaching and learning. The recorded interview below picks up with our discussion of how, when the learner is at the centre, the teacher does not have the kind of power over the learner that is asserted in a conventional teacher-centred Western classroom.

OUR CONVERSATION

Lee Maracle (LM): So there [in an Indigenous model] the person is not dominate-able but they are teachable. They also are teachers, so an exchange of discourse can happen. All heads are the same height. We know that the teacher or facilitator of learning has more information, but the purpose of that facilitator or that teacher is to develop the expertise of the whole and not just to transmit information. That information came from that specific person, whoever the teacher is—the way that they were going at birth and from their specific gifts. Since no one else has them, it would be useless to try and get everybody to swallow what that person knows.

The only thing that that teacher has to do is set up a discussion that's general enough to inspire thinking from all kinds of directions, all four directions. Your lecture must be from all four directions. It has to be lean enough so that there are holes that can be filled. It's not that there are holes in your lecture, but you don't say everything that you need to say.

Aubrey Hanson (AH): There are opportunities.

LM: Yeah, opportunities for other people to develop their thinking and contribute to creating the whole. That's a little bit of a trick. It requires that you really believe that there's an infinite number of pathways to the centre of the circle and that you come to that circle, like everyone else, wanting to learn something, because there's some knowledge missing. You're aware that you have the bulk of the contribution to be made, to setting up finding it. That's what you're doing: you're setting up the finding of knowledge. You have the biggest head start, so you give as much of a head start as you can. If you sort of think of a spiral, you get them halfway to the centre and they can fill out the rest and find the missing knowledge. It's always beautiful when a student does that.

I remember we were talking about Indigenous healing methods and this guy says, "Theirs is a military method." Everybody sat up and looked at him. "Of course it is," I said. "Isolate, examine, quarantine, destroy." [*Laughs*] We just started laughing. It was like the lights went on and then the discussion got very animated about the difference between Indigenous healing methodology and European methodologies. People realized that the class is also military. We were sitting in a circle. As long as I was standing up, lecturing, everyone was small. It felt that way. They were making notes and all that and they were all looking for what struck them. And, you know, you can try and say, "Don't take all this so seriously that you can't think straight. Don't be kicking at your own ass." But, in the end, you're bigger than them. You're standing up higher. There is a hierarchy, and you're the tip-top and everybody is beneath you. That's a set-up that's not tenable. They need to use the symbols that you use to get there. So I have to have the blackboard to draw, to use the symbols, and so then I have to be standing.

It all depends on how the next part goes. If everybody starts with what struck them, then they'll go in their own direction automatically. You get them to do response papers with what struck them, and then their essay is all about whatever struck them on the subject in the end. Their oral presentations are about what struck them, and all the way through, they're going for the finish line. They're going for the goal post. So it becomes part of a whole. In my particular English literature class, it was where the story took them. Which direction did the story take them? How did it guide them? That's the essay. They talk about what struck them in the story, how this character related to that character on this issue, say.

One of the things that struck my students is the empathy for the "snake" that I had in *Ravensong*. It was really irritating to see that empathy. He's walking out of the village, and he's holding his head up and walking almost military-style, holding his pride together because that's all he's got left. They've ostracized him. And Stacey, the main character, *so* wants to look back. She's arguing with herself because of what he did, but she wants to look back. She doesn't, but she really wants to. And, so, this girl said she was really struck by that, but then halfway through she says, "Oh God, I get it." And everybody says, "What?" you know, because they want to know what she got. And she says, "That's the feeling women have when they let the violent man back in the door." They want to bring him back in. It's a disbelief in what he was. You just can't believe someone that's related to you or that's connected to you could be that terrible. You can't believe that the women or girls who suffered suffered as much as they did. There's a disbelief in women and a stronger belief in men. So then it goes around, and that girl ended up doing a master's degree in that very subject: the strength of the belief in men as opposed to women. The belief in men is where they get their strength, regardless of what they've done. The disbelief in women is where the weakness comes from, and that's the nature of the patriarchy. It's not the nature of gender abuse; it's the nature of the patriarchy that holds up the gender abuse. She became a theorist on the subject because of the way a class went.

Now *they* wouldn't accept that as a way to teach literature, and that's the trouble, because then the stories don't help us. They don't hold up society. That's why stories are belittled—storytelling is belittled—as opposed to *studying literature*. Studying literature is finding the metaphor, and the hermeneutics, and the post-colonial this and that. If you read those essays, those dudes who write like that, you sort of think, "What a waste of a good education." As opposed to Vine Deloria, who's obviously read all kinds of literature and got miles more out of it than the rest of the English literary crowd of Aboriginal scholars. You think, "Yeah, that's the way to read a story, all right." I think Tom King is the same way. How he reads a story is completely different—and of course that shapes how he writes it, too—than anybody else I know who has an English degree.

That's the important thing that you need to know about what it is you're doing. And you're the only person that can know it.

AH: That's what I came in to ask you, really. Thank you for knowing my question in advance [*laughs*]. I'm trying to talk to people who write and teach. I'm talking to teachers who teach Indigenous literatures in Calgary, who may not be Indigenous, and I'm also speaking with writers, asking them how they think about what it means and why it matters. You've answered that question in a lot of ways. I'm wondering how people think about what literature does and how it matters for communities. And I'm reading things like that book there by Leanne Simpson [*I point to the book* Lighting the

Eighth Fire, *which sits on Maracle's desk*]. I'm listening to people who are talking about that stuff.

LM: I think we're talking about what it *did* for communities, and we're not there yet. I think she's great at mapping the journey to get there, though, because we're recovering from residential school. People call it healing, but we weren't the sick people, really. We're recovering from the sickness of colonization and struggling to become decolonized. That's not going to happen anytime soon, because decolonization is, of course, a physical thing, not just a mental, emotional, and spiritual thing. It's a physical thing of having back the property, so it's not just going to happen anytime soon. It's also a government-to-government thing. Canada's got to know that its reason for being here is to hold up these Treaties, and of course it doesn't do that. We're not to be dominated. That's not the point of Treaties. There's nowhere that says, "I'm going to give up all my rights to just be and have access to this land."

That's all part of the colonial picture that's not going to be solved in a hurry, but the emotional and the spiritual and the intellectual stuff is going to get us to the physical stuff. It's going to get us to fighting for the physical domination of our own lives. I have a lot of faith in it. The lighting of the Eighth Fire is a prophecy, and it means that we're going back toward home again. We're getting there. I think it's important to know that we're going in that direction. People like Leanne Simpson are mapping that direction. Glen Coulthard is another one. Marie Battiste contributed quite a lot to it.

[*In this next portion of our conversation, Maracle is holding the book* Lighting the Eighth Fire *and reading brief excerpts. The individual quotations are cited in the endnotes.*] I love this business of to fish "as formerly,"[10] which is what these people wanted, just to be able to fish as formerly. Here we go, "Kulu danced in the sky, / with stars and moon."[11] Who's Kulu? And why Kulu? Why would we want to start with Kulu, I would want to know. If I were stuck somewhere along the line "the ocean heaved as her essence / flew in infinite directions, through the stars"—I could get stuck on that line: What exactly does that mean? I go back to "Kulu danced in the sky." So, we're starting in the sky, and Kulu is there. So it's a sky-world person. What do we actually see in the sky? Well, we're seeing a singular galaxy and there's many of them. So where is Kulu? He's in one of the infinite directions—its infinite number of pathways to the centre of the circle. Infinite directions in the sky world—infinite, infinite, infinite. It's unrealizable. I have to let it go and just accept that the "ocean heaved as her essence / flew in infinite directions, through the stars"—that the ocean can heave itself and her spirit can roar up to the sky and fly about in all the infinite directions of the sky world. It's not realizable by a human being, but it's imaginable. Then we think, "Kulu's maiden-voyage was his last…. He fell in the vacuum of space." Oh my God, that's right, there's no air. That's why nature doesn't like a vacuum. That's why there's a ceiling on us. We're sealed in here; there's no getting out. If we get out, we're gone. We're going to float. Imagine floating infinitely in space, alive.

AH: I can't. It's terrifying.

LM: Yeah, exactly. Then you can know where you get stuck. If you go back to "Kulu danced in space": Why "danced"? Why not "floated"? Why not "perished"? It's a lot of why nots. You think, "No, it has to be 'danced.' " It just has to be "danced" because everything begins with song. We all have a rhythm. We all have a melody. It's personal. We each have a song, and the song inspires us to move. So, we all have dance, even a baby.

AH: [*Laughs*] Yeah. I've seen that.

LM: Hang on to the crib, you know, and shake their little tushies [*laughs*].

AH: Yeah! And it's beautiful.

LM: It *is* beautiful. And we so fall in love with it. We're alive again because of it. So, then we can know this poem. We can know this poem because it manifests in real life, and any piece of writing that doesn't manifest in real life is a pile of guck. That's what I think about all the stuff that's written about our work, that calls me monologistic, polyglot, post-colonial, postmodern, blah, blah, blah. It's guck. My writing comes from thousands of years, way before post-colonial or colonial. It's older than that. You want to tell them, "It's older than you, you turtle." Same thing with Tom King—he hates it when they call him post-colonial. [*Laughs*] "Not likely," he says.[12] It's so arrogant to think that everything begins with them.

That's what I call the "knower's chair." You have to remove your own knower's chair if you're teaching. You have to have a facilitator's chair. What I'm here to do: I know more, that's something that I have to just accept, because I've lived longer. I've spent my life learning, as opposed to these young people, who are just beginning. But that doesn't mean I know *better* than them. You can know *more*, but not *better*. I know about tsetse flies but it doesn't fucking help them a bit! [*Laughs*] You know what I mean?

AH: [*Laughs*] Yeah.

LM: So that's *more* [*laughs*]. I know about surgery but that doesn't help them a bit. [*Laughs*] There are a lot of things I know.

AH: And you can't know *for* them.

LM: Yeah, you can't know for them. And it's not necessarily better. Most of what I know is probably pretty useless. What you do know is *more*, and so once you can accept that, then you can say, "How will I make it easy for them to know for themselves?" That's where what you know becomes very limited. That limits it right away. As soon as you ask a question that's so specific as that, then what you know doesn't necessarily help you. It's thinking about it that's going to help you. "What helped me to learn? What helps so-and-so to learn?" You know, you have to find out what helps people to learn, and I think it's that business of what struck you. Because it's sharp. [*Claps*] Bang! This is what struck me. Then, when they start to talk about it, they automatically theorize. Even a three-year-old will theorize.

My little girl came back from day care and said, "The students are noticing I'm turning brown." I said, "Oh, really?" She wasn't turning anything, but I didn't want to say that to her. [*Laughs*] Obviously she had some idea, had thought about this. I wanted to know what her thinking was. And she says, "So I told them, 'everybody's born white, but if you're beautiful, you turn brown, and if you're really beautiful, when you grow up you turn Black.'" And I thought, "Oh, is she in for a big surprise when she gets older and she doesn't turn Black!" [*Laughs*].

AH: She's got a sophisticated system of—

LM: A very sophisticated system of reasoning. And it went right back to James Brown's song, "Say it loud! I'm Black and I'm proud!" We'd be dancing around—my friend was Black and Native, but she wasn't as Black as this other guy, and I wasn't as Black as them. So, she had it in her head. My friend was older, too, by ten years, and the other one was older by fifteen, so to her, the progression was toward Blackness [*laughs*].

AH: She was using the evidence at hand [*laughs*].

LM: And I just tried not to laugh. I didn't say a word, but I thought, "That's magnificent reasoning, and all I've got to do is keep *that* process alive." And so, I said, "Is that what struck you, when your classmate said that?" And she says, "Yes! And I was struck, just like you strike a tree and all the leaves scatter. All my thoughts started swimming around inside my head! All in different directions!" [*Laughs*] She was just cracking me up. It was even funnier than the first idea. I said, "Wow, that's magnificent. That's really magnificent. You're so lucky to have such a marvellous brain!" And she says, "Is that right, Dad? Is my brain marvellous?" And he says, "It definitely is." He was just agreeing with her.

I saw him and her together last week. It was in Vancouver. They went off for a bike ride. He comes back, and he's sitting down, and he said, "I really like bike riding with her." I said, "Yeah, you two have the same expression on your face as you're going out the door." Whatever his mood is, hers is the same, which I've always found sort of interesting. They go off together and he really appreciates how her mind works. And he reminded me that I once said she had a magnificent mind, and she asked him if her mind was magnificent, and he agreed. And he says, "I now understand why that was so true," and that he really appreciated that I saw it when I did. She pursued her own mind all her life and developed into this magnificent human being. She's so quick and incredible. If she ever gets to write down some of her thoughts, if she ever puts it into a book, it's going to be something else. She likes play writing; she's written millions of plays.

Her sister is the sort of intellectual like her father, too. She's an English degree person. And she's very much like myself. She doesn't like the way it's taught. First of all, the metaphors aren't the same. You can't translate metaphors, so the metaphoric language that they're using doesn't work. You have to find a new language for yourself in understanding the work. I think the key is what Huron Miller said one time. He was reciting Peacemaker. He said at the end, "If you see yourself in this story, come forward and make it right with Creation." That's the purpose of story. It's governance. You go and make it right. And governance has to be out loud. If you fucked up, you have to admit it [*laughs*].

AH: And maybe do something.

LM: Do something about it. Exactly, you have to make it right. First you have to say it out loud to everybody. Then you have to make it right, not just with the people there but the whole world. The whole earth, the animals, the plants, the sky—everything that's in the words that come before all else. That's magnificent, and it's so magnificent it makes me think a child said this. If you look at the Haudenosaunee messenger tradition, there was a group of children who made this plan. It was a group of children. You just want to laugh your head off because all these adults saw the brilliance in those children. That's love. That's love.

Nothing else is love, for a child. Just to see their brilliance: that's all you're there for. Of course, you have to feed them and clothe them and all that kind of stuff. You're not there to boss them. You're not there to teach them to be adults—none of that. Whatever it is they want to do, they do. They're going to play at being adults; let them play at being adults. They're going to play at being children; let them play at being children. They're going to play at being together. They're going to play at being separate. Whatever it is they're going to do, you do.

I was telling my son that. "How do I get him to stop throwing tantrums without hurting his spirit?" And I said, "Well, first of all, who are the tantrums hurting, you or him?" He says, "Well I guess it's me." [*Laughs*] So I said, "Yeah, so you need to find a way to get past that hurt. It has nothing to do with him." And he says, "Well, how did you deal with it with Columpa?" And I said, "Sid, she still throws tantrums and she's forty! Just not as often [*laughs*]." And they're way more adult than his. [*Laughs*] Our people say you can change conduct but you can't change character. I said, "Your son's tantrums are not hurtful, but your feelings got hurt because he didn't listen to you and he outsmarted you, Sid. Honestly, you've just got to be smarter than him."

I asked him, "Did you negotiate?" He says, "Yes, I made a deal with him before we went! And the deal was this," he says. "I'm going to town."

"Can I come with?" He's four.

He says, "No, because you're going to ask for something,"

"I won't."

"Well, I'm not buying you anything, and you can't ask for anything."

"Okay."

They shake hands. Off they go. So, he gets to the store. [*Laughs*] He goes in and grabs something. And he's looking at his dad. He says, "You know how we go to dance and we get down on our haunches, and we're ready to just rip?" And I said, "Yeah." He's down on his haunches and he's got the thing between them. He says to me, "I says, 'Put that back!' And he says to me, 'I'm not putting it back and I'm not listening to you!' " And he ran through his legs and out the doors of the store, with this thing in his hand.

Well, Sid ran after him, and the lady's saying, "It's okay, it's okay!" "No, it's not! He's taking it back!" [*Laughs*] So he goes to grab the thing, and they're fighting—literally. The boy is just trying to take his father on. He goes back into the store, and the poor store lady just wants all this shit to stop [*laughs*]. "It's okay, it's okay." "No, he can't!" [*Laughs*] So he makes him give it back. He gets in the car and he's furious, but he doesn't want to threaten his son. So, he's trying to calm down, and he says, "What happened, son?" And he says, "Well, you told me I couldn't ask, and that you weren't going to buy me anything." He says, "Yeah, I told you that, so what happened?"

"You didn't say that I couldn't steal it."

AH: [*Laughs*] "I didn't ask!"

LM: [*Laughs*] "I didn't ask and you didn't buy it. I just took it!" [*Laughs*] "You didn't say I couldn't take it!" That's what he said. So he says, "Okay." So, he gets home, and instead of talking to him he says, "I'm going to phone your grandma." And then he starts to cry. "You're going to make my grandma think ill of me," he said. And he went to his room and shut the door and locked it. So then he feels really bad, and he said that threw water on his fire, because that is the worst thing for a little boy. "Oh, Grandma's going to think ill of me!" And he was in there, not crying out loud but weeping, and his wife says, "What happened?" Sid says, "Let me phone my mom."

So, that's what he asked: "How can I deal with these tantrums, without hurting his spirit?" And I said, "He wasn't hurting anybody, and you did successfully get the toy away from him and restore it to the owner, which is the right thing to do, even though he doesn't like it. But telling him that you were going to phone me was a threat. And I don't think he deserved that. I think he was right that you didn't say he couldn't just take it. So he outwitted you. He was a little fox. And he needs a story about that, and a little bit of ceremony about that, but I don't think you're the person to do it for him." I said, "When I come up, I'll get some tobacco, and we'll go down to the beach and I'll give him a teaching about it, and I won't tell him that it's for him. I'll talk about it from my own perspective and see if he gets it. If he doesn't get it, then you have to deal with it again, until he's old enough to get it. He's got to be of good will toward you. The whole way to get a good relationship going is each of you has got to be of good will. You threatened to tell on him to me, which is a threat to him. He can't bear having me think ill of him." And I says, "Don't do that again. Don't use me to hurt him. And the other thing is, you just keep trying to outsmart him [*laughs*]. That's all it is, really. You have to be one step ahead. So, take your time. Don't make a decision like, 'No you can't come unless.' You know, take your time, think about it. And next time, get him in the car and then take the toy. Don't involve the store people and humiliate him in that way."

So, I went up there, and I went down to the water with him to throw rocks. And I was smoking then and I kept dropping this cigarette, so finally I said, "Well, obviously this is for the ancestors." So, I take it out of the package, and he says, "What are you doing?" And I said, "Well I'm going to lay out tobacco." And he says, "What do you lay out tobacco for?" And I says, "Well, sometimes I need guidance, you know, and obviously I need some now, or this cigarette wouldn't be falling on the ground." He says, "Is that what we do?" And I say, "Yeah, it's one of the things we do." And he says, "What does it do?" And I says, "Well it makes us have good relations. We need to have good relations with others to be truly happy. You can be content inside yourself, but you can't be truly joyful unless all your relations with your family are good." He says, "Yeah, I can see that."

And I said, "You know, I sometimes fight with my kids and, I don't mean to, but every now and then I say something, and I see the hurt on their face and I think, 'Oh crap.' So, I always ask my ancestors to look with discipline at my indiscretion, to look at me when I'm about to fall off a good wagon so that it will stop me before I say things that are hurtful." He says, "That's a good idea," and then he tells me the story of his tantrum with his dad. And he was sobbing and he was saying, "He was going to tell on me by telling you and I thought you were going to hate me because I was so horrible to him. And that's your son!" He realized that that was my son, and I started to cry. [*Laughs*] I didn't think of it as my son; I thought of it as my grandson. I wasn't thinking of my son at all, and I thought, "Oh, isn't that extraordinary, that when you face your grandchildren, you aren't thinking of your children at all? [*Laughs*] That's terrible!"

So there we were, my little grandson and I, sobbing. I was thinking about the way this boy is loved by me. It's not that I don't love my son, or other people in the world. I love a lot of people, but that's my grandson. [*Laughs*] It's very, very special. That's what they mean when they say, "I am here because I was so loved by my ancestors. Every line of them loved me." And that's what they mean by so many generations into the future. We're supposed to love our children seven generations into the future, so we created this body of story to guide those children so they will forever be loved by the living. Not just the dead. That's what our stories are for. That's the purpose of us studying the stories. It's not for determining metaphors and themes, or whatever it is. It's for the impact of that story on the lives of the people who read it.

[*Laughs*] And that's all I got to say about that!

"I HOPE MY WRITING CAN HELP OTHERS"
A Conversation with Sharron Proulx-Turner

SHARRON PROULX-TURNER WAS A member of the Métis Nation of Alberta and lived in Calgary. She traced her origins back to the Ottawa River Valley Métis and to Mohawk, Wyandat, Algonquin, Ojibwe, Mi'kmaw, French, and Irish ancestry. She was a two-spirit woman and a poet, an Elder and a storyteller, a grandmother, mother, and auntie. She engaged in social justice and community work alongside her creative practice in the literary arts. Having earned a BA and MA in English, Proulx-Turner taught courses in literature and creative writing at various institutions, for instance at Old Sun College, Mount Royal College (now University), and the University of Calgary. Sharron Proulx-Turner passed away in November 2016. One of my last memories of her was watching her—surrounded by family, friends, colleagues, and admirers—as she listened to her work being honoured at a special conference held at the University of Calgary in the spring of 2016. Knowing she was ill, the literary community had gathered around to celebrate her creative work and her beautiful presence.[13]

Proulx-Turner's first book, a memoir published under a pseudonym, was *Where the Rivers Join* (1995). In the following decades she published four books of poetry: *what the auntys say* (2002); *she is reading her blanket with her hands* (2008); *she walks for days / inside a thousand eyes / a two-spirit story* (2008); and *the trees are still bending south* (2012). The memoir *One Bead at a Time* (2016) was a collaborative project with two-spirit Lakota Elder Beverly Little Thunder that brought Little Thunder's oral life story into book form. Proulx-Turner's final book, a collection of prose poetry and expressive writings, is called *creole métisse of french canada, me* (2017).[14]

Proulx-Turner was an award-winning writer and a respected member of the literary community. Her early memoir was a finalist for the Edna Staebler Award for Creative Non-Fiction in 1995. Her poetry books have been shortlisted for such honours as the 2003 Gerald Lampert Prize for first book of poetry, for *what the auntys say*, and the 2008 Governor General Award, for *she is reading her blanket with her hands*. Her work has also been anthologized in various journals and magazines. As a member of the literary community, Proulx-Turner was appreciated for her engagement and teaching, for instance through her mentorship and support of young Indigenous writers. She is often named as a source of inspiration, whether by two-spirit artists or by others for whom her life story resonates.

On September 22, 2015, Sharron Proulx-Turner and I sat down for our conversation at Weeds Café, a quiet and artsy little coffee house not too far from the university, in northwest Calgary (the spot was her recommendation). Our time together unfurled over tea and treats on an especially sunny fall afternoon. Proulx-Turner asked me to listen and take notes during our conversation rather than use a mechanical recorder; that process gives this chapter a unique feel compared to others in this collection.[15] After our meeting, I sent Proulx-Turner my written notes, which she reviewed with care and expanded from note form into prose. In this way, the following interview took shape.

As we speak here, Proulx-Turner shares stories from her own personal and educational journey, including her process of becoming a writer. She explains that it is important to her to write for an Indigenous audience, and in so doing to benefit Indigenous people. This drive connects also to her belief that she can only tell her own story and that she must write from her perspective as a Métis person. When asked for advice for teachers who want to teach Indigenous literatures, Proulx-Turner offers a range of strategies, and she counsels non-Indigenous teachers not to be too sensitive as they learn, and as they will inevitably make mistakes in that learning. Holding a fair amount of hope for the work that education can do for Indigenous Peoples, Proulx-Turner emphasizes that young people need to see themselves in what they are reading. With this point, she issues a clear call for change in curriculum and pedagogy.

OUR CONVERSATION

Sharron Proulx-Turner (SPT): Before I begin I would like to thank the Creator for this beautiful day, for the sun coming up one more time in my life. For bringing us together like this. I would like to thank the peoples of Treaty 7 Territory—the Stoney, the Peoples from Tsuu T'ina, the Peoples of Eden Valley, the Blackfoot Peoples. Always, the Métis Peoples.

Aubrey Hanson (AH): What brought you to writing? How do you think about the significance of writing?

SPT: I will begin to answer by talking about when I started writing. I've always written; I had dyslexia and a severe speech impediment when I was small, and in the fifties they thought I was slow, but after passing an intelligence test, a lady in the school helped me and taught me language, writing, and speech skills.[16] Taught me to substitute a word I couldn't remember with a phrase or group of words without taking long, hesitant breaks in my natural speech rhythm. I think this would have been grades 1 and 2. Then in grade 4, I was required to write a poem for a poetry contest. I had a poem to hand in that I'd painstakingly written, and then woke in the night the night before the due date with another whole poem in my sleepy mind. I won the contest with that poem and I was convinced for years I'd cheated because I wrote a poem that came to me in a dream.

[*At this point, Proulx-Turner tells me a story about times in her life when she would write on tiny scraps of paper and then throw them out so as to protect her thoughts and words. She tells me that, after she returned to university in her early thirties, her marriage fell apart. In the process of leaving, she found dozens of those private notes that her ex had taken. She sat on the floor of the house weeping—for herself and her children and what they had endured, but also for all women who had been trapped in abusive relationships. She was afraid to be on her own and to face the palpable hardship and poverty that would ensue. However, she said, she began to feel hope as she read her own words on those notes: she knew that she would be able to tell her story.[17]*]

I sat on that floor and thanked the Creator for everything I had, took the notes, and threw them back into the garbage—not because of shame, but to begin to let go of the weight of that past. I knew I could. In that moment, I knew I would, through my writing.

And to speed up that letting-go process, I was going back to school, to university again. In my late teens I received a scholarship and went to Carleton. But I was pregnant. I had my son in March and didn't go back to school. I had a math professor who took a special interest in me. He said if I moved to Alberta I could get a student loan as a single mom. The where was an instant decision. [*She explains remembering what she had learned in sixth grade about Chinook winds and the rapid temperature changes.[18]*]

That is why I moved to Alberta: youth. The truth is, I wasn't especially interested in university. I was lost. So many people. So few Métis and Natives. To make matters more complicated, I was and am a very introverted person and I was super shy. What motivated me? My Métis grandmother wanted me to go to school, to university. I wanted to give back, to my family, to community. My grandmother said something like, "Ma petite, you have what it takes. It's your duty to go to school, for the generations who follow." I didn't know the first thing about post-secondary. It wasn't part of our family history, and like you said about yourself, I was interested in escaping into literature, not sharing my ideas—written or otherwise. Yet over the years, reading and speaking about my writing has helped me to speak and write better, and more.

When I returned to university in Calgary in my early thirties, I failed an effective writing test. I took two literature classes in grade 13, yet was uncertain as to how to write a post-secondary "essay." It was either take an English literature class or be expelled from university with grade 13, a scholarship, and excellent grades in high school and in university. I was taking fine arts at the time. I settled on a literature/composition class with Aritha Van Herk. Not that I knew who she was at the time, I'll admit. The lady frightened me, even though she was my age. She was an icon and she was, let's just say, a firm teacher. But she did something that changed the course of my life. Aritha Van Herk got us to write an essay in exam booklets at the beginning of term. A couple classes later, she returned the booklets by first slamming them down on her desk and declaring in a broad-stroked, booming voice that only two people passed. I was one of them. She wrote a comment in red ink on a recipe card—which I wish I still had—that said, "This is no essay, but you sure as hell can write." I learned later that she was a writer. I had no idea. I borrowed a paper from a woman who was getting straight As, and copied the way she wrote it—not the paper, but her form and structure. There is a formula, I was convinced. And there was/is. I got mostly As for the rest of my degree based on this what I call "formula."

Later in my degree, I took creative writing courses with poets Chris Wiseman and Fred Wah. Chris Wiseman taught me to lose my fear and Fred Wah, another icon with firm mannerisms, was very good at helping people to understand the strengths in their writing. I was shocked at first that we had to read our writing out in class, and I guess that was when I really started writing. Both of the men were excellent at getting us to think through our role as writers. But most of my knowledge and understanding about my writing came from the other students in the classes. I took the courses in the later 1980s and it was 1990 before I published. To this day, I am a slow writer, so I have written five books. The sixth is coming out in the spring, 2016, a memoir spoken orally to me by Lakota Elder Beverly Little Thunder. It will be in her name and the royalties will be hers, of course. It is her story as told to me. I kept to the spirit of her oral story, all verbatim, transcribed, and then brought the text from almost nine hundred to around two hundred and fifty pages. Hers is a beautiful story. I am fortunate to have had this experience.

AH: In thinking about writing and why it matters, how do you think about community, or about representation, when you write?

SPT: I am a Métis writer; I can't write from another perspective. Each of us is unique; our experiences are different.[19] My history has affected me, and my children, and my grandchildren. Yet it amazes me how much our community is growing and has grown—despite the internalized hatred, the pain. As my mom used to say, these memories are caught in our DNA. They are part of us. We are walking miracles, she would say. We survived the brutality. We can and we will survive the healing. So I'm a Métis writer; I can't be anything else.

I've edited some collections of Native, Inuit, and Métis writing. Some white, mainstream editors I have worked with have asked, "Why do all Indigenous writers write about the same things, over and over again? It's just so boring, and bad writing." I've sat on granting juries, and the lowest ratings are consistently given by mainstream jurists to the Native writers. I figured out how to have the Indigenous writers discussed on the juries I was on. Native writing is pigeonholed. A round peg in a square hole. Non-Native people's expectations of Native writing are generally extremely myopic. In some ways you can't fault people for that, because they are trained that way. But what of people on juries? What of people who really *should* know? It's important for many people to understand that Western education is limited, let's say, in its scope. It's dead/live wealthy white men and women (on juries and in the texts read), and that has not changed much: my grandkids are reading the same books I read when I was a kid, and that was fifty-something years ago. It's still a big problem. I can see now where things are beginning to shift, but from within the Indigenous communities themselves more than from anywhere else. Having mandatory Indigenous studies courses throughout school—for everyone—from the beginning with the little ones to the end of university would be a good beginning.

One time I was invited to do a smudge in a social work course by a woman who was meant to conduct the circle but was sick. I wanted to know why, because it's not something to be showcased. It was a huge class and I asked them, "How many of you are planning to work with Native people?" Almost everyone in the room put up their hands. "How many of you have Native friends?" Nobody. "What are the reserves around here, and what are the demographics of Native people in Calgary?" Not one person in that room knew. Didn't even know whose land they were on or what Treaty territory they were living on. Had not read a Native author, but knew of the radio program "Dead Dog Café" hosted by writer, educator, and university professor Dr. Thomas King.

At the time I did my master's, I was not allowed to refer to Indigenous women's theories of writing or theoretical works. I was told, and I quote, "Women of colour are writing 'high theory.' Native women's work is merely highly theoretical." That door was closed. Today I understand that has changed, otherwise you would not be working on your thesis today, my young friend.

When I completed my master's, I taught at Mount Royal College. I taught in both the Aboriginal Education Program and in mainstream beginner critical writing classes. I introduced the first Indigenous literature course in Mount Royal's more than ninety-year history, but the filled-up course was cancelled before the term began, and before the previous term ended I was fired. I was fired because of racism, because of the way I chose to conduct my classes. I wasn't listening to the unspoken words, "We know what's best for you." The students sat in a circle in my classes. They had to know one another's names. They had to examine their values, the institutions that influenced the ideas and beliefs they internalized. They were asked to find their true voices. And their reading list was made up of Native writers and of-colour writers, of white theorists who were writing about white privilege, oppression. All the reading materials for these classes were in essay format, as the students were learning to write the different forms of essay. Each essay chosen for the reading list fit a certain form of essay. Mainstream students complained to the English department head about these classes. Their complaints were consistent—that they did not sign up for either a Native studies class or a class on racism.

At the time, the department head was very supportive of my pedagogy. Told the students to come see me, talk to me. She told them they were lucky to have a class taught this way. She special requested that I teach in mainstream classes after she sat in and witnessed my teaching in the all-Native classes. Most of the students in the subsequent mainstream classes were from social work and the content alone would benefit them throughout their lives, she would tell the complaining students. All difficulties with complaining students were resolved this way for the first few years. The department head also implemented something for the department in terms of Indigenous awareness, including the Indian Act and the Treaties, residential schools, posters on the walls, and race awareness overall.[20]

But after a short time, a new department head took over who did not agree with my pedagogy or with "student complaints." Felt strongly about both. He felt that if a student was complaining, the teacher had a problem.

Period. So, he told me to change my approach in the classroom. To stop sitting in circles. Teach from a "traditional" perspective and teach from an agreed text generally used by the English department for the course I was teaching—it was a composition/critical writing course. Follow a syllabus designed by him and the dean. He said all this behind closed doors, alone in interview with him—I learned from that one not to go in alone again. He admittedly wanted to censor me and possibly even the messages being planned for faculty and support staff through racism training. What followed from there is a long story. Most importantly, the university leadership agreed to take Indigenous sensitivity training and racism awareness training from professional organizations outside university staffing; yes, they existed way back in the late nineties and early Y2K). I was happy. As my auntie would say, "What is the use in living if you don't speak out and do good with your words?"

AH: Do you have an intended audience when you write?

SPT: I do. My intended audience is Indigenous—Native, Métis, Inuit—and whoever else may benefit. It was the same when I was teaching. The students I was concerned with first were the Indigenous students. If they were comfortable enough in any classroom then I knew it was a good environment. Generally, when the Native students were comfortable, the non-Native students were not. But I have to say overall—I taught a lot of classes at Mount Royal—students were appreciative of what they learned. I still hear from people today—new people and ones I continue to hear from—and it's been a long time, fifteen years at least. I hear from both Indigenous and non-Indigenous students. They all say their experiences in the classroom were life-altering, in a good way.

AH: Some of the teachers I have spoken with have brought up the idea of risk. They know they could be reading more Indigenous literature with their students but there is a perception of risk. What would you say to a teacher who wants to teach this but is afraid of risk or backlash?

SPT: The first thought that comes to my mind is don't work alone. Find someone who is like-minded, and if they are non-Native, seek out those true allies. There are some. Check out the Indigenizing education efforts across Canada that stem from the Truth and Reconciliation recommendations. I would say, too, look up the texts that are recommended by community members, by Native educators and Elders who are helping in the education area. Most urban schools, for example, have advisory Elders and Native support workers who advise teachers and students. I would say if you are urban, reach out to them. There are lists and some Indigenous texts there that are recommended by Native writers and educators. Google Native writers. Almost all Native writers, from the most humble to the most famous, will take the time to talk to you. You just have to reach out.

Non-Native parents may complain, but then a book written by a Native author is no different from this or that other recommended text. I would say to teachers, too, get yourselves a thicker skin. Be diplomatic and kind, but firm. Sometimes the most unexpected people will complain and sometimes a thick collective skin is needed. So, again, I recommend, don't work alone. Also, if you are white, put your white guilt in the cupboard. If you are a person of colour, watch out that guilt doesn't creep up on you, too. In a three-day workshop for Native women and women of colour several years ago, the facilitator, Lee Maracle, guided the women to come together in solidarity and understanding. During that workshop, Lee Maracle declared, "*guilt paralyzes.*" Having been raised Catholic, the truth of this stuck with me. Guilt is something that takes away both passion and compassion. Guilt is a waste of time. Guilt paralyzes.

There are non-Native teachers who are afraid they're going to do something wrong when they teach "Native content" in the classroom. They might even get continuous pressure from certain parents about what they're doing. It's so important for the teachers to stand their ground, to remain sensitive to the material. Parents and other teachers who have issues can always come and visit. Come to the classroom. Invite the Elder and the Native support workers. In Native cultures, we do things in an active and participatory way, in an experiential way. People expect to sit back and be lectured to in Western classrooms, but that ain't gonna happen in some Native teachers' and allies' classrooms.

Decolonizing is the first concern from my point of view. We have all been colonized. It's hard work, this decolonizing. Demystifying our different ways is a start. As a student of literature, as a reader and writer, I ask, What better way to help begin that decolonizing process than to read a book? And talk to real people. As I mentioned, urban schools all have Aboriginal teams that teachers can bring in and consult with. That would really help them if they were having problems: to get to know those Native people on the Aboriginal teams. Try not to be afraid of making mistakes. We all make mistakes. If we didn't make mistakes we would never learn. That sounds corny, and can be difficult to accept, but as a writer of poetry and prose, as a Métisse woman in today's world, I'll quote my auntie, who has said to me, "A mistake is a gem—like turquoise or ammolite or sweetgrass or sage. A mistake is a learning tool for success, my girl, so suck it up. It is what it is."

AH: Another teacher in the study said that she works with other people, for instance with Aboriginal education resource people and Elders. She knows that if she makes a mistake, someone will tell her. She finds this is something that enables her to do this work. This is an experienced teacher who has been doing this work for decades.

[*We discussed some other topics at this point, including the danger of academic work preying upon student's stories. This topic brought us back to Proulx-Turner's writing.*]

SPT: A close Métis relative recently asked me, "Do you make a lot of money from writing?" I said, "No, I sure don't make a living, I don't make any money," and my relative says, "Really?" There was another relative sitting there, who scrunched up their face and raised their voice to a lowish boom: "Then why the hell do you write? It's a complete waste of time and you're not making money, so why are you writing?" Not what I expected to hear on that snowy day. My immediate comeback? "That is a good question." A pause while I brought my thought to words, "I write because I *have* to."

And even as I said it, even as I'm in my sixties, I had doubt. Western values kicked in. I felt shame. Shame that I might be wasting mine and readers' time. Then I remembered what Elder and artist, writer and photographer Shirley Bear once told me: "It is your duty to write." She went on to say that, like all the arts, writing is a gift. When Creator gives a gift, it is our duty to share that gift. My auntie said the same thing. My grandmother. Did I say any of this to my relatives? No.

Since I'm sharing a very vulnerable moment, I will share this: Deepest truth be told, I write because I *have* to and I write equally because I *love* to. It's because I write a lot of autobiographical material that the process of both the writing for me and the reading for the reader can be difficult in the extreme. I experienced more trauma than most people and I am able to share some of that trauma, to be a witness to atrocities in my lifetime that involved not only me, but too many others who are not able to write, but who are readers. I find reading the stories of others helps me in my life in deep and meaningful ways. I hope my writing can help others and at the same time be not too frightening to endure. According to my mom, living through heinous childhood experiences changes our DNA. We must get it out, she would say. Through the arts is one important way. I feel this in my bones.

In all this, I try not to write about others. I was taught that you do not tell or write somebody else's story. It's one thing if you have permission, like you do in this project, in writing. But, for example, I work with many Indigenous students. I don't write about their stories; they are theirs. If they choose to tell or write about their experiences later in life, that is theirs to do. Of course my story has been shaped by my experiences with these amazing young people, but their stories are not going to be a monolithic thing. I'm not suggesting you are suggesting this, but it makes me think about the acronyms—the TRC, the RCAP, the RCMP. The work that has been done and then undone, undone and then undone some more in the last fifty years, in my memory and lifetime, the conversations of our Peoples that have been recorded and transcribed and put into print and on the World Wide Web. Personal stories. Traditional stories. Literally volumes. Government-run programs.

In our communities, we are generally open, honest. If you are going to tell your story, you tell your story. And now among all the acronyms there are all of these available stories and histories; it's almost as if, in several large rooms—I'm going to say on Parliament Hill in dimly lit vaults—is all of this knowledge-making theft. A new kind of Canadian/Canadienne/ien museum.

Most good work is being done in education. I don't mean as in engineering, or even in literature—I mean education (from my experiences). Generally, teachers in schools know so much more concerning Native histories than the teachers who are teaching those teachers (in universities). When you did your literature degree, did you learn about yourself?

AH: I would say I did, but similarly to the way I said before I felt like I was connecting to people when I was reading literature. I definitely learned about myself in a different way when I did my education degrees.

SPT: I would say that Indigenous ways of knowing are more respected in education disciplines overall, though my own knowledge in this area is limited. There are texts to refer to, like *Pedagogy of the Oppressed* and many, many others. Indigenous ways of knowing are not respected in the other disciplines in the same way, at least in this town. I know at U of C they are trying to implement change, to great opposition still, though there is more support than ever. A great and difficult conundrum that is kept going by a few committed and devoted individuals. Brings me back to decolonization. Where does decolonization fit in reconciliation? Now that's a whole other topic.

[*Proulx-Turner shares some stories from her early days as a student at the University of Calgary, including the lack of support she experienced in the institution at that time. We come around to the topic of strength and resistance.*]

SPT: I am from the Eastern Ottawa River Valley Métis, from Ontario, but my earlier ancestry reaches out to many parts of Quebec back to the late 1500s. Our Métis people there were not a part of the fur companies; there was a law against being Free People punishable by death. It takes fortitude to be Métis. Always has.[21]

People learn about Indigenous Peoples from Indigenous literature—through all the arts. People who hold Western values don't realize, when reading the "classics," people are learning about white people—mostly dead, male, British/American ones. If only people could get a sense of love and pride for who they are (all peoples) instead of having their backs up and backlash at the ready. I think it's key to people's understanding of where we are and whose land we are on, to be able to understand that the future holds the potential for something very different for partnerships between non- and Indigenous Peoples, government aside. Through the arts. Nobody's going anywhere: There are no white people going back to Europe or other, newer immigrants going anywhere else; we're all here to stay.

And the Native population is growing at an exponential rate. We are going to have a much larger number of artists and writers and dancers and actors and singers, teachers and lawyers and doctors and judges and even politicians, mommies and daddies, nokomises and mosoms and aunties and uncles and cousins, sisters and brothers—you name it—twenty years from now. And still more people will be coming out of the Métis closet and claiming their identity, more Algonquin Peoples and other oppressed Nations.

The important thing for me is to have a child go into a classroom and see themselves represented in something they're reading. Even with all the books and all the arts available in this glorious system, for example, my granddaughter has not read about herself in school. Except for her couple closest friends in school (she and them the only Native students in her grade), her friends who are of-colour kids from school (the small group in her grade chum together), she is surrounded by a sea of white faces.

My granddaughter gave me permission to tell this story with her guidance. In her language arts class, she was writing a futuristic story about the effects of pollution on all peoples. Her story was about what can happen, but also the character development was powerful and the plot was complex. The story took a few weeks to write and she kept showing me her progress and her process. I was fascinated by her level of understanding, not just of the world around her, but of the mechanics and structure needed to write a good story. I was humbled by her talent. When she was ready to include her conclusion she was so proud the audience was still uncertain as to what would happen next. I said to her something like, "You're almost finished your story and your audience doesn't know your character is Native." Her response was, "What if they aren't? Native?" "What else can they be?" I wondered aloud. I said to her, "You pick up a book by a Native writer and they will say who they are and where they're from somewhere in their bio. If they don't say, the reader can assume the author is white and the story is appropriated by a non-Native person." "That's true," was my granddaughter's response.

In the end, though, she decided her character would just blend in, like they do at school. She just wanted to give back, she said. She was embarrassed to represent the main character(s) as Native in her story. Yet in the end, she showed her main character and her main character's family is Native after all. "Why, Kokum?" my granddaughter wanted to know when I read the rest of her story. "How?" Several characters from the same family pass away from a rare cancer caused by the level of pollution. When the main character passes, the way her passing is represented by the author is something taught from the character's (and the author's) culture. What the character experiences at her end-time would be foreign to a white person.

Shame. There's that shame again. A beginning solution is to have students see themselves represented in what they are reading in school, and that way be "given permission" to insert themselves into their work in a conscious way.

In Native classes (at Mount Royal), when I asked students, "Why are you in school?" the answers from Native students almost always were just like my granddaughter's: "To give back"—whether they were urban, rez, or from wherever. In non-Native classes, the answer from all the students to a one was something like, "I want a house, a two-car garage, to provide for my family." Values are already so different (and *real*) at the beginning of post-secondary education, in junior high already. Not to mention graduate school. A friend of mine recently graduated from a master's degree in law from the University of Saskatchewan in Saskatoon. The man who is the chancellor for the University of Saskatchewan, Blaine Favel, is an influential Plains Cree leader. At the graduation he had on his chancellor clothing, of course, with beautiful medicine wheels on the front. His speech he gave was powerful. Among many empowering ideas and ideals, he talked about how Native students see their role in education, giving back to community, giving back to family. He said, "How different would this place be if everybody saw their role that way?" Now that would change the world!

So, our voices are small, but they are large. You are going to influence a lot of people, my young friend, and that's what we do as writers. I hear from you that you already see the value of a small act of kindness, for students.

AH: I told you a bit about how I went to Indigenous literatures—for example, poetry by Métis authors—as I grew pride in my Métis heritage and learned what it meant to me and how to live it out well. Reading helped me to connect to the perspectives of other Native people and want to be responsible, to connect to community. I believe that literature is powerful and can enable that kind of process. That is the core piece I started with in this project.

SPT: Yes, literature can do that! Really work hard at getting your audience to be Native. Having a Native audience matters. Think about what you can do to build a Native writing community in Calgary: it doesn't need to just be in Winnipeg and Toronto. You have a role and you can contribute, my girl. You are a force to be reckoned with in your writing. Keep your voice strong. Help keep our circle strong.

"INDIGENOUS LITERATURES MATTER"
A Conversation with Daniel Heath Justice

DANIEL HEATH JUSTICE, a citizen of the Cherokee Nation, was born and raised in Colorado. From a young age he was drawn to fantastical literature and popular culture, and increasingly to texts that enabled him to explore queer and Indigenous issues and identities. A gentle teacher and incisive thinker, Justice works a great deal in academic contexts but has also published a handful of compelling creative works. Pursuing his love of literature through his studies, Justice earned a BA from the University of Northern Colorado and subsequently undertook an MA and a PhD at the University of Nebraska-Lincoln. After moving to Canada in the early 2000s to take up a faculty position at the University of Toronto, he spent ten years in the city, working in the U of T English department as well as with the Aboriginal Studies Program. For the past decade or so, he has been at the University of British Columbia, where he now holds a Canada Research Chair in Indigenous Literature and Expressive Culture. He has held a number of academic leadership roles at UBC, including chairing the school's First Nations and Indigenous Studies Program for five years. As a professor at UBC, Justice has taught in English and in First Nations and Indigenous studies. Invested in nourishing community and relationships around Indigenous literatures and literary scholarship, he has served in a number of roles around that work: for instance, he was the submissions editor for the journal *Studies in American Indian Literatures* and was a founding member of the Indigenous Literary Studies Association, which he has helped to sustain since its inception. He has also been an active voice across social media, advocating for Indigenous, queer, and trans folks, women, marginalized people, and our other-than-human kin, calling for better ways of being together.

Justice's work and engagement in the Indigenous literary arts demonstrates an imaginative spirit. He is known for his personal motto, "imagine otherwise," which shapes his critical and creative work. While he openly names the damages caused by colonization and oppression, he also works to envision other, better ways for things to be. True to these intertwined impulses, Justice has written a three-part epic fantasy called *The Way of Thorn and Thunder: The Kynship Chronicles*, consisting of *Kynship* (2005), *Wyrwood* (2006), and *Dreyd* (2007). The graphic novel–style collection *Love Beyond Body Space and Time: An Indigenous LGBT Sci-Fi Anthology* (2016) features his short story "The Boys Who Became the Hummingbirds." He also published a short story called "Tatterborn" in the 2017 anthology *Read, Listen, Tell: Indigenous Stories from Turtle Island*. Bridging his creative and critical writing is *Badger* (2015), a cultural history of badgers, authored for Reaktion Books' Animal Series. Working largely in critical scholarship, Justice has published wide-reaching research in Indigenous literary studies over the past two decades, focusing on Cherokee studies, queer theory and arts, and a range of issues significant to Indigenous Peoples and creative practice. In our conversation below, Justice and I discuss his book *Why Indigenous Literatures Matter*, which has since been published (2018). He has also edited collections of Indigenous literary criticism, with several well-reputed publications compiled collaboratively with colleagues in the field, including *The Oxford Handbook of Indigenous American Literature* (2014), edited with James Cox.

Justice and I met on October 2, 2015, at the Bear's Inn at Six Nations of the Grand River. We were both at Six Nations for the Indigenous Literary Studies Association's inaugural community gathering, which was co-hosted in that territory. We had shared a long, rich day at Six Nations Polytechnic with the approximately one hundred participants. Okanagan writer and scholar Jeannette Armstrong had given a beautiful keynote on story and community. Indigenous literary studies scholars had shared work on wide-ranging topics, including orality and poetics, Haudenosaunee literatures, kinships and communities, hip hop and spoken word, and using digital media for decolonization. Near the end of the day, a special event was held at which author Joseph Boyden was invited to share a dialogue on his novel *The Orenda*. He responded to Haudenosaunee community members' concerns about his representations of their history in his writing, and he tackled questions of artistic responsibility. Justice had been selected to facilitate and contribute to that difficult conversation. Thus, when he and I started our conversation late that evening, we were very much continuing on with that long day's work, and were already deeply immersed in conversations about arts and community.

Speaking with me as a writer, critic, and teacher of Indigenous literatures, Justice raises a number of significant questions around writing. While writing is powerful, he agrees, that means that it can inflict harm as much as it can help or heal. As such, it is necessary for writers to move carefully, to consider how their work may affect others who have already been misrepresented in literature and across media and culture. Working with a humble spirit, Justice is careful to reflect on his own learning journey and to share his past mistakes. When I ask him what advice he would offer to teachers who are struggling to bring Indigenous literatures into the classroom, Justice channels that humble spirit toward some liberating advice: mistakes are inevitable, and no one can be held to the standard of getting things right all of the time. As I share with Daniel in this conversation, many teachers I have spoken to—within my research and in teacher education classrooms—are afraid of making mistakes with Indigenous education, and I believe that it is helpful for educators to hear this forgiving advice from Indigenous writers. Mistakes are likely inevitable, but we as teachers can do our best, moving through our mistakes to keep learning and working in a good spirit so that we are not hurting others, as much as possible. There is, as Justice shares, still a great deal of work to do, which requires many hands: fear of mistakes need not preclude teachers from doing this work.

Another key strand in this conversation is the need for more stories that speak to those of us who feel under- or misrepresented in much literature and popular culture, such as sexually and gender-diverse people, realistic and full-bodied women, Indigenous people, and so on. Justice has a strong personal enthusiasm for fantasy works that open up space for diverse folk, and articulates both the riskiness and significance of writing outside of his own positionality (e.g., around gender). In articulating his approach to responsible writing, he turns to his kinships: for instance, sharing that the women in his life have made it necessary for his imagined worlds to include strong women, as well as how he has connected with other queer folks and women in his drafting process in order to craft and sustain positive characterizations. In discussing these issues, the infectious imaginative spirit that lights up Justice's creative writing is prevalent, as is the fierce sense of responsibility and community advocacy that shapes his writerly and critical sensibilities.

OUR CONVERSATION

Aubrey Hanson (AH): You are working on a book called *Why Indigenous Literatures Matter*. I smiled when I saw the title, because my big question for this project is the same: Why do Indigenous literatures matter?

Daniel Justice (DJ): Indigenous literatures matter because *we* do. Because Indigenous people matter. And Indigenous Peoples matter. Literature is our voiced expression of being in the world, and it enters a world where we are presumed to already be erased or where we are expected to disappear. Our stories, our fiction, our plays, our poems, our songs, all of these embodied story-ways affirm the rightness of our belonging in a world that is so wounded, and so ruptured, but to which we still hold a significant claim. When it comes down to it, that's why our literatures matter: because we do.

AH: Is there a piece of your creative work that you'd like to talk about, in terms of how that work has been taken up or what you hoped it would achieve?

DJ: My creative work is more fantasy work. I do creative non-fiction, which is a little bit different, but I'm thinking about the fantasy stuff, and its ambitions are modest. What I have really appreciated in readers' responses is that people who feel like they are not included in mainstream fantasy have responded very nicely to these stories, because they see themselves in it for the first time. The best response I ever got—I don't remember who wrote it—was an email from a woman and it was just one line: "Thanks for thinking about us chunky chicks." That made me cry. It was just the most beautiful thing. It was because my female protagonists in my world are not Barbie dolls; they're not skinny little twigs. They are full-bodied women. I want my books to speak to Indigenous people, to queer folks, to women, and to all of us who, in various ways, feel in some ways like freaks and outsiders and weirdos, and the people who don't feel like they have a place in the world, but who are fundamental to the beauty of what this world is. If my fiction does anything, I hope that's it. I would love to have a larger readership, but, if that doesn't happen, that's okay. I just want it to find its way to the people who need it. I write, in a lot of ways, to thirteen-, fourteen-, fifteen-year-old me, who would have just loved to see himself in fantasy worlds that were not written for him.

AH: Certainly, for Indigenous folks, for queer folks, and for real women, it's great. I told you before about the two-spirit gathering and conference at the University of Alberta.[22] One of the people who spoke there was Chrystos. She shared with us that she often felt she had to bring one part of herself or another to gatherings, and so to go to an Indigenous and two-spirit space, bringing her whole self to the conversation, was powerful. That's definitely something I find very validating in your work. If somebody gets it, I can relax and be all there. Often, I have to pick my politics in one context or another. It's more than just validating identities; it's feeling reflected in this. That's one of the important connections for education. It's not just reflecting people. It's not just, "You're here, so we put some Indigenous content in the curriculum."

There's something more. I would ask you this: I know that imagination, imagining otherwise, is one of the ways that you think that through. How is that imaginative work more than just showing that people exist?

DJ: I used to struggle, because I had students who were really resistant to Indigenous literature. One day in class I had this student who said, "I just can't relate to it." So I thought, "I'm going to probe that a little bit more." I said, "What is something that you relate to? Tell me what you're looking for." This was a non-Indigenous student. She said, "I'm looking for something that talks about my experiences." And I said, "Okay, so something that connects with you. It's got to sound like your experience. Something that reflects your life and your way in the world." And she said, "Yeah," and we just kept going like that. "So, if you're looking for something that reflects your experiences, you're looking for a mirror, right?" And she said "Yeah," and I said, "Well, if you're looking in a mirror, you only see yourself. You're reading these Indigenous works to only see you. Where's the Indigenous person in that?" And she kind of stopped, and the whole class was like, "Whoa." And I said, "No, really, I'm not being facetious here. Should literature be a mirror or should it be a window?"

That's dangerous, too: the window metaphor can also be problematic. Even through a window, depending on the light, you can see yourself, but it's not only about you. It's about others in that relationship and it's about another world beyond you. Even for those of us who want to see something of ourselves, I don't think we're looking for a mirror. I think we're looking for a window into a world that includes us. I think we're looking for stories, and images, and possibilities, and dreams, and visions of reality, wherein we are part of the narrative. We are part of the story. We are part of the experience. I think looking just for a reflection can only really lead to narcissism, if it's not about something beyond. Sometimes we need that; sometimes we need just to see what we're comfortable and familiar with. That's totally fine, but if that's the only thing we're looking for, it's not actually about engaging ourselves in the world. I think we're not looking only for ourselves. I think we're looking for ourselves within a bigger context.

AH: I'm smiling because I want to test the strength of this metaphor and see how far we can take the window [*laughs*]. If literature is a window, or could be a mirror, but we want it to be not only a mirror, what are the teacher's responsibilities? You teach Indigenous literatures, too. What are the teacher's responsibilities in mediating that relationship between the person who's trying to look through the window, or looking for a mirror? What are our responsibilities in bringing students to think about how they look through, and think about how they see, and show them how to navigate that space, which in itself is a mediation or a creation? I like how you ask questions about responsibility. Thinking through responsibilities is something important that you've taught me over the years. So, what are the teacher's responsibilities in setting up that relationship between the student and the text and the world?

DJ: I think one of the things that we are called upon to do is to make sure that we are preparing students for the work of that window. You don't take students to the eightieth floor and throw the window wide open and push them though. That is doomed to failure, and it's catastrophic for the student. You can say, "Oh, I'm just throwing you out into experience." Well, you're going to kill them. You're going to do real harm. You don't necessarily only want to do it on the first floor, either, because if you just throw the window open there, they're like, "Yeah, I've seen this before." I think part of the teacher's responsibility is to take a look through that window first. Make sure it's safe. Make sure there's something to see. Make sure that you're giving them everything they need for that. I don't think it's enough just to have the window there. You have to open it up, smell the breeze, experience what's beyond it. And what you may have is smoke and smog; it might be an unpleasant experience, but that's also appropriate sometimes. But make sure the students are prepared as best you can and then give them the opportunity to figure what they want to do with that.

AH: In reading a text, it's not just like, "Let's hang out with this text for a long time." It's also about thinking beyond the text and the classroom and engaging with people and the things that exist outside of books and classrooms. Do you think that's important pedagogically, too, in terms of our responsibilities as readers or teachers? To connect with real people and communities?

DJ: If we don't, then we're just in a gallery. Even galleries now are more interactive. Honestly, if we're not engaging with the world, we're probably in a sarcophagus. We're probably not even looking through a window. We're looking at an epitaph, or we're looking at a headstone. You can learn things from that, but it's probably not going to be something that takes you very far. I've got a lot of mixed metaphors thrown around here.

AH: [*Laughs*] Well, I was thinking about what if it's a peephole-sized window, because sometimes what's through there might be difficult for young people to see; it might be too much. You can have a smaller window. You can have a big window [*laughs*]. That's where I was going.

DJ: That's part of the teacher's job to figure out. Which window do we want to take students to? And why? And are they prepared? Sometimes the peephole is the safest one, because there's just too much danger on the other side. And sometimes the whole damn wall is glass. Instead of a window you have a door. That's part of the teacher's job, to assess as best we can. We're not always going to get it right. We're often going to screw it up, but as long as we are prepared to look after the student, no matter what happens—oftentimes if it doesn't go well and teachers haven't prepped themselves or their students. That's when things can get really challenging.

AH: I want to give you a chance to answer a question that you asked earlier tonight, in another way. As a writer, how do you think about responsibility? Knowing that works can be taken up in certain ways, and given the context that we're all in—in terms of what Indigenous communities are doing, and Indigenous scholarship and Indigenous arts—how do you think about responsibility as a writer?

DJ: Writing is dangerous. Even at its best, it's dangerous. Fundamentally I think we are called upon to do the best we can with what we've got, to learn the lessons we can, but to not go into the world with the intent of harm. It doesn't mean we're going to be successful. It's an old chestnut for a reason: "The road to hell is paved with good intentions." The best of intentions can go awry. It's sad, and it's scary, but it's true. Any power can be a power for evil just as well as for good. The way I think about responsibility is, first, tell the truth as best you can. If you get it right, great. If you don't, learn from it and do better. Do no harm. I try. I haven't always had that philosophy. Some stuff I wrote and published early in my career was pretty ugly and unkind, and I regret that now. I wish I hadn't done that, and I don't do it anymore. You're not always going to get it right, but I think you try.

I'm not a writer who believes that it's my right to write anything I want to. I think that's actually a really dangerous presumption. There are some stories that I have wanted to tell that I decided not to tell, because the hurt it would cause was bigger than the help it would bring. It's not just about me. I now think very carefully about what I write. You can't control how people are going to take it. Some people like my stuff; some people don't; but I don't think many people would say that my work creates harm. I hope they don't. If it does, I want to know so I don't do it anymore. You have to think about responsibility—partly because if you are an Indigenous writer, no matter what your connections are to your community (and I wasn't raised in community), you have to write in the context of settler colonial realities that have already misrepresented Indigenous Peoples and other marginalized peoples to a horrifically negative degree. If you don't understand that context, you're going to hurt people. You may still hurt people understanding that context, but at least, keeping that in mind, you're less likely to be sloppy. I think that context matters. No work of art exists in a vacuum. You have to understand it in the context of a larger conversation, some of which we have some control over but a lot of which we don't.

AH: Is literature always teaching? Story has a long history of being peda-gogical. Is literature—reading and taking it up and talking about it—is that always an educational thing?

DJ: For somebody, yes. Even the most hastily written hack novel will connect to somebody in some way. I think you don't go into it necessarily expecting that you're doing teaching, but you have to go into it knowing that you're influencing somebody's life. If your work is actively working to hurt people, you're going to hurt somebody. If it's actively working to heal, it may heal. The thing about words and stories, even entertainment, is that they are teach-ings. Even fun, silly stuff. I'm working on a book about raccoons now, so I just recently re-watched *Guardians of the Galaxy*. I loved it, but it's a silly movie. You have a talking, genetically modified raccoon who blows things up. He's awesome. And a talking plant man who only says one thing, and apparently the raccoon knows what he's saying. It's an awesome movie. It's very fun. It's well written. It's not deep, but it's cool. Some people have been deeply moved by it, and some people just enjoyed it. That's how it works. I think art will always be educational for somebody, even if it's educating them not to do something that way [*laughs*].

AH: There's a question of audience, too, in terms of that teaching. You were talking about acknowledging the settler colonial context when writing. If I'm an Indigenous writer, and I'm writing knowing there's going to be folks of all walks who take it up, possibly Indigenous folks and non-Indigenous folks, and that sometimes those audiences don't necessarily speak the same language, that's a question of responsibility, too. I might be able to write something for one audience that the other audience won't be able to take up in a positive way. Is that something you think about?

DJ: I'm not writing for a non-Indigenous audience, first of all. If they read it—great, I love it, it's awesome. But they're not the ones I want to get it first. I want *us* to get it first. They *can* get it. There's no great deep mystery or magic in any of the stuff I write.

AH: Well, there's some magic [*laughs*].

DJ: A different kind of magic! But I think it's the kind any thoughtful reader could find. Everybody's going come to it with their own context, and I have my own gaps, too. I try to be really conscious and reflective, especially in terms of gender—just to make sure, as best I can, that I'm not writing problematically about women and trans folks. That I'm thinking about gender in a way that is not furthering misrepresentations that are already out there. Actually, going back to *Guardians of the Galaxy*, I love the movie up until the very end, when Ronan the Accuser is dying and he says, "Who are you?" and Peter Quill says, "We're the Guardians of the Galaxy, *bitch*." I'm like, "Really?" After all of this, and we've really challenged all these stereotypes and presumptions and clichéd templates, and the best insult he can hurl is a misogynistic one? That shot me right out of the movie. For me that's a big one. Women have been so central to my coming to consciousness, whatever consciousness I have. I have a lot to learn, and I don't ever want my work to be something that a woman or a trans woman or trans person reads and feels like they are less human as a result of having read what I wrote. Certainly, I don't want that to be the case for any Indigenous person either, or for queer folks. But gender is a particularly complicated space of accountability for me as a pretty privileged cis-male-identified person. I don't want my writing to ever make already marginalized people feel further dehumanized.

AH: You still take the risk of writing them into your stories, right?

DJ: Oh yeah.

AH: Because they need to be there, and that is the story. I would argue, for you, that you try to create these—I just about said "empowering," which I think is wrong, because your characters are already powerful. It's not like that kind of liberal "Let's lift you out of your disempowered position" idea. But it is a risk—you take the risk of writing these characters in, knowing that it's a powerful thing, because of your own alliances and politics and personal beliefs. If it were done wrong, it could do harm. If it were done well, it could open up a space that needs to be opened up. This space needs to be opened up. There needs to be representation. I am relying a lot on that word, "representation," which I don't love, but these characters need to be there, speaking and living and being awesome.

DJ: My friend Alice Te Punga Somerville, who is a Māori literature scholar, talks about her work as always opening up space. Her job isn't to close down space; it's to open up space. That resonates deeply with me. I think that's my job, too. I'm not there to shut down conversations—unless the conversations are abusive, and, even then, I don't know that we are there to shut them down as much as to change the conversation to something better. I think that's what this is about. If I don't write female and trans characters into my world, then my world actually is not a world that speaks to a huge number of people in my life. If I don't write Indigenous people into my world, obviously it's completely lopsided. If I don't write those characters in, then we're back in worlds where—90 per cent of fantasy worlds do that already, so why would I need to replicate those exclusions? I may get it wrong, and if I get it wrong I'll certainly work to do it better the next time. I'll try my best not to get it wrong, and I'll always test it with readers for their experience.

When I wrote my trilogy, I think all of my beta readers were women, and most of them were queer. And one of them was my mom [*laughs*]. That was scary, because she's a good reader and she didn't tell me what I wanted to hear, which was that it was brilliant and wonderful. She let me know that there were some problems, and I fixed a lot of them. I didn't agree with some of the problems she saw, and I still don't, but most of them needed attention, and the book is better because of her insights. I will always make sure that it's being tested by readers. Hopefully it's good, but if it's not, then I will really work hard to do better the next time. I won't go with the expectation that I'm going to get it right and then be surprised when people call me on it. I'm going in the hope that I did the best I could, with the expectation that people will let me know.

AH: I want to bring you into dialogue a bit with the teachers I talked to. Generally, the teachers I've spoken with are non-Indigenous, English teachers or social studies teachers or Aboriginal studies teachers. They're working in high schools or maybe with younger kids, but the context I usually talk about is secondary education. All of them are in Calgary, and we're talking about how they take up Indigenous content, whether literatures in English classes, or different kinds of things in social or Aboriginal studies. I ask them, "How do you as a non-Indigenous teacher, given this task, how do you position yourself in taking up that teaching work? Whether it's from the curriculum, from your school, from your own sense of ethics, or all of the above. Do you feel comfortable doing it?" We talk about resources; we talk about supports. We talk about a lot of things.

I want to share with you two examples of what people said. One teacher says that she has a lot of connections with people and she knows that, if she makes a mistake in the teaching that she does, somebody will tell her and guide her. She's in connection with lots of supports. That's one example. I had another teacher who said she is intimated to do this kind of work. She articulated very thoughtful ideas about the teaching she does do with Indigenous texts. One of the things that struck me is she said it's intimidating work. She's afraid of getting things wrong. She said the reason it's intimidating is because it matters. She knows enough to know it's important. She's afraid of getting it wrong. Looking at those two teachers and all the spaces in between them, what would you say to non-Indigenous teachers who are struggling with that question? They know teaching Indigenous lit to high school kids is the right thing to do. What would you tell them about that struggle, of how to do it well?

DJ: The first one is yeah, you're going to screw up. You're totally going to screw up. Just like Indigenous teachers screw up. That's the nature of the beast, the reality of teaching. We're going to mess it up. And what's going to work for one group of students is not going to work for the next one. Part of it is to own your imperfection. No one expects that they're going to get it right on other stuff all the time. In some ways that fear of it being perfect can work to lull teachers into a sense that the fear is the work. But the fear isn't the work. The fear can keep you from doing the work.

You're going to screw up, but you're probably not going to destroy your students. If you say "Indian" instead of "First Nations," a student might get irritated at you; you're probably not going to destroy their entire lives. So, I think it's also about keeping things in perspective. This is important work, but it's important in the big picture. You might screw things up one day. Own it, come back, apologize, fix it, if you can. On the one hand, the work we do is important. On the other hand, we're not that important. That's one thing I tell students I work with when they're teaching. Yeah, you may mess up, but there's a huge difference between messing up honestly, being a thoughtful, nice person, and doing something that destroys a student's sense of self. There's a whole world of difference between pronouncing names wrong once or twice and, after being corrected, either repeatedly getting them wrong or outright mocking their names. One error is a mistake; multiple errors are a pattern. There's a whole world of difference between focusing too much on violence in the work by an Indigenous writer and normalizing that violence as though that's the only thing about Indigenous people. You're going to screw it up, and you're going to get it right. You can't learn to get it right if you don't risk screwing it up. You learn, you work, and you do better, and you cut yourself a break. You cut your students a break.

If you go in with the expectation of perfection, you've already failed. You will convince yourself not to do the necessary work, because it's not perfect. In what other thing are we expected to be perfect? It's an easy out. I don't intend this in any negative way toward the person you talked with, who sounds really awesome—and I'm not actually presuming about the teacher; I'm thinking about it just in general—but I think there's a way that some guilty white liberal folks feel like the guilt is the work. Or they're scared. They don't want to get it wrong, because Indians are so mean, right? That's the implication. "I might get it wrong." And? For goodness' sake, no one's going to scalp you! There's this implicit expectation of offence or violence or rage in response to error. Most folks are not unreasonable—once in a while there's going to be somebody who has an unreasonable reaction. In every population, there are people who have unreasonable reactions to things. I get a little impatient with that, not because I don't think that it's a fair or a real response, but I think that it's a response that can disempower. It's a response that can make people feel like what they need to do is just feel guilty or just feel scared and they've done the work. Well no, that's not the work. That's your shit you have to deal with. And then again, sometimes what might seem unreasonable at the moment is actually an entirely reasonable response to relentless microaggressions that diminish and dehumanize. It's complicated. Always. It's always scary. And frankly, if we're too comfortable, we're probably doing something wrong.

AH: There are a lot of factors they shared with me, like contingent employment, funding for resources, and so many things. The material pressure on teachers—or teachers may have something that they want to do, and then the effort it takes to push beyond those canonical, tried-tested-and-true texts: the books are on the shelf; the materials are made; they know the terrain; they know the text; they've studied it in university; they have had communities of dialogue around it; they know what students will ask; they've had their own discussions with instructors; they know the stuff. So, for Indigenous literatures, the uphill climb to get to know the literary criticism, get to know the conversations, understand the cultural investments, have conversations with people, make resources, talk, convince somebody with money to buy the books for the school—all of those uphill things that teachers have to do to do this work, why should they do that? The teachers I have spoken to know why they should do that, but why would you say they should do that?

DJ: Well, first of all I'm glad you pointed that out, because I'm also speaking from a position of real institutional privilege. I can get impatient because I don't have those kinds of obstacles in the same way. We have our own obstacles but they're not the same.

I think the reason they should do that is because the only way things will be better is if we do that. It won't happen otherwise. If they truly believe this is what we have to do, then we've got to do it. If it was easy it would have been done by now. They are being called to carry that bundle. It was never a call that was meant to be easy. They will not see it change in their lifetime to the degree they want to, but if they don't carry that bundle, it won't be lighter for those who come after. They don't have to take it up, but they can't say they believe in the cause if they're not going to do the work. But they're not doing it alone. There are a lot of resources out there, and your work is out there now, and will be out there in a more substantive way. There's a lot of good stuff that's out there, so part of it is to build those networks, to make those connections, and to draw on the expertise of the people who are there. And to risk it. If they really want to change things, they've got to do the work. It can't only be on our shoulders. The problems weren't started by us. The burden wasn't created by us. The solution cannot be left only to us. But the directions to something better have to be led by us.

"A BEAUTIFUL BOMB"
A Conversation with Tenille Campbell

TENILLE CAMPBELL IS a Dene and Métis artist from Saskatchewan. As she explains in our conversation here, she comes from the English River First Nation, in the northern part of the province. At present, she lives in Saskatoon, where she is working toward a PhD in English at the University of Saskatchewan, focusing on Indigenous literary arts. Campbell previously completed an MFA at the University of British Columbia and a BA (honours) in English and Native studies at the University of Saskatchewan. With one foot planted in the academic world, Campbell engages in research and teaching on Indigenous storytelling, kinships, erotics, gender, and visual arts. She was recognized as an up-and-coming artist by CBC Saskatchewan with a 2017 Future 40 award.

Campbell shimmied onto the Indigenous literary stage in 2017 with her breakout poetry collection *#IndianLovePoems*, which emerged from a series of social media posts. Several poems from this book have since been published in various volumes, including *kisiskâciwan: Indigenous Voices from Where the River Flows Swiftly* (2018) and *ndncountry* (a 2018 special issue of the journal *Prairie Fire*). *#IndianLovePoems* was featured in CBC's Great Canadian Reading List in 2017. In 2018, it was recognized with two Saskatchewan Book Awards (the First Book Award and the Indigenous Peoples' Writing Award). That year it was also shortlisted for both the WILLA Literary Awards and the Indigenous Voices Awards.

Campbell's photographic work—which she conducts under the banner of Sweetmoon Photography—has also appeared in a range of magazines, zines, and news publications, as well as in Mary Beth Leatherdale and Lisa Charleyboy's edited collections *Dreaming in Indian: Contemporary Native American Voices* (2014) and *#NotYourPrincess: Voices of Native American Women* (2017). She also did the cover art for the second edition of Kim

Anderson's book *A Recognition of Being: Reconstructing Native Womanhood* (2016). In addition to these projects, Campbell shares her visual art and storytelling through the collective blog *tea&bannock*, an online forum tended by and for Indigenous women that she co-founded.

Tenille Campbell and I met on July 23, 2018, at Weeds Café in Calgary, chatting on the patio until a summer thunderstorm chased us indoors. (And yes, jokes were made about getting wet.) Our conversation explored the connections between the various media in which Campbell works, highlighting the storytelling practices that manifest through her blogging and photography as well as her poetry. By celebrating her own experiences and those of her fellow emerging artists, Campbell suggests that it is powerful, and expected, for young artists to work across diverse platforms. We mention, for instance, the 2018 Indigenous Voices Awards inaugural gala event, which featured poetry and prose readings alongside dance, singing, spoken word, and other kinds of performance in English, French, and various Indigenous languages. Across the multiple modes through which she chooses to share her stories, Campbell considers her kinship responsibilities and what it means to enact good relationships—for instance by representing people with love in her photographic work and creating space for Indigenous women to come together and share experiences through her blogging. Her sensual poetry, likewise, creates opportunities for readers and listeners not only to be titillated and entertained, but also to engage in the important work of connecting around erotic experiences; opening up about their own sexual journeys; asking questions about relationships; and examining what it means to be sexual, contemporary, and Indigenous.

In that same vein, Campbell's poems in *#IndianLovePoems* are more than entertaining and more than confessional. Certainly, as she outlines in our discussion here, the poems reflect very personal experiences along her own sexual journey. In this interview, and elsewhere in the media take-up of her writing,[23] Campbell has described her experiences re-entering the dating world, navigating dating apps and other modern realities, and processing those experiences with her friends and through her poems. (Notably, she does not claim to be the firsthand source of all the stories in her love poems.) Amidst these personal stories and reflections is a strong awareness that sharing erotic experiences—both in the embodied sense and in the sense of discussing and understanding them in community—is an empowering process. Campbell's writing and thinking here connects the erotic lives of Indigenous people to processes of reclamation and, I would argue, resurgence. Whether it's making jokes, speaking our languages, telling our stories, or outlining each other's bodies, Campbell knows how to put Native tongues to good use.

OUR CONVERSATION

Aubrey Hanson (AH): Do you want to start by telling me about yourself?

Tenille Campbell (TC): I am Tenille Kelry Campbell. I am Dene from English River First Nation and I am Métis from the Batoche region. I am the daughter of Ornella Campbell and Isadore Campbell. I have three brothers. I grew up on reserve. We're a very close family—too close! We're always in each other's business. I have one daughter who is seven. I have an ex who is also Dene and I'm very close to him and his family as well. They are my extended family. Academically, I'm in my PhD program at the University of Saskatchewan, studying under Kristina Bidwell. As a writer, I'm the author of *#IndianLovePoems*, published last April through Signature Editions. I'm also a blogger of *tea&bannock* and a photographer with Sweetmoon Photography—storytelling on multiple levels.

AH: Awesome. I want to ask you about all of those projects and how they fit together, but why don't I start by asking you a bit more about *#IndianLovePoems*.

TC: *#IndianLovePoems* was a project that came out of me being very generous with my time and spirits and emotions with multiple, multiple, multiple men and women, and writing about that experience of casually engaging in sex, being emotionally available to people when usually very closed off. That process of healing through sex, healing through relationships, through kinship, but also having one-night stands and making it not a big deal. Reclaiming that space in a lot of ways. For me, writing about it was this automatic expression of myself and my story. So I started writing these little things, probably around early 2013, and sending them to my friends, sending these short little poems to people I thought would get a laugh or connect to the idea I was presenting. I was very lucky that an editor got wind of a couple of poems and was like, "I want to publish this." He was pretty persistent and got me a contract with Signature Editions and worked with me. I made sure he was Indigenous, because I wanted this to be Indian love poems for other Indians. I wanted it to be cultivated in our languages and our sense of humour. I was really lucky with that. A lot of the poems are tongue in cheek. They're meant to make you grin and laugh and blush and feel uncomfortable, but humour's such a great gateway into talking about sex that I found it really worked for us.

AH: Nice. And the hashtag comes from the Twitter history. Is that like—I'm not on the Twitter and I don't understand it.

TC: The Twitter [*laughs*].

AH: The Twitter, the tweeting.

TC: I'm not on the Twitter. Now you have me saying it. *#IndianLovePoems* came out of Instagram usage for me, because I'm big on Instagram.

AH: Okay, you can put a hashtag on an Instagram, too?

TC: Yes! I wasn't trying to make big, traditionalist love poems. I wanted to talk about here and now, how we make love, how we make mistakes, and how we connect with each other. These were born on a computer being texted to my friends. It was a nod to that urban experience, urban love, modern love.

AH: How does that fit with your photography and the kinds of stories you're trying to tell through that work?

TC: They fit together, just natural reflections of each other. Sweetmoon, my photography business, is a visual love story to Indigenous people. That's what I specialize in; that's where I'm welcomed most; that's where I feel connected to most. Sweetmoon was born of me wanting to get images that reflected my experiences as an Indigenous person. I wanted the joy and the laughter; I wanted the beauty and the chaos; I wanted the culture and the traditional ceremonies; and I wanted us shopping at the mall and wearing stuff other than ribbon skirts. I wanted to show the modern experience that we have as Indigenous people.

AH: There's a lot of history of not being represented by yourself, right? Of non-Indigenous people telling Indigenous stories.

TC: Exactly. Being Indigenous is foundational to Sweetmoon and the views that it reflects. I wouldn't be invited into a lot of spaces—I wouldn't be given the trust and the community and kinship—if I wasn't Indigenous and couldn't claim my spot there.

AH: What about your blog? Where did that come from?

TC: *tea&bannock* is definitely born of love. We started in January 2016, me and Joi Arcand, a Cree artist out of Muskeg. I contacted her and I literally was just like, "Joi, I want to start this blog. I'm a writer, I'm a photographer. I want to combine them and I want to work with you." She's a visual artist who also works with photography. She's amazing. She's this great storyteller, and she's also a graphic designer; she has an amazing eye. She designed my Sweetmoon logo and our *tea&bannock* logo. I was like, "I think we just need to do this." I thought I'd have to woo her a lot because I'm actually quite intimidated by her, but she was just game right away—like, "Okay, let's do it." Then between the two of us, we just started naming women that we wanted to work with. We wanted it to be women's stories; we wanted to have an Indigenous women's space. A lot of them were women I had never met. They were just people I followed on Instagram: I was like, "They could tell a good story, they can take a great picture. Let's do it." I wanted a mix of urban and northern and we're trying to go more east, although it's harder because we don't have many contacts out there. It's all word of mouth and it's slow going still. We wanted to feature other artists, not just photo artists, and we wanted to have guest bloggers to give space for other women to come onto the blog and tell their stories. It just kind of took off. People loved it. We're growing every day. It's my labour of love.

AH: What would you say—in all the art that you do across these various projects—what brought you to your art?

TC: I grew up with storytelling—and I'm not talking about the traditional Wesakechak and Trickster and Sky Woman. I'm talking about the family stories. Dad would tell stories about his youth and baseball and hockey and slow-pitch before he would read us a book. Mom would tell us about Uncle Charlie and chuckwagon races and growing up on the farm before she would read us a book. We learned to speak and listen, and speak and listen well. I think that definitely affected how I engaged through life. Writing was an escape for the ideas always floating in my head. I was a writer before I was a photographer. Reading was always this thing that I could do well and imagine and lose myself in. Writing was just a natural extension of who I was. It wasn't something I had to work hard for; it wasn't something that I had to sit down and force myself to do. It was a joy; it was an expression.

Photography came later. I always kind of stole my mom's camera, back in the film days. I still have those pictures. They're amazing. When I graduated my first degree and then I took my master's at UBC, my dad asked me what I wanted. I was the first in my family to go to a graduate program. I was like, "Oh, I want one of those cameras I can't use, because I'll learn how to use it." And he was like, "Okay, my girl. Sure. That makes no sense to me, but okay." So he bought me my first camera. Then when I was at UBC, I took some godawful pictures. They were so bad. Then, when I came back to Saskatoon in 2010, I was better at it. I put it out there that I was going to do this. It felt weird to shift from "I'm going to be a writer" to "I'm a photographer." Definitely my identity switched, but once I realized that this was just another form of storytelling, it sat more comfortably with me. I was like, "Okay, I can do this." I took it from there, and haven't stopped since.

AH: It's neat to hear you talk about all of them as storytelling. How do you think about what stories you're telling, or who you're telling them for, when you're doing all that work?

TC: That European idea that you can be neutral when you're telling a story—as a photographer, you're still supposed to step aside and just document the moment—that's bullshit. Who we are is foundational to the stories that we tell through writing or literature or art: how we place ourselves in the story. Being Indigenous, working on Indigenous stories through photography, I'm always someone's daughter. I'm always related somehow, and if I'm not related, they know me through someone. I have responsibilities far beyond "I took your picture." I have responsibilities to make sure that these pictures are no longer used online in memes or in any hurtful way, that they aren't stolen. I take care of them. These are my people and my images of my people.

AH: I feel like the word *community* gets used a lot, and it's one people put a lot of weight on, and it means a lot of different things to different people. How do you think about community when you're doing your work as an artist, as a writer? What would you say community means to you?

TC: *Community* is definitely a buzzword nowadays. Community, for me, is pretty neutral. Community means a lot of different things—a lot of different spaces, land, culture, identity, education, job, art type. It can go as big as the community of Turtle Island to the community of my family and who we allow in. I find I work more with the idea of *kinship* right now. I find having to have that personal responsibility to do well by those around you, and to have them do well to you, is important, especially as I raise my daughter. I want her to understand that. And the idea that kinship can be ended. I think a lot of people don't like that idea, but I'm a huge advocate of not having toxic people in your life—again, especially now that I'm raising a daughter. Growing up, I was always told, "Be nice." And I'm like, "Baby girl, you don't have to be nice. Be strong, be powerful, be your own advocate. And if someone's not treating you right, I don't care if they're a distant auntie, you have the right to leave." So, I think that's what works for me—*kinship*.

AH: That kind of language has meant a lot to me, too. I've learned a lot from people like Daniel Justice over the years and his work on kinship.[24] There's a lot to be learned from that way of remembering that relationship is an ongoing set of give-and-take responsibilities. It's not just a free pass to anything, or something that you can take for granted.

TC: You're more aware of your actions and your words and how you represent when you're aware that it not only affects you, but the space that you're in. I'm in an Indigenous community no matter what, because I'm Indigenous. But am I accepted in someone's kinship circle, because I'm a good person?

AH: What is it that you hope that your work will do? If you think about your kinship relations, your people, what do you want them to get out of it?

TC: #*IndianLovePoems* opens up a space for women, and men, and people, to explore their own ideas of love: what it means for Indigenous love and what it means to love. It's already doing that. I get DMs on the daily from people sending me poems—or pictures, Lord help me![25]

AH: Oh my gosh. I guess you would, hey?

TC: Yeah, I do. It's creating this beautiful kinship community where just by being online and presenting the work and stories that I do, I'm already engaged in their lives in a very intimate way. They're giving back to me by sharing what they create with the energy that I'm giving them. I did not expect that. I did not expect to create that kind of intimate change in people.

AH: I heard an interview on the radio with Tracy Lindberg;[26] she talked about how books enter your home, and that's an intimate space. Your book is in people's bedrooms and they're probably reading it, like—

TC: Oh, I literally had a DM from, like, a guy two days ago saying, "My partner gave me your book. Every day we read a couple poems. Thank you for the gift of the poetry and thank you for the sex that comes after." I'm like, "You're welcome."

AH: Did that make you feel proud?

TC: Yeah. These are things that people say that they would never say to anyone else.

AH: It's public but it's a private exchange, right? Talking about intimate encounters, I wanted to ask you: Why sex? Why is that an important site for you of creativity and possibility? [*Laughs*] And action?

TC: [*Laughs*] Action! Well, I was in a long-term relationship from age seventeen to twenty-nine, twelve years with the same person, completely loyal, never even thought of another person. I was very monogamous; that was the one. Then, when we broke up, I gave myself a lot of emotional time to heal, to kind of just work through what I had to work through. Then came the physical stuff, of "I need to take this step," and I chose someone completely opposite of who he was, just for sex. I didn't want a relationship; I didn't want anything beyond one night. And the sex itself was amazing. It was great. My friends still laugh at the stories I'll tell about it, because it was wonderful.

But then I went home and I bawled. I cried so hard. It wasn't about the sex or the casualness of it. It was the grief of physically moving on from this relationship. As casual as I am about it now, sex at that time was very much a deliberate step, very much part of my healing, part of what I wanted to reclaim—my body, my pleasure, for myself.

And when I was telling my girlfriends about this, it kind of amazed me, the varying reactions I got. I felt super judged by a couple of them. I love them, and they're great. I understand this was completely 180 from who I was before, so of course they were questioning it. But I was like, "We should be able to talk about sex in a way that it brings people together, in a way that we don't feel embarrassed or shamed about it, in a way that we have safe spaces where we can be like, 'What do you think about this idea?' 'I feel like it's a little far-fetched but I'm curious.' "

I didn't know if I wanted to be that person, because that's a lot of energy to give people. I had to figure out a way that I was going to do it. The poems were an automatic expression—at first it was just me telling my stories. Once I started sending them out and people started to know what I was doing with them, there was more engagement. Like, "I can't believe you're doing this, but thank you." Or, "My auntie thinks you're so funny." Then you see the multiple generations, because, like, let's not pretend that grandma with thirteen kids doesn't know what sex is. And the idea of having sex and refusing to leave the bed until you orgasm, like *refusing*. There were all these layers that I didn't know I had that I was working through in bed. I had thought I was pretty well adjusted. I *was* fine, but I also never pushed boundaries, I never engaged beyond monogamy. I had never invited someone else into the bedroom with me and my partner. I told myself, "You know, this is like a bucket list. Let's just do some things, and try some things, and understand what consent is, and what your limits are." When I was really deep in exploring sex, I always had my own set of rules to make it safe for me. It was never about having sex while drunk or high. It was always about having a safe space, letting people know who I was with, where I was, phone numbers, addresses. It kind of humbled me that I had to do this. "You're not sixteen anymore and you're not in the North. People aren't going to know about it at the bar the next day!"

There were so many layers to work through, but sex is just one of those things that we all experience or know about, and it's unifying. When you throw in Indigenous culture on top of that, it becomes very tricky and hard to navigate. It becomes very layered. I just wanted to be that person that my friends, at first, can come to and talk to. I wanted them to be that person as well. Even the casual conversations between me and my friends had to really push boundaries and open up. There's been negative pushback—like, "All we do is talk about sex." I'm like, "Cool, I have a kid. I have a blog. I have photography. We can talk about many other things. But do you want to hear the stories, but don't admit you want to hear the stories? Do you want to ask questions but are too shy?" It was really learning to take that criticism and seeing what they're saying underneath that.

AH: And everyone has their own histories and feelings. I know, for myself, any new conversation can raise things that I might not be ready to share—or I just haven't thought through yet. I do tend to talk pretty openly about sex, relationships, history, things like that. I find sometimes it's a bit infectious and people are like, "Oh my gosh, I've been wanting to talk about this," and it catches on. And other times it's like, "Ah, no thank you." In the reception to the book, I can imagine you've gotten a lot of reactions. I'm curious what people think about that relationship between being open and the cultural piece?

TC: For the most part, after a performance, I get a lot of praise and positive feedback, and laughter and giggling and nudging. I get a lot of new Facebook friend requests.

AH: You have to figure out how to navigate that.

TC: Yeah. I'm pretty secure in my Facebook and in my private Snapchat. If you want to find me and engage me, Instagram is actually the way to do it. Plus, I have a private Instagram of just friends and family stuff. I've really had to set some boundaries. My daughter's kind of my guideline for that.

In terms of feedback, usually the negative stuff comes privately. It comes in DMs. It comes in being pulled aside, and usually it's older Native women who are just like, "We don't talk about this." I've learned, again, to step back. It's not personal; it's never personal. It's their own issues with sex and they're on their journey. Often, I'm like, "Thank you, I don't agree. Let's carry on, on our different paths," because it's not my job to educate them. You can't change someone's mind if that's what they think. Everyone's on their own self-awareness journey.

AH: The last time we saw each other, you were being recognized through the Indigenous Voices Awards program. Could you say a little bit about what that experience was like?

TC: It was really great. I know the origin of where the IVAs came from, so I was really proud to be nominated. I also knew that I was sharing space with Billy-Ray and I was like, "Sit down, Tenille."[27] Billy-Ray's work is so foundational and so important. I always laugh because I'm like, "This is serious poetry." It's not that mine isn't, but mine is definitely meant to catch you with Indian humour and catch you with the shared reminiscence while you read it. Billy-Ray's is so personal, and this is his journey, and if you connect, wonderful, but you're reading his diary.

AH: I don't mean to set you up to compare. What I love about the richness of your work—and I see it in how all your different modes connect, like the photography and the blog—you're getting out into people. There's a real openness to sharing that kind of intimacy with everyone. I personally see it as a kind of service.

TC: [*Laughs*] There are a lot of services in that book!

AH: [*Laughs*] You're offering something to people. It's a different way of engaging. I get excited about the IVAs program, because I think it has poten-tial to bring some spotlights to people who really deserve it.

TC: Yeah! It was great, and there is no comparison of Billy-Ray or any author. We're all very different, and I think that's one of the things that non-Indig-enous people in mainstream society don't really get. It's not a competition. We're here telling our stories and they're all so different, and that's what I love about it. This idea of Pan-Indianism, or "Indigenous experience"—yes, there are unifying factors, but foundationally, it's all so varied. There's so much storytelling and so many forms and genres to share.

AH: That builds us up to my last question, the big question that I ask every-body: Why do Indigenous literatures matter? Your art, your photography, your blogging—why does the art matter?

TC: For mainstream society, for settler society, I think it matters because we are claiming the space that we should have rightfully inherited from the start. We don't need any more Grey Owls. We need Billy-Ray and Smokii Sumac and Brittany Catherine and all these young emerging writers standing up,[28] and not giving any fucks about structures in place, and saying, "No, *this* is how we're expressing ourselves, in multiple formats." All these artists that I admire and work with are not just writers. The way that they're claiming space on all these different artistic expressions brings me so much joy. The fact that I carry multiple forms of storytelling within me didn't surprise me, but it made me laugh how often it surprised other people. I was like, "Who has one job title?" [*laughs*].

I think it matters for Indigenous people, for our communities, because they see reflections of themselves in the work. When I read these poems in Cree territory—[*laughs*] I'm laughing at this poem. There's a poem where I'm having sex and I count, "peyak, niso, nisto, newo." And the guy asks, "What does that mean?" I'm like, "You're my sun, my moon!" Cree people know it means "one, two, three, four." So it's hilarious, and there's Cree and

Indigenous humour right in the poem. I was reading these poems up in La Loche; I was there for a writing camp. There are poems that obviously say dirty things: one of them is "bénachulé nezu," which means "I like your big penis." They lost it, because there's never Dene in poetry; there's never Dene in a published book, unless it's old archaic history books. I think seeing reflections of our words, our stories, our humour, our laughter, our celebrations—that's what important, that's why our stories matter.

AH: That space—it's risky, vulnerable, and it's so powerful when we open it up—it's such a vital place. You're talking about reclaiming, and people telling their stories, and taking up space in ways that they should. In academic work, we stick a lot of labels on things, like *decolonizing, Indigenizing, resurgence, reclamation*—all of those words. I think whichever one of those you're working on, that intimate space, that sexual space is a powerful place to be working on that from. And it's alive—you're bringing the language out in these really vital ways.

TC: It's important to note that I'm not the first. I'm not alone in this. Tracy Bear and Janet Rogers and Kim TallBear and Gregory Scofield and Drew Hayden Taylor, Richard Van Camp—the list goes on. I'm just one of those people who has a very savvy knowledge now of social media. Let's not underestimate the power that social media gives us to reach people. I think that's what has helped it, because when a lot of these books were coming out, Facebook was new or non-existent. Instagram was not a thing. So the combination of social media, plus a slightly taboo topic, plus humour, was just a beautiful bomb to go off.

"TO WRITE MYSELF BACK INTO VISIBILITY"
A Conversation with Marilyn Dumont

MARILYN DUMONT IS MÉTIS and lives in Edmonton. Her family has a long history in the area, as she explains in this interview; she is also ancestrally tied to the Dumont family, which has played a significant role in the history of the Métis homeland. She has built up her writing career alongside a formal education, earning a BA from the University of Alberta and an MFA from UBC. Currently, she is an associate professor at the University of Alberta, jointly positioned in the Faculty of Native Studies and the Department of English and Film Studies. Her teaching at U of A focuses on creative writing, particularly on poetry and Indigenous writing. Beyond this current role, Dumont has taught creative writing in a number of capacities: as a writer-in-residence at five different Canadian universities as well as the Edmonton Public Library, and as a mentor at the Banff Centre, for instance in its Aboriginal Emerging Writers' Program. Dumont also interned with the National Film Board of Canada in video production, and has served with the Public Lending Rights Commission of Canada.

Marilyn Dumont's first published book of poetry was *A Really Good Brown Girl*, first published in 1996. This book has since gone through numerous reprints, and in 2015 Brick Books published a second edition in its "Classics" collection. The book has also been translated into French. Dumont followed her debut with *green girl dreams Mountains* (2001) and *that tongued belonging* (2007). Her most recent poetry collection is entitled *The Pemmican Eaters* (2015). Widely taught and anthologized, Dumont's writing has also won multiple awards at both the provincial and national level. She was awarded the Gerald Lampert Memorial Award in 1997 for *A Really Good Brown Girl*, and in 2007 *that tongued belonging* earned her the McNally Robinson Aboriginal Poetry and Aboriginal Book of the Year Award. She has also won the Stephan G. Stephansson Alberta Book Award for Poetry from the Writers' Guild of Alberta twice, once in 2001 and once in 2016, for *green girl dreams Mountains* and *The Pemmican Eaters*, respectively. In 2018, she was also awarded a lifetime membership in the League of Canadian Poets.

I met Dumont in her office in the U of A Faculty of Native Studies on October 2, 2018. As with many of these meetings, I was both excited and nervous to be meeting with a literary idol, a Métis writer whose words had shaped my own experience to such an immeasurable extent. It helped that she and I had met before at a few literary gatherings, at least in passing. We had once been thrown together in a drama game at an ILSA workshop, forming neighbouring pieces of an imaginary machine, whirling our limbs and emitting regular beeps and whirs, advancing some unknowable mechanical operation. Going into this conversation, then, I had an idea of her as playful and good-spirited, in addition to admiring her stature as a substantial figure within the Métis literary scene.

Our conversation begins with me getting to know Dumont a bit better, connecting my questions about her writing to her personal background and to her emergence as a writer. With her current university teaching role at the fore of her mind, she speaks about the significance of writing for young Indigenous people, and women particularly, who, she explains, do not often grow up with a sense that their stories have literary merit. In this way we move straight into the question of why it matters for young people to see their experiences reflected in literature and to feel that their own stories are worthy of belonging there, to feel that they, too, are worthy of a sense of importance and belonging in the world. Dumont connects these experiences for young writers to the need for mentorship work, caring labour that she points out is disproportionately done by women.

In addition to reflecting personal and cultural experiences, Dumont suggests, literary works can illustrate the depth and breadth of Indigenous knowledge. That is, the historical lack of respect for Indigenous stories also reflects the lack of respect for Indigenous knowledge systems. Dumont speaks to her own parents' wealth of knowledge, living in a "traditional" manner, in the bush and speaking Cree, for instance. Part of her work as a writer has been to voice those experiences and validate the knowledge that they represent. These aspects of Dumont's writing—and of other writers' work that demonstrate, describe, and validate Indigenous ways of knowing, being, and doing—are an important site where artistic and educational work come together for Indigenous communities.

In responding to my questions about community, Dumont highlights the centrality, for her, of Indigenous people and Indigenous poets, particularly Métis people, but she also explains that the non-Indigenous audience is an important one for her, in that her writing often aims to resist or push back against racism and colonialism; those poems are also for a settler readership. We discuss the educational effects of her writing, the fact that reading Dumont's poems can draw people into learning more about the Métis, about Métis presence and history, about the strength and vitality of Métis people, as well as about experiences of oppression, dispossession, discrimination, and violence. For Indigenous readers, this learning is important in that, when they learn more about themselves through literature or their studies, they are better able to connect to their families and ancestry and develop a grounded sense of self in relation. For a mainstream readership, Dumont voices the need for readers to learn from Indigenous literatures so that public consciousness can change. This point is timely, given recent shifts in the Canadian literary scene: people are now excited about reading work by Indigenous writers, people of colour, women, and so on. Dumont expresses the hope that, at the very least, such learning could encourage non-Indigenous people to treat the Métis, as well as First Nations and Inuit Peoples, with more respect—a necessary step for relationships to change.

OUR CONVERSATION

Aubrey Hanson (AH): Do you want to start by telling me a bit about yourself?

Marilyn Dumont (MD): I see Edmonton and area as my homeland, but it's taken many years to come to that, with family moving around and displacement and all kinds of things. Over the last seven or more years, I've been doing more reading about this area and recognized that this really is my family's homeland—not only in the Dumont name, but, on my mother's side as well: Dufresnes and Vanesses were also in this area. Two years ago, I found out that the little research we did on my mother's side has been a blind spot for my family, because we now know that Francois Dufresne, our great-grandfather, was the illegitimate son of Chief Factor Rowand, who was the chief factor here in Edmonton. I'm sure he's not the only illegitimate child, but knowing that now, I think that's kind of amazing. This really is my homeland, in terms of my ancestors on both sides now.

Who am I as a writer? I've been really struggling. I'm going into my third year here,[29] and I've been really struggling trying to find time and space, and head space, to do any writing. I just haven't found it. It's getting to the point where I'm really having to say, "Okay Marilyn, we're going to have to buckle down; you have to find time." It feels like I'm being totally drained by this job. I love the teaching. I love the teaching of creative writing, especially to Aboriginal students, because they have never been asked to write about themselves. They've never had the opportunity. If you can imagine—some of them have gone through twelve years of school and then maybe four years of university—and it's the first time they even write about themselves. I just think that's crazy. To me it's indicative of how much work there is to do in reconciliation—if that's even a possibility. If Indigenous people are so distanced from their own sense of self, how can things possibly change? For many of them, it's a really empowering kind of experience to say, "This is who I am, and I stand behind my words." Maybe it's the first time they've ever had to do that. So, for me, as a writer, that's also a really big part of what I do, is to encourage and support other writers.

I find that that's quite a different role from what male writers inhabit. There is, I think, very little sense from male writers that they have to give back to the community. Somehow, we're all supposed to run to them and fawn over them, like, "Wonderful, wonderful, wonderful." They go off and do their own writing or creative stuff, but I don't see them supporting other writers.

AH: Whereas you feel called to be an auntie, to help support everybody?

MD: Yeah, because it's so important. One voice is great, but hundreds of voices is so much better, because it will give people who don't know Indigenous people a much broader perspective of who we are. There isn't any one writer who can write all that. But there are hundreds of writers out there who could, and that's one of the things I'm really interested in, is making sure that the Indigenous students that come into a creative writing class with me, that they leave with something meaningful and substantial about themselves, about their culture, about their kinship to other people. They've never had the opportunity, never been allowed, never been required to do that kind of self-reflection. I just think it's so important. Yes, it's a position of being an auntie, but it's more than that—it really is part of the professional role of being a writer. Not all writers are like that, I know.

Particularly for Indigenous women writers to support one another is critical, because there is no Native guy out there who is an author who is going to be singing our praises. They just don't do it, and they're not expected to. Maybe Indigenous women aren't either, but I think it's really important that we also focus on the writing community, and not just on the individual or the exception. So, that's a really big part for me of being a writer as well: to support, nurture, and encourage Indigenous women writers.

AH: I want to pick up on the part you're saying about people being able to reflect on themselves and think about who they are, and to be able to speak about their own story or identity. To understand themselves and be able to express that, but also to recognize kinships and do that in relationship and in context. I think as an educator, and as somebody who works with teachers, that's so central to what I do. If you're going to be teaching other people, you have to go through that reflective work. Know your story, and know where you come from, and be grounded and positioned. We could talk all day about the complexity of reconciliation work, but being able to understand who you are in a relationship is necessary. We're all journeying, and learning, and it's complicated, but that work of being able to tell your story—for our young Indigenous people, to validate who they are and where they come from—is huge.

MD: It's huge, yes.

AH: I like to ask people how they think about community when they're writing, whether it's Indigenous communities or the writing community—or there's often an invocation of campus community or academic communities. What strikes you as important about *community* when you think about your writing?

MD: I definitely think about other Indigenous people, but also other Indigenous poets—as opposed to novelists or people who write memoirs—because poets do a particular thing with language that nobody else does. Those are two big communities for me, the Indigenous community, Métis particularly. But in the past, there's been so few Métis writers, particularly in Alberta. Poets and the Indigenous community are my two main audiences, but it is also the non-Native audience. When I'm writing about resisting things, quite often I'm talking to the non-Native audience.

AH: Like in "The White Judges."[30]

MD: Yeah.

AH: I try to keep this project grounded in Indigenous perspectives and working for Indigenous communities, but there's often this call to a mainstream Canadian readership. Do you kind of think about what people, Indigenous or non-Indigenous, are learning from reading your poems? Do you think about it that way?

MD: Absolutely. Especially being in Alberta, where people are just not educated about the Métis. Even though it's an exceptional province in terms of its land tenure for the Métis.[31]

AH: People don't know about that.

MD: No, people don't know about that. Nor do they know how powerful our Métis organizations are.

AH: Do you think about if, or what, people are learning when reading your work?

MD: Definitely. This last book, *The Pemmican Eaters*, all Canadians—I think the reason the book got attention was that people were surprised. Like, "Oh my God, there's actually Métis history here in Alberta." It's definitely educating people about the Métis—and not only the Métis, but also First Nations people. Quite often we're just forgotten. People say, "Treaty 6," and that's it. There is also the Métis Nation that you have to acknowledge.

AH: People say, "We are all Treaty people," and you say, "Okay, but ..."

MD: No, we're not.

AH: What about the Métis? How do we fit in that?

MD: Yeah. And it's naive to think the First Nations people are going to say, "Come on, yeah, you come on in." They don't want us to be competing for their resources.

AH: If it was a situation of abundance it'd be different.

I'm always interested in the young person finding poetry, partly because that's my own experience—although I didn't run into Métis writers until my second or third year of an English degree. There was a CanLit prof at UVic who was dedicated to putting Indigenous writers on the syllabus—a couple of my profs there did a good job. Your work, and Gregory Scofield's work, and *In Search of April Raintree*—those were the first three things I remember reading that really struck me, in terms of listening to Métis voices through the page. Did you have an experience like that, or what brought you to writing? When did you start, or why did you start?

MD: I started because I felt like I needed to vent. I needed to get stuff out, and I needed to try to figure things out on my own, because it didn't seem like anyone in my family knew, and nobody at school. I had to try to write my way out of confusion, really. Only in retrospect did I realize I grew up in a pretty traditional lifestyle. We were a big family: I'm the youngest of nine. The only way my parents could feed us was to have wild meat—we couldn't go buy that stuff; it was impossible. So, that's what I grew up with, eating wild meat and, when my father worked in the bush, we lived in a little trapper tent. Only in retrospect did I find that I actually lived a pretty traditional upbringing, with both my parents speaking Cree, and speaking Cree to my relatives, who would come and work with my dad or come and visit from the settlements.

I didn't see any of that in any reading that I had done. Zero. So, I thought, "Well, I'm going to write about this." It really was a way to bring sanity to me. I really did need to express those emotions, those feelings, those confusions. I needed some kind of understanding of it for myself. Then, in the process of writing my first book, I realized, maybe this isn't just about me. Other people were giving me feedback on this saying, "Wow, this has really struck me—it resonates with me." Then I really did understand that what I was writing was not just about me; I was writing about other people's experience, too. I didn't really know it at first. When I wrote my first book, my ideal reader would've been a young, Indigenous, Métis woman who said to herself, "Wow, I feel this way, too." That was the person I was writing to in my first book, *A Really Good Brown Girl*. Yeah, I saw nothing in what I read or that was in the media about myself. It was one way of making myself real, to write about myself, to make myself visible. To say, "Yes, I do exist in this province, even though it has tried to erase me, and has done a pretty damn good job of erasing anything Métis."

AH: So it's safe to say you didn't see yourself reflected in what you learned at school or what you were given to read?

MD: Nothing, no. In fact, the general feeling I went away from school with was that I was deficient. I needed to be something different; I needed to be white, or more white. I always felt like there was something wrong, something just not quite good enough. I had to fight against that, and I did it through my writing. Really it was to write myself back into visibility. I don't think people realize how damaging that whole colonial legacy is, when you feel like a zero and a nothing, or not important, not interesting. You have no knowledge; you come from a culture that is not important. That hurt me.

It really hurt, because when I looked at my parents, I thought, "They know a lot of stuff." Growing up in the bush, my dad could easily make a camp for us. He'd go out with his little hatchet or saw and cut things down, and set up a camp perfectly, so it wouldn't blow down in the wind. My mom was the same. She could cook over an open fire. She could bring out that frying pan and make bannock right there. It seemed to me like that's stuff other people don't know how to do. It was something that they possessed as knowledge. And both of them speaking Cree—that was always seen as backward or not important. Like, "That's of no use whatsoever" and, "What good is that?" kind of thing. That was really painful for me, to have people think that my parents were like blank slates, that they had no knowledge. It was ridiculous. Those kinds of ideas were perpetuated in the school system. Those kinds of things hurt me to the core, and then I had to get them out and write about it.

AH: Do you remember when you first found other Indigenous writers to read?

MD: Maria Campbell's was one of the first books that I read, when I was seventeen or eighteen. She had just published it. That was pretty amazing, to read that. Then I started reading Lee Maracle, Jeannette Armstrong, anyone whose books I could happen upon. Then also writers from the States, like Joy Harjo, Leslie Marmon Silko, Simon Ortiz.

Also, I started to read Black women writers: like in the US would be Lucille Clifton or Gwendolyn Brooks, Zora Neale Hurston, but also, in Canada, Marlene Nourbese Philip and Dionne Brand. What resonated with me with their writing was—I didn't know at the time, but it felt like, "Wow, they know about living in poverty, or they know about living in or some kind of oppression." So I was really drawn to their work as well. I could relate to what they were pushing back against, in all kinds of ways.

I read everything I could get my hands on that was Indigenous; it would've been in the eighties when I started reading, I guess. Then I taught a course up here—just a non-credit course through the women's centre (which was part of the Faculty of Extension in the eighties), because they weren't teaching anything in the English department about Indigenous anything. I had grad students come over and take that course, a non-credit course, because they offered nothing in the English department.

AH: Was that course focused on Indigenous writing?

MD: Yeah, Indigenous women's writing. We read everyone that I've mentioned, plus Kimberly Blaeser, Linda Hogan, Wendy Rose.

I just read as much as I could possibly read, and then I also started to read writers from other countries that had experienced colonialism. I read people like Ngũgĩ wa Thiong'o and Chinua Achebe. These people really influenced my writing, particularly when Ngũgĩ said, "I'm not writing in English anymore, I'm not writing in the colonizer's language," and I was blown away by that—"Oh my God, you're my hero." What a risk to take, for a writer to say, "I'm not writing in English anymore. I'm not writing in the colonizer's language. I'm going to write in my own language." Those kinds of things really made a really big impact on me. Finding Indigenous writers to read—I was just so grateful they were out there. In my undergrad, I read as much Indigenous lit as possible and tried, in different courses, to propose it as a paper. Some profs were interested, and most weren't—they couldn't care less.

AH: You've been teaching creative writing for so long, and in touch with other writers—do you feel like you've seen changes in the writing community, for Indigenous people, Indigenous women?

MD: Absolutely, it's changed dramatically. Look who won the last three Griffin prizes; there were all Indigenous poets: Liz Howard, Jordan Abel, Billy-Ray Belcourt. It's changed the landscape of publishing in Canada. Publishers are now interested, because they know there's a market for it. For example, when I started writing poetry, there was this organization called the League of Canadian Poets, and I thought to myself, "I'll never be part of that; that's way out of my league." At that time, it was—not all, but pretty much—white, male poets. They were interested in the Confederation poets and that kind of thing. So, I thought, "I'll never reach it." But then, last year, they asked me to give the Anne Szumigalski lecture for the League of Canadian Poets. The whole organization has changed; it's no longer white, male poets. It's now women of colour, younger women really driving the energy of the organization. So, just in that one organisation, how much it has changed is unbelievable. I don't think anyone in Canada necessarily wants to read anything from a settler point of view about Canada, because it's now meaningless.

AH: With all these other conversations going on, there's a lot of other things to talk about. One of the things I say, sort of as a joke, but it's true, is that I don't remember hearing the word *Métis* outside my house until I was in my twenties, which is a long time. And now, I feel like I run into it every day. That's partly because I work in Indigenous education, so, in my day-to-day a lot of people are talking about First Nations, Métis, and Inuit perspectives in curriculum, and so on. But I think that there's a lot more presence in public dialogue. And I always have CBC on; they do a good job of reflecting back what's going on in Indigenous conversations, like around reconciliation.

So, thinking about the kinds of shifts you've described in writing, I want to bring it back to questions about learning. I'm interested in what you think the impact of that is on Indigenous communities.

MD: It's huge, because more and more young women now see the potential to actually write and be heard, be seen. Prior to this, it wasn't a possibility; they didn't see it as a possibility. Now, young writers see a future in it, where there was nothing open to them before. The publishing, the awards, the media attention on Indigenous writers has really encouraged young men and women who are Indigenous to consider the arts, consider writing, consider telling their story or their ancestors' story.

AH: I'm always thinking about kids. When I was a teacher, I was teaching teenagers. Being a teenager is hard anyway, but if you're looking for a sense of belonging, or—I've taught a lot of kids who were struggling with poverty and racism. Even in a city like Calgary, if they come from a really poor family, that's enough to make them feel like they don't belong or have opportunities.

MD: Absolutely.

AH: I think that it really matters for young people to see, to hear something that gives them a sense of that possibility, to be who they are and then pursue something. Even if it's just feeling like they can be here, that's a start.

MD: Yeah, and that there might be a place for them in the literary world. As I say, for me, when I started writing, it was like, "No chance, absolutely none. I won't be in that group of people." But it's all changed, which is great. And more and more people going back to university, too—this thing about "Who is Métis?" People focusing on, "Okay, well, who are my relatives; how do I find them; and how do I make a connection with them?" It's been pretty instrumental in getting people to want to discover more about their ancestry.

AH: What do you think can come from that, if people are connecting into their families?

MD: There's a greater sense of identity and being grounded. For example, when I talked about how I grew up and not really knowing that it was traditional, until I got to university, and I talked to other people, and I realized that they didn't grow up like that. They grew up maybe on a reserve, and maybe they had a bit of wild meat, but it wasn't the same. I met more Indigenous students, and that gave me perspective on what my early life was like and what kinds of things I learned from that experience.

AH: It shows you the significance of what you know in more dimensions.

MD: Yeah, precisely.

AH: I remember, when I first started to talk about my Métis ancestry, a lot of people asked, like, "Okay, but you're not really Native" kinds of questions. I was ready to accept that I had grown up "without my culture," because that was what I was told. "You didn't grow up in a Native place; you didn't grow up with any culture." They're looking for these markers of authenticity or experience. So, like, seeing the significance of what you know in more dimensions, I see myself being able to look back at my childhood and see the Métis-ness in what I was raised with. And to love those things that I'm seeing, instead of seeing it all as this narrative of loss or of fraudulence. When I was young, even just debating getting my card and that kind of stuff,[32] I was always thinking about it. People would say the thing, like, "Just because you have one Cree grandma somewhere in your family tree …" And that's not my story; this whole branch of my family tree is Métis, not like just one Cree grandma. But even still, I was always listening to that and thinking, "But what if that one Cree grandma takes up a lot of space, and has a really loud voice, and she's telling me not to forget her, not to erase her?" When I was really doubting and people were telling me, "You aren't really Native," you're just white, let it go, I was like, "Well, no, I need to not be erasing that," because then I'm the next one in line to perpetuate those acts of erasure. I should say, these were non-Indigenous people voicing these questions. Even when I didn't really get it yet, I kind of was like, "I don't think that's the right thing to do." All that was happening around the same time I found your poetry, and other people's writing that opened up that space—just being, and voicing experience, and connecting in that way.

MD: I also find, with the Métis, it might not be tangible information, but attitudes around relationships with the opposite sex, or with the same sex, attitudes around money, attitudes around food, attitudes around material wealth, attitudes around child rearing. Those things are so evident. People may not tangibly say, "Oh that's Métis," but it's quite a different way of relating to child rearing, material wealth—

AH: Sense of humour …

MD: Sense of humour, yeah!

AH: Yeah, I think I know what you mean. I might not be able to sit down anthropologically and say, "Here are the things that are Métis about this," but I kind of know it when I see it. There's a familiarity when somebody starts teasing in a certain way, and I'm like, "Okay, I feel comfortable now," because that's just what I was raised with. My mom's one of nine and, I have a zillion cousins on that side, and they're like siblings. We raise each other's kids, and there's all this kind of stuff that's just normal.

MD: Exactly.

AH: And of course you can go into your cousin's house and make yourself at home. You expect to be hosted in a certain way—i.e., teased and left to get your own food [*laughs*]. Just ways of being. It sounds so stilted to talk about "Indigenous ways of being and knowing," but actually validating those things and seeing those things matters to people's sense of who they are; I really think of it as a well-being issue—being able to read and write and express who you are and connect to others in terms of community. People talk about writing for survival, too. Do you ever think of all of that in terms of wellness?

MD: Yeah, I do now; it is definitely a part of my wellness, too. I don't think I did in the beginning; as an early writer, no I didn't. I knew there were certain things that were going to come from it, but not as much as what has come to fruition by publishing.

AH: I have a big question that I ask everyone. Why do you think Indigenous literatures matter?

MD: One thing is affirmation and acknowledgement that Indigenous knowledge exists. The other is educating the broader public about Indigenous people. I think it's the best way to do that. People often will say, "Oh, did you read *Marrow Thieves*?" They're not asking that about the most recent scholarly text that's come out about the Métis or about Indigenous people, but they will ask that about a piece of art or writing. That's why it's so important. People who won't read theory, as in a scholarly text, will be influenced by that theory in a story or a poem. It's critical to any kind of relationship of respect and understanding between non- and Indigenous people in Canada, to acknowledge, "Yes, you do have something to say, and it's different than what I think about the world." It's critical. What happens is that it encourages that discussion amongst Indigenous and non-Indigenous people, when a lot of the times we don't have to interact. We don't want to. We're separated so nicely and neatly in the Canadian social order, that oftentimes Indigenous people don't even have to talk to a non-Indigenous person, unless they're going out to public services or doctors or that kind of thing. I think it's fundamental to the growth of a country, for them to acknowledge the literature of the Indigenous people.

AH: That big question about why it's so significant to create and to listen to Indigenous literary arts is really central. I have thought a lot about it as a teacher. I think it's really important for people to listen to artists about why they create what they do, and why they engage in the ways that they do.

MD: I think what's happened, too, with the publishing, it really has decentralized our centre of literature. People looked to Central Canada, with the old guard, saying, "This is literature." But that's not where the energy and excitement is in Canadian literature anymore. It's with writers of colour, Indigenous writers; people are excited about Indigenous lit.

AH: Is there anything in particular that you hope, in that big picture, that your work can contribute in the future?

MD: I feel very grateful that my work has made even a mild mark, because when I started writing I didn't think there would ever be a chance of that.

I'm extremely grateful that my books have gone as far as they have. I can't really ask for any more.

AH: Is there a piece that you've been happy to see how it's landed or where it's gone?

MD: Well, my first book, *A Really Good Brown Girl*, has done amazing things. I think it was last week or the week before, Kitty Lewis said that we have to do another printing.[33] So, it would be close to its seventeenth printing. I'm amazed, myself, how far that book has gone. I think it has made an impact because the writing is raw. It kind of grabbed people by the jugular and shook them up a bit and then, "Okay, on your merry way. You just read some Indigenous lit." I'm so glad that it is taken up in a lot of different courses and that kind of thing. I'm beyond kind of amazed at how the book has done.

AH: I told you I talked to teachers about the work they're trying to do, sharing Indigenous lit in their classrooms, even if it's just one story, one poem, making some space in mainstream schools. This was before all the professional standards, which say that everyone has to demonstrate a foundational knowledge of Indigenous perspectives, and everyone has to put it in their classrooms. Things are already going to be different from when I did the interviews with the teachers. These teachers were fighting to do it. Some of them were even stealing resources to make sure that they had Indigenous texts. Of course, you want to see those things paid for, but they were fighting to make sure Indigenous writing was represented. As a last question, is there anything that you would hope for, if you have teachers who are trying to do the work, trying to share Indigenous lit?

MD: I would really hope that they would make sure to include the Métis. To not only teach writers who identify as First Nations, but writers who identify as Métis and Inuit. They're always an afterthought. I would hope that that reification of the First Nations status can be open enough now for people to see there is more than one kind of Indigenous person in this country. And no, they're not merely an afterthought; they are a part of this core that we have to teach. I think quite often, because people don't know who the Métis are, they don't know how to teach it. They might think, "Oh, it's just a watered-down version of First Nations, right?" So, I would hope the teachers go deeper, at least in terms of understanding what the difference is between the three status groups.

AH: Something I've heard you say today, too, is not just teaching the text, but I would hope teachers would also engage with what it means to be responsible or engage with community. Talking about women and mentoring younger writers, and that degree of support, awareness of youth, that kind of thing. There's a *way* of engaging with Indigenous writing, too, not just content teaching.

MD: Precisely, exactly.

AH: Those insistences you've made on those parts really resonate with me. It matters for learning, too. So, at this time where there's so much insistence on reconciliation, what do you hope that people will carry forward out of this work in the long term, out of these conversations?

MD: I would at least hope that people begin to show some more respect for Indigenous people—that we do have extensive knowledge about all kinds of things in the world.

LISTENING TO WRITERS

THE AUTHORS IN the previous chapters have shared perspectives on and personal stories of writing. They have spoken about their own educational experiences; their experiences reading and becoming writers; their conceptions of community; their beliefs about teaching and learning, in diverse forms and venues; their investments in political or social change; and, ultimately, their understandings of why Indigenous literatures are important to Indigenous Peoples. I began this project because I believe it is valuable to listen to Indigenous writers speak about their work, their beliefs, and their experiences, and I for one have learned a great deal from listening to them.[1] I hope that readers of this book have gained something as well.

Listening to writers' deeply held beliefs and attending to their careful thinking fits within a broader initiative to engage meaningfully and responsibly with Indigenous literatures, for readers and particularly for teachers. I maintain that, for teachers to engage well with Indigenous texts—as the readers, learners, educators, and leaders that they all are, however diversely positioned—they are called to engage also with Indigenous contexts: with Indigenous communities, histories, knowledge systems, and contemporary social and political realities. This call involves engaging with Indigenous people and moving beyond the page.[2] It also involves interrogating some of the assumptions that we as educators accumulate through our literature degrees, teacher education programs, and time in professional practice, as some of what we know as teachers do not serve us well when we engage ourselves and our learners with Indigenous literatures.

In thinking with authors about literatures and learning, I have been particularly interested in the ways in which Indigenous writing extends far beyond the material text and into people's thoughts, choices, relationships, beliefs, and actions. Writing represents, reflects, influences, shapes, and changes the world around it. Communities are made up of stories. Writing by Indigenous people unfurls in relation to its surroundings, amidst the persistence of settler colonialism and the ongoing efforts of Indigenous communities and allies to precipitate political and cultural change. Indigenous writing speaks to its context but it also affects it. Along the strands that form the relational webs between writers, words, and the world are a host of connected relationships between readers, knowledges and beliefs, attitudes and frameworks, kin and community. The complexity of these relationships and dynamics is encapsulated in the simple notion upon which many of the writers included in this volume insist—that it is important for Indigenous people to see themselves reflected in the things they are reading, and for non-Indigenous readers to recognize difference, to build understandings, and to step into respectful action. Explicitly educational settings are excellent sites for transformative learning to take place, but learning and relationship-building work can happen anywhere. If you are reading this book to think about literatures and learning, cognizant of who you are, how your experiences have shaped you, and where your responsibilities lie, I hope that you can imagine a way to allow Indigenous writing to influence you and, in turn, how you influence those around you, in a good way.

By listening to these authors' perspectives on their work, readers can gain an understanding of what matters to them. This work of listening is particularly important right now, at a time when Indigenous literatures are prevalent in the public eye, having gained attention through publishing, literary awards, media coverage, and the rising stardom thrust upon many emerging writers. Some of these dynamics are concerning: for instance, it can be problematic when authors are pushed to speak for other Indigenous people, extending beyond their own perspectives and experience; or when Indigenous writing is taken up only as a means of achieving token inclusion or superficial reconciliation work, rather than for its literary merit or its informed engagement with social contexts. Such problems affect artists and their communities. Authors in this collection have pointed to issues across the literary landscape: appropriation of voice or culture, dismissal of Indigenous literary craft, marginalization of Indigenous people in academic or publishing contexts, negative educational experiences affecting academic and artistic growth, lack of promotion of Indigenous literatures for Indigenous families, and the commodification of Indigenous stories, to name a few. At this time of increased reception for Indigenous literatures, it is important for readers to listen to authors' concerns.

These issues matter to Indigenous writers, because they affect these writers' work, but also because they affect Indigenous communities—from the youngest children encountering the world and forming their identities, all the way on up to Elders seeking to share the wealth of knowledge and experience they carry. Contemporary issues concerning Indigenous writers are inextricable from more fundamental issues impinging on the well-being and self-determination of Indigenous communities in Canada. The removal of Indigenous Peoples from their lands and traditional, healthy lifeways; the colonization of sex and gender systems, marching arm-in-arm with the oppression of two-spirit and LBGT people and the squashing of Indigenous erotics; the colonization of Indigenous languages, cultures, and onto-epistemological frameworks; the forcible separation of Indigenous families and targeting of Indigenous kinship systems; the erasure and erosion of Indigenous governance systems; and the continuing physical and spiritual violence perpetrated against Indigenous bodies, from gendered and sexual violence to incarceration—each represents an enduring concern for Indigenous communities. For Indigenous writing, the interplay between creative expression and worldly contexts takes particular forms because of the extensive scope of colonial violence that Indigenous people have endured—and continue to endure. Indigenous artistry is also shaped by the exceptional resilience, creativity, ferocity, patience, and beauty that Indigenous people have sustained and shown in enduring and resisting such violence. One way or another, Indigenous literatures exist in relation to colonialism, and readers of those literatures walk in a world where what happens next truly matters.

My conversations with the authors presented in this volume are, in so many ways, just a few threads out of a much larger fabric. They are inevitably limited. Most obviously, I only spoke with a small number of people: enough to fill a book but nowhere near enough to reflect the diversity of experiences and perspectives of Indigenous writers. This book does not speak to all of the diversity that exists across genres, genders, sexualities, ages, or leadership capacities; degrees of cultural knowledge, religions, and spiritualities; urban, rural, and reserve homes and migrations; academic, professional, and community involvements; or among First Nations, Métis, and Inuit Peoples with home territories spanning this vast land known as Canada. Further, while these conversations invoke a degree of dialogue between the perspectives of educators and Indigenous writers, this project does not bring writers and teachers into each other's spaces to see what work might be done together. I leave for future scholars the work of pursuing what seems necessary or valuable in what has been missed here. This project is just one snapshot, inevitably partial and limited in scope.

Likewise, the authors I spoke to are human, and I do not intend to suggest that they have all the answers or are getting everything right. Each conversation is simply a dialogue between two people who care about Indigenous literatures: I sat down with these writers to ask them about their work, experiences, and beliefs, not to set out any kind of proclamation for Indigenous art. I add this cautionary note because the context surrounding Indigenous people and communities in Canada is complex, and requires some work to understand. I would not want anyone to come away with too-simple answers when so much is at stake for Indigenous knowledge systems, cultures, self-determination, and well-being. I hope that readers will continue to engage with the plentiful scholarship that addresses Indigenous literary arts and Indigenous education. Further engagement might also take the form of reaching out in support of Indigenous initiatives; showing up to community events to listen and learn; strengthening understandings of one's own kin, communities, and histories; or, indeed, seeking out other works of Indigenous literature, performance, music, visual art, or artistic expression. Individual writers cannot be oracles speaking to all Indigenous experience, but as these writers have shown, they do have something to say about why literatures matter to the well-being of their communities.

READING FOR RESURGENCE, READING FOR RECONCILIATION

One of the main takeaways from this book is that engaging with Indigenous literatures means engaging with the contexts and communities from which these literatures spring. Here, I would like to consider how the explorations in this volume have taken up this theme, and particularly how these conversations have responded to the two guiding frameworks I established in my introductory chapter: resurgence and reconciliation. Resurgence is insistently rooted in Indigenous communities, while reconciliation focuses on relationships between Indigenous Peoples and Canadian society. Many of the worldly contexts that these writers and I have explored—in relation to literatures, communities, and learning—call for attention to the latter work, as when we are thinking about non-Indigenous teachers and learners, for instance. Depending on what conversation is taking place, this can take the form of a positive insistence on relationship and engagement, or a dangerous re-centring of non-Indigenous perspectives—a reassertion of a Canadian mainstream at the centre of the critical frame. Perhaps public education in Canada might focus on relationships between Indigenous Peoples and settlers, as in reconciliation, because that is what is asked of teaching and learning here. For Indigenous communities, however, resurgence is a vital framework for considering Indigenous literary work.

I began this project with the notion of resurgence as an organizing and motivating concept: I described it as the growth of Indigenous communities from their roots upward; as the revitalization of Indigenous ways of being and knowing; and as the expression and celebration of Indigenous humanity in defiance of colonial oppression. I understood that resurgence could take place through everyday ways of being Indigenous, and that it was in many ways about the health and well-being of communities. Existing discourse on resurgence insists on particular Indigenous communities as sites of revitalization. That is, it is not a generic, pan-Indigenous concept, but one that takes shape in particular ways in particular places. I also understood that processes of artistic creation, as in the writing of Indigenous literatures, were integral to inspiring and enacting such regeneration and expression: creative expression, after all, is inseparable from ways of living. I knew that stories and literatures were important to the growth of healthy, self-determining, vibrant communities, and that learning was a vital part of that importance. I wanted to find out more about why all of this was so—how learning through literatures might foster community resurgence. In so doing, I set out to attend to particular instances of how this phenomenon manifests in the everyday work of writers. I set out to investigate what certain writers' particular experiences and perspectives might reveal about how learning through Indigenous literatures can affect community resurgence.

It is absolutely vital to see the resurgence at work in Indigenous literary arts, and to focus on the creativity, learning, and shifts that are internal to Indigenous Peoples. In these conversations, some authors insist that serving their own communities is a priority—for instance, that they write primarily for Indigenous readerships. Sometimes that community focus means not focusing on non-Indigenous people. Some artistic work does not fit within the mandate of reconciliation. In these cases, artists are creating what Métis artist David Garneau calls "irreconcilable spaces of Aboriginality" that exist "without settler attendance."[3] Indigenous communities' processes of self-understanding and the Canadian nation-state's understanding of reconciliation may be incommensurable, just as Indigenous histories may be at odds with the prevailing national myth that Canada is a nation of peacemakers.[4]

When it comes to the well-being of Indigenous communities, it is often necessary to focus primarily on these communities, to centre the critical frame in Indigenous territory. Failing to do so might mean losing some of the depth and specificity of understanding. I mean this in the sense that Simpson evokes when she says that she has "grown tired of explaining" to non-Nishnaabeg audiences: "I felt the need to create a space for myself to vision and to live, where my primary pursuit was *doing* or *making stories* grounded in contemporary Nishnaabeg ontologies and animating contemporary Nishnaabeg poetic and narrative consciousness rather than writing *about* those things. In making that decision, I realize that ultimately I have chosen to write for a Nishnaabeg audience."[5] Simpson's perspective highlights the conflicting

demands placed on Indigenous writers—to write from and for their communities, and to write so that non-Indigenous readers can understand. It is
vital to recognize that focusing on the latter might jeopardize the former. At
the very least, respectful engagement between distinct groups requires genuine recognition of difference.[6] Framing what learning through Indigenous
literatures means *for Indigenous communities* means respecting the need
for Indigenous writers, readers, and communities to focus on their particular concerns, without necessarily asking that those be made intelligible for
non-Indigenous audiences. Serving Indigenous communities sometimes
requires readers and learners to see through a framework of resurgence,
rather than of reconciliation.

Reconciliation, meanwhile, is a mobilizing framework when it comes to
relationships between Indigenous and non-Indigenous people. Many authors
in this volume have shared that they write with non-Indigenous readers and
learning in mind. Whether as a form of resistance or as a direct desire to
educate, many of these writers are working to teach the broader population,
in order to improve things for their communities. Reconciliation is one way
of framing that work, although some authors are quick to qualify that terminology: *reconciliation* discourse may not be unproblematic enough for
substantive change. In the most hopeful sense of fostering more respectful,
reciprocal relationships between Indigenous Peoples and settler society—not
forgetting the *truth* emphasized in the work of the Truth and Reconciliation
Commission for instance, or the Calls to Action that the TRC has sounded—
reconciliation work may be beneficial for many.

While my own focus has been on resurgence, I do not, ultimately, have
to reconcile these two frameworks: reconciliation has a role to play, as does
resurgence. Change for Indigenous communities can happen from within
and from without, with different roles for differently positioned people. But
if building better relationships between Indigenous and non-Indigenous
communities is one of the desired goals of teaching Indigenous literatures,
it is necessary to formulate what it means to build better relationships with
resurgent Indigenous communities. Indigenous Peoples' flourishing is a
necessary component in reciprocal relationships. Reciprocal relationships
between settler and Indigenous people in Canada require non-Indigenous
people to develop positionings that respect Indigenous resurgence. Ethical
engagement between distinct parties requires each to be "supported and
informed by their own autonomy."[7] In simultaneously doing education work
for non-Indigenous people while working for Indigenous resurgence, I am
pulling myself in different directions, but I hope that readers will see how
these distinctions come across in the conversations. I am not here to translate

Indigenous resurgence so that non-Indigenous folks can understand and participate in it; simply put, that is not what resurgence is for. Rather, I encourage non-Indigenous learners (of all ages) to recognize the importance of resurgence work for Indigenous communities, to respect that it may be irreconcilable with a settler status quo, and to develop and enact respectful ways of being in relation with Indigenous Peoples. Indigenous community resurgence is about fostering community well-being first. That well-being is a requirement for fostering healthy relationships between Indigenous communities and others. This is an important lesson as reconciliation movements take place across Canada, and part of the broader learning required when Canadians engage with Indigenous literatures.

LITERATURES AND LEARNING

The conceptions of *learning* outlined in this book have addressed formal education and schooling, but they also extend more broadly to learning that happens outside of formal settings. It is always a priority for me to point to traditional models of Indigenous education, which are holistic, based in land and kinships, and inseparable from stories; remembering these traditions demands a conception of *education* that by far transcends the structures of schooling. For non-Indigenous Canada, shifts in mainstream literary studies, many of which have sought an increased responsiveness to Indigenous literatures, are paralleled by shifts in education that seek a similar responsiveness to Indigenous knowledge systems. And, as has been articulated in this volume, *education* writ large also takes place outside of formal settings. Any reader is also a member of society who may be connecting with others, participating in dialogue, expressing opinions, sharing knowledge, showing up to events, voting, reading more, listening and witnessing, going to work, parenting or supporting loved ones, engaging with media, or otherwise influencing others in innumerable ways. Any of these relational pathways is a venue for potential engagement with Indigenous writing and Indigenous communities—for better or for worse. As well as non-Indigenous readers, I am including Indigenous readers in these broad strokes, too—again, both are varied and unsustainable categories full of individual humans with complicated stories and diverse communities marked by complex histories, connections, and disconnections. It is important to me to see also the educational aspects of broader social engagements, from the scale of the individual right up to national and international levels. Any reader can do the work to step into ethical and meaningful engagements with Indigenous literatures, and can have an impact on others' ability to do so. The conversations in this volume have illustrated this notion in intricate and colourful ways.

While I have tremendous optimism about people learning from Indigenous literatures—I think it is mostly inevitable that more widespread engagement with Indigenous writing will serve Indigenous communities and foster more reciprocal relationships between Indigenous and non-Indigenous people—I recognize the potential for such endeavours to go awry. As has been so thoughtfully explored in the preceding conversations, anything that is powerful can create positive or negative effects, healing or hurt. Likewise, the creation and teaching of Indigenous literatures can be done in harmful ways. Consequently, I am not only calling for engagement with Indigenous literatures; I am calling as well for responsible, relational ways of engaging with Indigenous literatures.

In the context of education, for instance, I think it is likely of minimal benefit for Indigenous texts to be *included* in the mainstream classroom, in the sense that a text is brought into a prior and privileged epistemological-pedagogical framework, such that the classroom and the mainstream do not shift. Some learning and affirmation might still happen in that case, but the potential is smaller. I think it just as likely that inclusion in this sense—meaning without ethical or reciprocal engagement, without a willingness to shift *how* learning happens and influences learners rather than just *what* is being learned and the desired outcomes of learning[8]—will not serve Indigenous communities in any significant or meaningful way. Superficial inclusion is akin to a picture drawn on an Etch A Sketch: one shake and the image disappears. If colonial frameworks and systems are not also challenged, Canadian consciousness resumes its amnesia, its common-sense racism, or its self-perception as a peaceful multicultural country.[9] In educational settings, strong learning means being attentive to the multiple dimensions of Indigenous education I outlined in my introductory chapter: not just teaching *about* Indigenous literatures, but, rather, being attentive to teaching *with* Indigenous pedagogies and *for* social change, for instance. Strong pedagogical practice, or strong engagement by readers outside of educational settings, can help Indigenous writing to have powerful and positive effects.

As Indigenous communities continue to work for and enact self-determination, and as a (hopefully) growing number of Canadians work to unsettle what they know, to confront colonialism, and to co-conspire toward decolonial transformations, the arts can foster learning and inspire the ensuing labour of implementing change. The artistry of Indigenous literatures, the compelling voices that speak through them, the human connections that they depict and catalyze, and the truths, dreams, histories, alternatives, and visions that they convey can lure readers into learning and into deepening their relationships with Indigenous communities. This draw can materialize regardless of whether the community is one's own or is separated from one's known by vast differences, geographies, or emotional barriers. As so many writers in this collection have suggested, literatures can be a way in: to learning, to relationships, and to transformation.

So much has been expressed in these conversations about why Indigenous literatures matter to Indigenous communities. The beauty of literary writing and the pedagogical ancestry of story within oral cultures both beckon and bind individuals into relationships and learning. While learning through or teaching Indigenous literatures is no simple process, strong directions on how to engage have been set out by people who care deeply about what literatures can do. People can come together around an Indigenous text—a text that emerges from the experiences and imaginings of a particular person, in relation to Indigenous communities. If readers remain open to the text and to the relationships in which they are implicated, they may see promising possibilities and responsibilities for next steps. Once the learning is picked up, it cannot really be put down again. Some kind of response will ensue, in the sense that Cherokee author Thomas King reiterates at the end of each story in *The Truth About Stories*: "Do with it what you will…. But don't say in the years to come that you would have lived your life differently if only you had heard this story. You've heard it now."[10] As I have reiterated throughout this book, the growth and brilliance of Indigenous literary arts have much to contribute to social, cultural, and political change. Continuing along those paths is both possible and necessary. I hope that this book inspires and motivates others to move forward in good ways.

NOTES

INTRODUCTION

1   I delve deeper into these pedagogical issues throughout this volume, but readers looking to expand on this point might consider visiting Marie Battiste's *Decolonizing Education*, Susan Dion's *Braiding Histories*, Jo-Ann Episkenew's "Socially Responsible Criticism," and Sharron Proulx(-Turner) and Aruna Srivastava's "A Moose in the Corridor," as well as the volume *Learn, Teach, Challenge: Approaching Indigenous Literatures*, edited by Deanna Reder and Linda Morra. I also conceive of "educational settings" very broadly, as I explain later on.

2   At a very basic level, the well-being of Indigenous youth is a focus for me because their well-being is essential for healthy Indigenous futures, and at the present moment Indigenous youth in Canada are disproportionally at risk of death by suicide, of encounters with child welfare and other state systems, of lower success in schooling, and a raft of other dismaying social issues that result from colonial histories and systems—including in education—in this country. See, for instance, Tanya Talaga's *Seven Fallen Feathers* and her *All Our Relations*, or Bernard Schissel and Terry Wotherspoon's *The Legacy of School for Aboriginal People*. It is also useful to look at the information gathered by Statistics Canada, such as in the report "A Portrait of Canadian Youth" and "Aboriginal Peoples in Canada."

3   For more on the distinction between these two terms and their significance for Indigenous Peoples, see Yvonne Poitras Pratt, Dustin Louie, Aubrey Hanson, and Jacqueline Ottmann, "Indigenous Education and Decolonization." According to this encyclopedia article, schooling is "institutionalized and systematically governed and legislated by provincial, state, or federal institutions"; further, it is "bounded within physical structures where the majority of learning is confined to specific temporal, legislative, and bureaucratic limitations." By comparison, *education* is much broader: "for Indigenous peoples," education has traditionally been "embodied in all of the cultural lifeways of a community."

4   Regan, *Unsettling the Settler Within*, 50.

5   Dion, *Braiding Histories*, 179.

6   Dion, *Braiding Histories*, 179.

7   Dion, "Disrupting Molded Images," 331.

8   Some prefer the term *accomplice*, suggesting that an ally will "join an effort to help a marginalized group or advocate for an issue of justice," while an accomplice will "work alongside" as a "colearner and coconspirator," to quote from Laura Roy, *Teaching While White*, 149.

9   See, for instance, Ashleigh-Rae Thomas's piece for *Vice*, "Who is a Settler, According to Indigenous and Black Scholars."

10 This fascinating Icelandic history also involved complex and conflicted relations with Indigenous Peoples in that part of what is now Manitoba; see, for instance, Ryan Eyford, *White Settler Reserve*.

11 One of my parents (I *think*—it could have been a grandparent) slipped me a copy of E. Pauline Johnson's poems at some point during my childhood. I still have it. (My mom's mom wrote her own poetry—that is another story.) Those were the earliest Indigenous writings I met, but they were very few compared to the number of other texts I encountered.

12 Battiste, *Decolonizing Education*, 24–5.

13 Battiste, *Decolonizing Education*, 175.

14 Hampton, "Towards a Redefinition of Indian Education," 8.

15 Hampton, "Towards a Redefinition," 8.

16 Hampton, "Towards a Redefinition," 10.

17 Hampton, "Towards a Redefinition," 35.

18 Battiste, *Decolonizing Education*, 29.

19 For more on the understandings informing this discussion of Indigenous education, see, for instance, Marie Battiste, *Decolonizing Education*; Eber Hampton, "Towards a Redefinition"; Susan Dion, *Braiding Histories*; Teresa McCarty and Tiffany Lee, "Critical Culturally Sustaining/Revitalizing Pedagogy"; Yvonne Poitras Pratt et al., "Indigenous Education and Decolonization"; Bernard Schissel and Terry Wotherspoon, *The Legacy of School for Aboriginal People*; and Linda Tuhiwai Smith, *Decolonizing Methodologies: Research and Indigenous Peoples*.

20 Louie, Poitras Pratt, Hanson, and Ottmann, "Applying Principles of Decolonizing Methodologies," 18.

21 See, for instance, the Canadian Council on Learning's report *Redefining How Success is Measured*.

22 Louie et al., "Applying Principles of Decolonizing Methodologies," 22. Leadership credit for this pedagogical work goes to Dustin Louie.

23 Armstrong, "Traditional Indigenous Education," 17–19.

24 Goulet and Goulet, *Teaching Each Other*, 110–11.

25 Battiste, *Decolonizing Education*, 116.

26 Regan, *Unsettling the Settler Within*, 37.

27 Battiste, *Decolonizing Education*, 112–17.

28 Battiste, *Decolonizing Education*, 114.

29 For more on strong models of Indigenous education, see, for starters, the following: David Bell, Kirk Anderson, Terry Fortin, Jacqueline Ottmann, Sheila Rose, Leon Simard, and Keith Spencer, *Sharing Our Success*; Linda M. Goulet and Keith N. Goulet, *Teaching Each Other*; Leanne Betasamosake Simpson, "Land as Pedagogy"; or Michele Tanaka's *Learning & Teaching Together*.

30 Battiste, *Decolonizing Education*, 116–17.

31 From "Governing Code for the Indigenous Literary Studies Association," para. 3–4.

32 The singular *literature* risks propagating the misconception of sameness across Indigenous Peoples and cultures. See, for instance, Janice Acoose's "A Vanishing Indian?" or Kristina Fagan's "What about You?"—both of which argue that it is problematic to generalize across the entirety of Indigenous writing as if it were a homogenous body of work. Likewise, Daniel Heath Justice argues, in *Our Fire Survives the Storm*, that "collapsing [Indigenous] affiliations and relationships into a generic claim of between-the-worlds Native hybridity is yet another act of colonialist displacement that has, as its ultimate

aim, the symbolic and physical erasure of Indigenous nations from the very memory of this land" (p. 215).

33 Fagan, Justice, Martin, McKegney, Reder, and Sinclair, "Canadian Indian Literary Nationalism?," 36. For more on literary nationalisms, see Jace Weaver, Craig Womack, and Robert Warrior's 2006 book *American Indian Literary Nationalism*.

34 Cariou, "Who is the Text in this Class?," 475.

35 See, for instance, Jo-ann Archibald, *Indigenous Storywork*.

36 Smith, *Decolonizing Methodologies*, 146.

37 See, for instance, Waubgeshig Rice, "Joseph Boyden's The Orenda Fuels Important Conversation," and Hayden King, "Joseph Boyden's The Orenda Faces Tough Criticism from First Nations Scholar."

38 Boyden, Justice, and Monture, "Authors, Communities, Responsibilities: Conversation with Joseph Boyden."

39 See Jorge Barrera, "Author Joseph Boyden's Shape-Shifting Identity."

40 Barrera, "Boyden's Shape-Shifting Identity."

41 Barrera, "Boyden's Shape-Shifting Identity."

42 Barrera, "Boyden's Shape-Shifting Identity."

43 McMahon, "What Colour is Your Beadwork, Joseph Boyden?"

44 Kinew, "There is Room in Our Circle for Joseph Boyden."

45 Kinew, "There is Room in Our Circle."

46 Kinew, "There is Room in Our Circle."

47 Taylor, "Can Joseph Boyden Make Amends with First Nations?"

48 CBC Radio, "Joseph Boyden Addresses His Heritage in Exclusive Interview with Candy Palmater."

49 Boyden, "My Name is Joseph Boyden."

50 Ono, "11 Indigenous Authors You Should Be Reading Instead of Joseph Boyden."

51 Niedzviecki, "Winning the Appropriation Prize."

52 See, for instance, Ashifa Kassam, "Canadian Journalists Support 'Appropriation Prize,'" and Marsha Lederman and Mark Medley, "Writers' Union of Canada Editorial Sparks Outrage, Resignations."

53 CBC News, "An Emotional Jesse Wente on the 'Remarkable Arrogance' of an Appropriation Prize."

54 CBC News, "The 'Remarkable Arrogance' of an Appropriation Prize."

55 Akiwenzie-Damm, "The Cultural Appropriation Debate Is Over."

56 Akiwenzie-Damm, "The Cultural Appropriation Debate Is Over."

57 See, for instance, Deborah Dundas, "Editor Quits Amid Outrage after Call for 'Appropriation Prize.'"

58 For further discussion of these events in Canadian literature, see the collection *Refuse: CanLit in Ruins*, edited by Hannah McGregor, Julie Rak, and Erin Wunker.

59 More on these debates and on the Indigenous Voices Awards' backstory can be found through Twitter by searching the #appropriationprize hashtag. For more information on the Indigenous Voices Awards, see the awards' pages on the Indigenous Literary Studies Association website, available at http://www.indigenousliterarystudies.org/

60 Episkenew, *Taking Back Our Spirits*, 193.

61 Episkenew, *Taking Back Our Spirits*, 193.

62 Bidwell, "What Stories Do: A Response to Episkenew," 109 (emphasis added).

63 Bidwell, "What Stories Do," 109.

64 In my article "Relational Encounters with Indigenous Literatures," I explore these points in relation to the notion of "response-ability," which, as Anishinaabe scholar Kimberly Blaeser illustrates, accompanies Indigenous storytelling, in that listeners/readers are

expected to understand their need to respond to the story in some way, to take up what it has taught them. I describe this process as one of recognizing relationship.

65 Justice, *Why Indigenous Literatures Matter*, 208.

66 I see this insistence that literatures and communities are deeply interconnected as emerging from central critical principles in Indigenous literary scholarship over the past few decades. For instance, Jeannette Armstrong's 1993 collection *Looking at the Words of Our People* drew together Native critical voices in order to build upon the premise that interpreting Indigenous literatures is a process that must be undertaken from within the Indigenous cultures that formed them. Within that collection, Kimberly Blaeser, in "Native Literature: Seeking a Critical Center," called criticism arising from within Indigenous cultures and tribal stories a significant critical framing, insisting that Indigenous literary criticism must be deeply intertwined with Indigenous Peoples. In that same collection, Kateri (Akiwenzie) Damm's chapter, "Says Who," challenged the negation of Indigenous perspectives and identities through criticism originating outside of Indigenous communities. Renate Eigenbrod and Jo-Ann Episkenew's edited collection *Creating Community*, published in 2000, contributed another set of essays exploring the connections between Indigenous literatures and communities, such as cultural specificity and community accountability. These critical perspectives within Canada are also related to Native American scholarship that connects story to survival, such as Robert Warrior's *Tribal Secrets* and Jace Weaver's *That the People Might Live*. Another critical trend within Indigenous literary studies that insists upon linking literatures, criticism, and communities is Indigenous literary nationalism, as discussed above.

67 King, Introduction to *All My Relations*, xv.

68 Justice, "Go Away, Water!," 154.

69 Justice, "Go Away, Water!," 149, 150.

70 Justice, "Go Away, Water!," 150.

71 Ermine, "Aboriginal Epistemology," 106.

72 Justice, *Why Indigenous Literatures Matter*, 87.

73 This emphasis on connecting healing, resilience, and story is strong in Indigenous literary studies. For instance, I look to Jo-Ann Episkenew's book *Taking Back Our Spirits*, which engages with the role of Indigenous literatures in fostering healing from the impacts of colonial policies in Canada. Daniel Heath Justice's essay "Literature, Healing, and the Transformative Imaginary" dialogues with Episkenew's work and adds an important consideration of literature's ability to harm as well as heal. Sam McKegney's book *Magic Weapons* explores how stories can foster collective healing, helping writers to remake community in the wake of residential schooling. Deanna Reder takes up themes of survival and regeneration in "Stories of Destruction and Renewal." Jace Weaver also addresses healing and community through literature in *That the People Might Live*.

74 Episkenew, *Taking Back Our Spirits*, 2.

75 King, *The Truth about Stories*, 92

76 Justice, "Literature, Healing, and the Transformative Imaginary," 106.

77 For more on how Indigenous literatures must be taught responsibly, see Jo-Ann Episkenew, "Socially Responsible Criticism" and "Indigenizing Author Meets Critics"; Aubrey J. Hanson, "Through White Man's Eyes"; Daniel Heath Justice, "Literature, Healing, and the Transformative Imaginary"; and Sharron Proulx and Aruna Srivastava, "A Moose in the Corridor."

78 For more on how literary forms of resistance connect to other forms, such as political or cultural resistance, see Jo-Ann Episkenew, "Socially Responsible Criticism"; Sam McKegney, *Magic Weapons*; Daniel Heath Justice, *Our Fire Survives the Storm*; Leanne

Betasamosake Simpson, "Our Elder Brothers" and *Dancing on Our Turtle's Back*; Jace Weaver, *That the People Might Live*; and Craig S. Womack, *Red on Red*.

79 LaRocque, "Teaching Aboriginal Literature," 216.

80 Weaver, *Other Words*, 12.

81 Cranmer, "Exploring Voice and Silence in the Poetry of Beth Cuthand, Louise Halfe and Marlene Nourbese Philip," 125.

82 Eigenbrod, "'For the Child Taken, for the Parent Left Behind': Residential School Narratives as Acts of 'Survivance'," 280.

83 Maracle, *Memory Serves: Oratories*, 205.

84 Maracle, *Memory Serves*, 203.

85 There is plenty of work to go around. Decolonization is another avenue, alongside reconciliation, that can open up opportunities for non-Indigenous folks to move into the work. I am interested in what it looks like for non-Indigenous people to work on decolonization in a parallel process to Indigenous resurgence work. For some discussion of these complexities, see Lynne Davis, Jeff Denis, and Raven Sinclair, "Pathways of Settler Decolonization."

86 Simpson, *Dancing on Our Turtle's Back*, 148.

87 Friedel, Archibald, Big Head, Martin, and Muñoz, "Indigenous Pedagogies," para. 12.

88 Simpson, *Dancing on Our Turtle's Back*, 70.

89 For more on resurgence and cultural specificity, see, for instance, Jeff Corntassel, "Re-Envisioning Resurgence," or Leanne Betasamosake Simpson, *As We Have Always Done*, "Bubbling Like a Beating Heart," *Dancing on Our Turtle's Back*, and "Our Elder Brothers."

90 Simpson, *Dancing on Our Turtle's Back*, 147.

91 Simpson, *Dancing on Our Turtle's Back*, 146.

92 Simpson, *As We Have Always Done*, 49.

93 Corntassel, "Re-Envisioning Resurgence," 89.

94 Corntassel, "Re-Envisioning Resurgence," 89.

95 See, for instance, Jeff Corntassel, "Re-Envisioning Resurgence," and Leanne Betasamosake Simpson, *Dancing on Our Turtle's Back*, "Our Elder Brothers," and *As We Have Always Done*.

96 Corntassel, "Re-Envisioning Resurgence," 89.

97 Tuck, "Re-Visioning Action," 48.

98 Dion, in *Braiding Histories*, addresses the relegation of Indigenous people and perspectives to the past; relatedly, Paulette Regan, in *Unsettling the Settler Within*, addresses the notion of *moving on* or failing to recognize the need for substantive processes of truth and reconciliation.

99 Regan, *Unsettling the Settler Within*, 11.

100 Truth and Reconciliation Commission of Canada (TRC), *Reconciliation*, 3. For a land-based reflection on the notion of atonement, see Trevor Herriot's lovely little book *Towards A Prairie Atonement*.

101 TRC, *Reconciliation*, 3.

102 For further considerations in Indigenous studies scholarship of *reconciliation* and the Truth and Reconciliation Commission, see, for instance, Margery Fee, "The Truth and Reconciliation Commission of Canada"; David Garneau, "Imaginary Spaces of Conciliation and Reconciliation"; and Keavy Martin, "Truth, Reconciliation, and Amnesia."

103 Martin, "Truth, Reconciliation, and Amnesia," 49.

104 Martin, "Truth, Reconciliation, and Amnesia," 49.

105 For further discussion of these issues, see *Reconciliation*, volume 6 of the TRC's report, as well as the TRC's *Calls to Action*.

106 Garneau, "Imaginary Spaces of Conciliation and Reconciliation," 30.

107 Garneau, "Imaginary Spaces of Conciliation and Reconciliation," 32.

108 Garneau, "Imaginary Spaces of Conciliation and Reconciliation," 33.

109 Garneau, "Imaginary Spaces of Conciliation and Reconciliation," 34.

110 The conversations presented in this book are a major component of a broader project. This book does not represent the entirety of that project, but rather focuses on the conversations I held with Indigenous writers. Between 2015 and 2018, I met and spoke with a total of seventeen people—teachers and Indigenous writers—as part of that research. The other half of the project engages with the perspectives of secondary school educators teaching Indigenous literatures. I take up those conversations elsewhere rather than here, largely because the teachers' contributions must remain anonymous because of their professional contexts, and so they cannot be shared in this same format. For an exploration of teachers' perspectives, see, for instance, my article "Relational Encounters with Indigenous Literatures." It is helpful to describe their participation here because this book of conversations is still often in dialogue with those teachers' perspectives.

111 In pursuing this question, this book is participating in the same conversations and explorations as Daniel Heath Justice's book *Why Indigenous Literatures Matter*, which I recommend to readers. In our conversation in this volume, we talk about how our two projects meet in this phrasing.

112 Donald, "Indigenous Métissage," 543.

INTERVIEWS

1 These two stories were since published as the opening pieces in *Moccasin Square Gardens*, so readers can enjoy them, too.

2 As detailed earlier, these numbers are from 2015. He has published many more since!

3 By "GG," Van Camp means the Governor General's Award.

4 Beatrice Culleton Mosionier, the author of *In Search of April Raintree*.

5 Vermette is referring to winning the 2013 Governor General's Award for Poetry.

6 The book Vermette is talking about is *North End Love Songs*.

7 Cariou co-facilitated this workshop, entitled "Editing Indigenous Manuscripts: A Publishing Master Class," with these other three scholars at Wanuskewin Heritage Park in June 2015.

8 Cariou is referring to Anishinaabe writer, storyteller, and scholar Basil Johnston's "One Generation from Extinction," in which Johnston makes an urgent case for Indigenous languages and oral knowledges.

9 Jesse Archibald-Barber edited the collection *kisiskâciwan: Indigenous Voices from where the River Flows Swiftly*, which came out in 2018. This volume showcases the Indigenous literary presence in what is now Saskatchewan.

10 Maracle is reading from page 47 of Claxton's essay in *Lighting the Eighth Fire*.

11 In this section, Maracle reads from pages 5 and 6 of Sark's essay in that volume.

12 Lee Maracle's Thomas King impression is quite remarkable.

13 This chapter has become part of this book with the support of Proulx-Turner's family: I offer my sincere thanks to them.

14 Proulx-Turner was working on this book around the time we spoke, and there are some resonances between this conversation and her pieces in that text. Where her stories here intertwine with those in her last book, I have made notes to refer readers to passages there, so that they can gain a fuller sense of those moments in her life.

15 I listened carefully to Proulx-Turner's words as we spoke, but neglected to take good notes on my own side of the conversation, such as the questions I asked. I have recreated these

in a minimal but representative manner. There are a few spots, as well, where the conversation may seem to jump topics, as Sharron and I talked in between my note-taking. To help make this chapter more readable, I've provided some transitional information in italics.

16 See Proulx-Turner, *creole métisse of french canada, me*, 17.

17 See Proulx-Turner, *creole métisse of french canada, me*, 49–50.

18 For more on Proulx-Turner's story about the Chinook winds, see *creole métisse of french canada, me*, 34.

19 Here she shares with me a little of her mother's story. Readers can hear more in *creole métisse of french canada, me*, 14–15.

20 For other stories that fit in this part of Proulx-Turner's experiences, see *creole métisse of french canada, me*, 75–76.

21 What Proulx-Turner tells me here is intertwined with the stories she tells in *creole métisse of french canada, me*, 7–10.

22 This was the 2012 AMIQAAQ conference hosted by the University of Alberta, at the St. Jean campus, entitled Born This Way: Two-Spirit Voices. It featured fabulous keynotes by writers Chrystos, Gregory Scofield, and Craig Womack, Dr. James Makokis, and youth activist Jessica Danforth, as well as a range of presentations and discussions on two-spirit-related topics like community, identity, health, and activism.

23 For instance, she was interviewed in 2018 by Rosanna Deerchild on *Unreserved* and has a segment in a 2017 episode of *New Fire* hosted by Lisa Charleyboy, both on CBC Radio.

24 See, for instance, Justice's essay " 'Go Away, Water!': Kinship Criticism and the Decolonization Imperative," or his book *Why Indigenous Literatures Matter*.

25 If you are also not on the Twitter, you might find it helpful to know that "DMs" are "direct messages."

26 This was the January 8, 2016 episode of CBC Radio's *The Current*.

27 Tenille Campbell, Billy-Ray Belcourt, and Joshua Whitehead were nominated and shortlisted for the same Indigenous Voices Award, namely Most Significant Work of Poetry in English by an Emerging Indigenous Writer.

28 Billy-Ray Belcourt is a Cree poet and currently a PhD student in English and film studies at the University of Alberta. Smokii Sumac is a Ktunaxa poet and PhD student in Indigenous studies at Trent. Brittany Catherine, or Brittany Johnson, is a singer/songwriter, creative writer, poet, burlesque performer, and doula, and is also in doctoral studies in English and film at the U of A.

29 Dumont is referring to being in her third year as a member of the Arts and Native Studies Faculties at the University of Alberta.

30 This poem is in *A Really Good Brown Girl*, 11–12.

31 Dumont is talking about Métis settlements in Alberta. Alberta is the only province that recognizes a land base for the Métis.

32 In this section, I am talking about my decision to join other members of my family in getting a "Métis card," which comes with formal membership in the Métis Nation (of Alberta, in my case). This felt like an enormous and symbolic decision for my young self.

33 Kitty Lewis is the general manager at Brick Books, which has published both the 1996 edition and the 2015 Brick Books Classics edition of *A Really Good Brown Girl*.

CONCLUSION

1 If you want to hear a great deal more about my personal and professional learning journey, please feel free to read my doctoral dissertation, "Reading for Resurgence," as well as my master's thesis, "Decolonizing Pedagogical Approaches to Aboriginal Literatures in Canada."

2 I have developed these arguments about teaching and responsibility elsewhere as well, as I suggested in the introduction to this volume. See, for instance, my articles "Relational Encounters with Indigenous Literatures," "Reading for Reconciliation? Indigenous Literatures in a post-TRC Canada," and " 'Through White Man's Eyes': Beatrice Culleton Mosionier's *In Search of April Raintree* and Reading for Decolonization." In making these arguments, I am building upon an extensive scholarly foundation, but as a starting place I would direct readers to the work of Jo-Ann Episkenew, including "Socially Responsible Criticism" and *Taking Back Our Spirits*.

3 Garneau, "Imaginary Spaces of Conciliation and Reconciliation," 27.

4 Garneau explores the notion of incommensurability in the above-cited essay. Regan combats what she calls the "peacemaker myth" in her book *Unsettling the Settler Within*. Tuck and Yang critique what they call "settler moves to innocence" in their essay "Decolonization is Not a Metaphor."

5 Simpson, "Bubbling Like a Beating Heart," 113.

6 In thinking through ethical relationships, I continue to appreciate the frameworks that Willie Ermine provides in "The Ethical Space of Engagement." Sam McKegney's "Writer-Reader Reciprocity and the Pursuit of Alliance through Indigenous Poetry" is also helpful for framing engagement between writers and readers of Indigenous literatures.

7 Ermine, "The Ethical Space of Engagement," 200.

8 Proulx and Srivastava made this call for the *how*, not just the *what*, back in 2002, and I am still listening to their cautionary advice about teaching.

9 For more on amnesia, see Keavy Martin's essay "Truth, Reconciliation, and Amnesia"; for more on common-sense racism, see Himani Bannerji's "But Who Speaks for Us?"; and for more on national myths, see Paulette Regan's *Unsettling the Settler Within*.

10 King, *The Truth about Stories*, 29.

BIBLIOGRAPHY

Acoose, Janice. "A Vanishing Indian? Or Acoose: Woman Standing above Ground?" In *(Ad)dressing our Words: Aboriginal Perspectives on Aboriginal Literatures*, edited by Armand Garnet Ruffo, 37–56. Penticton, BC: Theytus, 2001.

Akiwenzie-Damm, Kateri. "The Cultural Appropriation Debate Is Over. It's Time for Action." *Globe and Mail*, May 19, 2017. https://www.theglobeandmail .com/opinion/the-cultural-appropriation-debate-is-over-its-time-for-action/ article35072670/.

Archibald, Jo-ann. *Indigenous Storywork: Educating the Heart, Mind, Body, and Spirit*. Vancouver: UBC Press, 2008.

Archibald-Barber, Jess Rae, ed. *kisiskâciwan: Indigenous Voices from where the River Flows Swiftly*. Regina: University of Regina Press, 2018

Armstrong, Jeannette, ed. *Looking at the Words of Our People: First Nations Analysis of Literature*. Penticton, BC: Theytus, 1993.

Armstrong, Jeannette C. "Traditional Indigenous Education: A Natural Process." *Canadian Journal of Native Education* 14, no. 3 (1987): 14–19.

Bannerji, Himani. "But Who Speaks for Us? Experiences and Agency in Conventional Feminist Paradigms." In *Unsettling Relations: The University as a Site of Feminist Struggles*, edited by Himani Bannerji, Linda Carty, Kari Dehli, Susan Heald, and Kate McKenna, 67–107. Toronto: Women's Press, 1991.

Barrera, Jorge. "Author Joseph Boyden's Shape-Shifting Indigenous Identity." *APTN National News*, December 23, 2016. http://aptnnews.ca/2016/12/23/ author-joseph-boydens-shape-shifting-indigenous-identity/.

Battiste, Marie. *Decolonizing Education: Nourishing the Learning Spirit*. Saskatoon: Purich, 2013.

Bell, David, Kirk Anderson, Terry Fortin, Jacqueline Ottmann, Sheila Rose, Leon Simard, Keith Spencer. *Sharing Our Success: Ten Case Studies in Aboriginal Schooling*. Kelowna, BC: Society for the Advancement of Excellence in Education, 2004.

Bidwell, Kristina Fagan. "What Stories Do: A Response to Episkenew." *Canadian Literature* 214 (2012): 109–16.

Blaeser, Kimberly. "Native Literature: Seeking a Critical Center." In *Looking at the Words of Our People*, edited by Jeannette Armstrong, 51–62. Penticton, BC: Theytus, 1993.

Boyden, Joseph. "Joseph Boyden Addresses His Heritage in Exclusive Interview with Candy Palmater." Interview by Candy Palmater. *Q*. CBC Radio, January 12, 2017. http://www.cbc.ca/radio/q/schedule-for-thursday-january-12-2017-1.3929478/ joseph-boyden-addresses-his-heritage-in-exclusive-interview-with-candy -palmater-1.3932161.

———. "My Name is Joseph Boyden." *Macleans*, August 2, 2017. http://www.macleans .ca/news/canada/my-name-is-joseph-boyden/.

Boyden, Joseph, Daniel Heath Justice, and Terri Monture. "Authors, Communities, Responsibilities: Conversation with Joseph Boyden." Panel discussion at the Indigenous Literary Studies Association Inaugural Gathering, Six Nations of the Grand River, ON, October 1–3, 2015.

Canadian Council on Learning. *Redefining How Success is Measured in First Nations, Inuit and Métis Learning*. Ottawa: Canadian Council on Learning, 2007. http://www.afn.ca/uploads/fileseducation/5._2007_redefining _how_success_is_measured_en.pdf.

Cariou, Warren. "Who Is the Text in This Class? Story, Archive, and Pedagogy in Indigenous Contexts." In *Learn, Teach, Challenge: Approaches to Indigenous Literatures*, edited by Deanna Reder and Linda Morra, 467–86. Waterloo, ON: Wilfrid Laurier University Press, 2016.

Claxton, Nicholas Xumthoult. "ISTÁ SĆIÁNEW, ISTÁ SX̱OLE 'To Fish as Formerly': The Douglas Treaties and the WSÁNEĆ Reef-Net Fisheries." In *Lighting the Eighth Fire: The Liberation, Resurgence, and Protection of Indigenous Nations*, edited by Leanne Betasamosake Simpson, 47–58. Winnipeg: Arbeiter Ring, 2008.

Corntassel, Jeffrey. "Re-Envisioning Resurgence: Indigenous Pathways to Decolonization and Sustainable Self-Determination." *Decolonization: Indigeneity, Education & Society* 1, no. 1 (2012): 86–101.

Cranmer, Laura Ann. "Exploring Voice and Silence in the Poetry of Beth Cuthand, Louise Halfe and Marlene Nourbese Philip." In *(Ad)dressing our Words: Aboriginal Perspectives on Aboriginal Literatures*, edited by Armand Garnet Ruffo, 125–33. Penticton, BC: Theytus, 2001.

Damm, Kateri. "Says Who: Colonialism, Identity and Defining Indigenous Literature." In *Looking at the Words of Our People: First Nations Analysis of Literature*, edited by Jeannette Armstrong, 9–26. Penticton, BC: Theytus, 1993.

Davis, Lynne, Jeff Denis, and Raven Sinclair. "Pathways of Settler Decolonization." *Settler Colonial Studies* 7, no. 4 (2017): 393–7. DOI: 10.1080/ 2201473X.2016.1243085.

Dion, Susan. *Braiding Histories: Learning from Aboriginal Peoples' Experiences and Perspectives*. Vancouver: UBC Press, 2009.

Dion, Susan D. "Disrupting Molded Images: Identities, Responsibilities and Relationships—Teachers and Indigenous Subject Material." *Teaching Education* 18, no. 4 (2007): 329–42. DOI: 10.1080/10476210701687625.

Donald, Dwayne. "Indigenous Métissage: A Decolonizing Research Sensibility." *International Journal of Qualitative Studies in Education* 25, no. 5 (2012): 533–55. DOI: 10.1080/09518398.2011.554449.

Dundas, Deborah. "Editor Quits Amid Outrage after Call for 'Appropriation Prize' in Writers' Magazine." *Toronto Star*, May 10, 2017. https://www.thestar.com/entertainment/books/2017/05/10/editor-quits-amid-outrage-after-call-for-appropriation-prize-in-writers-magazine.html.

Eigenbrod, Renate. " 'For the Child Taken, for the Parent Left Behind': Residential School Narratives as Acts of 'Survivance'. " *English Studies in Canada* 38, no. 3/4 (2012): 277–97.

Eigenbrod, Renate, and Jo-Ann Episkenew, eds. *Creating Community: A Roundtable on Canadian Aboriginal Literature.* Penticton, BC: Theytus, 2002.

Episkenew, Jo-Ann. "Indigenizing Author Meets Critics: Collaborative Indigenous Literary Scholarship." *Canadian Literature* 214 (2012): 117–27.

——. "Socially Responsible Criticism: Aboriginal Literature, Ideology, and the Literary Canon." In *Creating Community: A Roundtable on Canadian Aboriginal Literature*, edited by Renate Eigenbrod and Jo-Ann Episkenew, 51–68. Penticton, BC: Theytus, 2002.

——. *Taking Back Our Spirits: Indigenous Literature, Public Policy, and Healing.* Winnipeg: University of Manitoba Press, 2009.

Ermine, Willie. "Aboriginal Epistemology." In *First Nations Education in Canada: The Circle Unfolds*, edited by Jean Barman and Marie Battiste, 101–12. Vancouver: UBC Press, 1995.

——. "The Ethical Space of Engagement." *Indigenous Law Journal* 6, no. 1 (2007): 193–203.

Eyford, Ryan. *White Settler Reserve: New Iceland and the Colonization of the Canadian West.* Vancouver: UBC Press, 2016.

Fagan, Kristina. " 'What about You?': Approaching the Study of 'Native Literature'. " In *Creating Community: A Roundtable on Canadian Aboriginal Literature*, edited by Renate Eigenbrod and Jo-Ann Episkenew, 235–53. Penticton, BC: Theytus, 2002.

Fagan, Kristina, Daniel Justice, Keavy Martin, Sam McKegney, Deanna Reder, and Niigan J. Sinclair. "Canadian Indian Literary Nationalism? Critical Approaches in Canadian Indigenous Contexts—A Collaborative Interlogue." *Canadian Journal of Native Studies* 29, no. 1–2 (2009): 19–44.

Fee, Margery. "The Truth and Reconciliation Commission of Canada." *Canadian Literature* 215 (2012): 6–10.

"First Nations Authors Discuss Carolyn Bennett's Proposed Indigenous Book Club Month." *The Current.* CBC Radio. January 8, 2016. https://www.cbc.ca/radio/thecurrent/the-current-for-january-8-2015-1.3394962/first-nations-authors-discuss-carolyn-bennett-s-proposed-indigenous-book-club-month-1.3394986.

Friedel, Tracy, Jo-ann Archibald, Ramona Big Head, Georgina Martin, and Marissa Muñoz. "Editorial—Indigenous Pedagogies: Resurgence and Restoration." *Canadian Journal of Native Education* 35, no. 1 (2012): 1–6, 221–4.

Garneau, David. "Imaginary Spaces of Conciliation and Reconciliation." In *Arts of Engagement: Taking Aesthetic Action in and Beyond the Truth and Reconciliation*

Commission of Canada, edited by Dylan Robinson and Keavy Martin, 21–42. Waterloo, ON: Wilfrid Laurier University Press, 2016.

Goulet, Linda M., and Keith N. Goulet. *Teaching Each Other: Nehinuw Concepts and Indigenous Pedagogies.* Vancouver: UBC Press, 2014.

Hampton, Eber. "Towards a Redefinition of Indian Education." In *First Nations Education in Canada: The Circle Unfolds*, edited by Marie Battiste and Jean Barman, 5–46. Vancouver: UBC Press, 1995.

Hanson, Aubrey J. "Decolonizing Pedagogical Approaches to Aboriginal Literatures in Canada." MA thesis, Ontario Institute for Studies in Education of the University of Toronto, 2008.

——. "Reading for Reconciliation? Indigenous Literatures in a post-TRC Canada." *English Studies in Canada* 43, no. 2/3 (2017): 69–90.

——. "Reading for Resurgence." PhD diss., University of Calgary, 2016.

——. "Relational Encounters with Indigenous Literatures." *McGill Journal of Education* 53, no. 2 (2018): 312–30.

——. " 'Through White Man's Eyes': Beatrice Culleton Mosionier's *In Search of April Raintree* and Reading for Decolonization." *Studies in American Indian Literatures* 24, no. 1 (2012): 15–30.

Harvey, Alban. "Joseph Boyden." *Canadian Encyclopedia/Historica Canada.* Last modified January 13, 2017. http://www.thecanadianencyclopedia.ca/en/article/joseph-boyden/.

Herriot, Trevor. *Towards a Prairie Atonement.* Regina: University of Regina Press, 2016.

"*#IndianLovePoems*: Tenille Campbell's Dating Life Served as Inspiration for Poetry Collection." *Unreserved.* CBC Radio. February 8, 2018. https://www.cbc.ca/listen/shows/unreserved/segment/15519585.

Indigenous Literary Studies Association. "Indigenous Voices Awards." Accessed March 4, 2019. http://www.indigenousliterarystudies.org/-indigenous-voices-award.

——."Governing Code for the Indigenous Literary Studies Association." Accessed July 2, 2017. http://www.indigenousliterarystudies.org/governing-code/.

Johnston, Basil H. "One Generation from Extinction." *Canadian Literature (special issue: Native Writers and Canadian Literature)* 124/125 (1990): 10–15.

Justice, Daniel Heath. " 'Go Away, Water!': Kinship Criticism and the Decolonization Imperative." In *Reasoning Together: The Native Critics Collective*, edited by Craig Womack, Daniel Heath Justice, and Chrisopher Teuton, 147–68. Norman: University of Oklahoma Press, 2008.

——. "Literature, Healing, and the Transformative Imaginary: Thoughts on Jo-Ann Episkenew's *Taking Back Our Spirits: Indigenous Literature, Public Policy, and Healing.*" *Canadian Literature* 214 (2012): 101–8.

——. *Our Fire Survives the Storm: A Cherokee Literary History.* Minneapolis: University of Minnesota Press, 2006.

——.*Why Indigenous Literatures Matter.* Waterloo, ON: Wilfrid Laurier University Press, 2018.

Kassam, Ashifa. "Canadian Journalists Support 'Appropriation Prize' After Online Furore." *Guardian*, May 13, 2017. https://www.theguardian.com/world/2017/may/13/canadian-journalists-appropriation-prize.

Kinew, Wab. "There is Room in Our Circle for Joseph Boyden." *Globe and Mail*, January 3, 2017. https://www.theglobeandmail.com/opinion/there-is-room-in -our-circle-for-joseph-boyden/article33467823/.

King, Hayden. "The Orenda Faces Tough Criticism from First Nations Scholar." *CBC News*, March 7, 2014. http://www.cbc.ca/news/indigenous/ the-orenda-faces-tough-criticism-from-first-nations-scholar-1.2562786.

King, Thomas. Introduction to *All My Relations: An Anthology of Contemporary Canadian Native Fiction*, edited by Thomas King, ix–xvi. Toronto: McClelland and Stewart, 1990.

———. *The Truth about Stories: A Native Narrative*. Toronto: House of Anansi Press, 2003.

LaRocque, Emma. "Teaching Aboriginal Literature: The Discourse of Margins and Mainstreams." In *Creating Community: A Roundtable on Canadian Aboriginal Literature*, edited by Renate Eigenbrod and Jo-Ann Episkenew, 209–24. Penticton, BC: Theytus, 2002.

Lederman, Marsha, and Mark Medley. "Writers' Union of Canada Editorial Sparks Outrage, Resignations." *Globe and Mail*, May 10, 2017. https://www.the globeandmail.com/arts/books-and-media/writers-union-of-canada-editorial -on-cultural-appropriation-sparks-outrage-resignations/article34952918/.

Louie, Dustin, Yvonne Poitras Pratt, Aubrey J. Hanson, and Jacqueline Ottmann. "Applying Principles of Decolonizing Methodologies." *Canadian Journal of Higher Education* 47, no. 3 (2017): 16–33.

Maracle, Lee. *Memory Serves: Oratories*. Edited by Smaro Kamboureli. Edmonton: NeWest Press, 2015.

Martin, Keavy. "Truth, Reconciliation, and Amnesia: *Porcupines and China Dolls* and the Canadian Conscience." *English Studies in Canada* 35, no. 1 (2009): 47–65.

McCarty, Teresa, and Tiffany Lee. "Critical Culturally Sustaining/Revitalizing Pedagogy and Indigenous Education Sovereignty." *Harvard Educational Review* 84, no. 1 (2014): 101–24.

McGregor, Hannah, Julie Rak, and Erin Wunker, eds. *Refuse: CanLit in Ruins*. Toronto: Book*hug Press, 2018.

McKegney, Sam. *Magic Weapons: Aboriginal Writers Remaking Community after Residential School*. Winnipeg: University of Manitoba Press, 2007.

———. "Writer-Reader Reciprocity and the Pursuit of Alliance through Indigenous Poetry." In *Indigenous Poetics in Canada*, edited by Neil McLeod, 43–60. Waterloo, ON: Wilfrid Laurier University Press, 2014.

McMahon, Ryan. "What Colour is Your Beadwork, Joseph Boyden?" *Vice*, December 30, 2016. https://www.vice.com/en_ca/article/wnd97z/what-colour-is -your-beadwork-joseph-boyden.

Niedzviecki, Hal. "Winning the Appropriation Prize." *Write* 45, no. 1 (2017): 8. https://www.writersunion.ca/sites/all/files/attachments/WRITE_Spring2017_ Web.pdf.

Ono, Jaydon. "11 Indigenous Authors You Should Be Reading Instead of Joseph Boyden." *BuzzFeed*, January 12, 2017. https://www.buzzfeed.com/jaydonono/ indigenous-authors-canada

"Opening Up About Indigenous intimacy." *New Fire.* CBC Radio. July 20, 2017. https://
    www.cbc.ca/radio/newfire/opening-up-about-indigenous-intimacy-1.4181758.
Poitras Pratt, Yvonne, Dustin Louie, Aubrey Hanson, and Jacqueline Ottmann.
    "Indigenous Education and Decolonization." In *Oxford Research Encyclope-
    dia of Education* (January 2018). http://education.oxfordre.com/view/10.1093/
    acrefore/9780190264093.001.0001/acrefore-9780190264093-e-240.
Proulx-Turner, Sharron. *creole métisse of french canada, me.* Cape Croker Reserve,
    ON: Kegedonce Press, 2017.
Proulx, Sharron, and Aruna Srivastava. "A Moose in the Corridor: Teaching English,
    Aboriginal Pedagogies, and Institutional Resistance." In *Creating Community: A
    Roundtable on Canadian Aboriginal Literature*, edited by Renate Eigenbrod and
    Jo-Ann Episkenew, 187–208. Penticton, BC: Theytus, 2002.
Reder, Deanna. "Stories of Destruction and Renewal: Images of Fireweed in Auto-
    biographical Fiction by Shirley Sterling and Tomson Highway." In *Creating
    Community: A Roundtable on Canadian Aboriginal Literature*, edited by Renate
    Eigenbrod and Jo-Ann Episkenew, 276–94. Penticton, BC: Theytus, 2002.
Reder, Deanna, and Linda Morra, eds. *Learn, Teach, Challenge: Approaching Indige-
    nous Literatures.* Waterloo, ON: Wilfrid Laurier University Press, 2016.
Regan, Paulette. *Unsettling the Settler Within: Indian Residential Schools, Truth Tell-
    ing, and Reconciliation in Canada.* Vancouver: UBC Press, 2010.
Rice, Waubgeshig. "Joseph Boyden's The Orenda Fuels Important Conversation."
    CBC News Blog, March 1, 2014. http://www.cbc.ca/news/indigenous/joseph
    -boyden-s-the-orenda-fuels-important-conversation-1.2555541.
Roy, Laura. *Teaching While White: Addressing the Intersections of Race and Immigra-
    tion in the Classroom.* Lanham, MD: Rowman and Littlefield, 2018.
Sark, Charlie Greg. "Kulu, Cops, and You." In *Lighting the Eighth Fire: The Liberation,
    Resurgence, and Protection of Indigenous Nations*, edited by Leanne Betasamo-
    sake Simpson, 5–8. Winnipeg: Arbeiter Ring, 2008.
Schissel, Bernard, and Terry Wotherspoon. *The Legacy of School for Aboriginal Peo-
    ple: Education, Oppression, and Emancipation.* Don Mills, ON: Oxford Univer-
    sity Press, 2003.
Simpson, Leanne Betasamosake. *As We Have Always Done: Indigenous Freedom
    through Radical Resistance.* Minneapolis: University of Minnesota Press, 2017.
———. " 'Bubbling Like a Beating Heart': Reflections on Nishnaabeg Poetic and Nar-
    rative Consciousness." In *Indigenous Poetics in Canada*, edited by Neal McLeod,
    107–19. Waterloo, ON: Wilfrid Laurier University Press, 2014.
———. *Dancing on Our Turtle's Back: Stories of Nishnaabeg Re-Creation, Resurgence
    and a New Emergence.* Winnipeg: Arbeiter Ring, 2011.
———. "Land as Pedagogy: Nishnaabeg Intelligence and Rebellious Transforma-
    tion." *Decolonization: Indigeneity, Education & Society* 3, no. 3 (2014): 1–25.
    https://jps.library.utoronto.ca/index.php/des/article/view/22170.
———."Our Elder Brothers: The Lifeblood of Resurgence." In *Lighting the Eighth
    Fire: The Liberation, Resurgence, and Protection of Indigenous Nations*, edited by
    Leanna Betasamosake Simpson, 73–87. Winnipeg: Arbeiter Ring, 2008.
Smith, Linda Tuhiwai. *Decolonizing Methodologies: Research and Indigenous Peoples.*
    2nd ed. London: Zed Books, 2012.

Statistics Canada. "Aboriginal peoples in Canada: Key results from the 2016 Census." 2017. https://www150.statcan.gc.ca/n1/daily-quotidien/171025/dq171025a-eng.htm.

———. "A Portrait of Canadian Youth." 2018. https://www150.statcan.gc.ca/n1/pub/11-631-x/11-631-x2018001-eng.htm#a3.

Talaga, Tanya. *All Our Relations: Finding the Path Forward.* Toronto: House of Anansi, 2018.

———. *Seven Fallen Feathers: Racism, Death, and Hard Truths in a Northern City.* Toronto: House of Anansi, 2017.

Tanaka, Michele. *Learning & Teaching Together: Weaving Indigenous Ways of Knowing into Education.* Vancouver: UBC Press, 2016.

Taylor, Drew Hayden. "Can Joseph Boyden Make Amends with First Nations?" *Globe and Mail*, January 13, 2017. https://www.theglobeandmail.com/opinion/can-joseph-boyden-make-amends-with-first-nations/article33618361/ .

Thomas, Ashleigh-Rae. "Who Is a Settler, According to Indigenous and Black Scholars." *Vice*, February 15, 2019. https://www.vice.com/en_ca/article/gyajj4/who-is-a-settler-according-to-indigenous-and-black-scholars.

Truth and Reconciliation Commission of Canada. *Calls to Action.* 2015. http://trc.ca/assets/pdf/Calls_to_Action_English2.pdf.

———. *Reconciliation.* Vol. 6 of *Canada's Residential Schools.* Montreal and Kingston: McGill-Queen's University Press, 2015.

Tuck, Eve. "Re-Visioning Action: Participatory Action Research and Indigenous Theories of Change." *Urban Review: Issues and Ideas in Public Education* 41, no. 1 (2009): 47–65.

Tuck, Eve, and K. Wayne Yang. "Decolonization is Not a Metaphor." *Decolonization: Indigeneity, Education & Society* 1, no. 1 (2012): 1–40.

Warrior, Robert. *Tribal Secrets: Recovering American Indian Intellectual Traditions.* Minneapolis: University of Minnesota Press, 1995.

Weaver, Jace. *Other Words: American Indian Literature, Law, and Culture.* Norman: University of Oklahoma Press, 2001.

———. *That the People Might Live: Native American Literatures and Native American Community.* New York: Oxford University Press, 1997.

Weaver, Jace, Craig Womack, and Robert Warrior. *American Indian Literary Nationalism.* Albuquerque: University of New Mexico Press, 2006.

Wente, Jesse. "An Emotional Jesse Wente on the 'Remarkable Arrogance' of an Appropriation Prize." Interview by Matt Galloway. *CBC News*, May 15, 2017. http://www.cbc.ca/news/canada/toronto/jesse-wente-appropriation-prize-1.4115293.

Womack, Craig S. *Red on Red: Native American Literary Separatism.* Minneapolis: Minnesota University Press, 1999.

Books in the Indigenous Studies Series

Arts of Engagement: Taking Aesthetic Action In and Beyond Canada's Truth and Reconciliation Commission / Dylan Robinson and Keavy Martin, editors / 2016 / viii + 376 pp. / illus. / ISBN 978-1-77112-169-9

Learn, Teach, Challenge: Approaching Indigenous Literature / Deanna Reder and Linda M. Morra, editors / 2016 / xii + 580 pp. / ISBN 978-1-77112-185-9

Violence Against Indigenous Women: Literature, Activism, Resistance / Alison Hargreaves / 2017 / xvi + 282 pp. / ISBN 978-1-77112-239-9

Read, Listen, Tell: Indigenous Stories from Turtle Island / Sophie McCall, Deanna Reder, David Gaertner, and Gabrielle L'Hirondlle Hill, editors / 2017 / xviii + 390 pp. / ISBN 978-1-77112-300-6

The Homing Place: Indigenous and Settler Literary Legacies of the Atlantic / Rachel Bryant / 2017 / xiv + 244 pp. / ISBN 978-1-77112-286-3

Why Indigenous Literatures Matter / Daniel Heath Justice / 2018 / xxii + 284 pp. / ISBN 978-1-77112-176-7

Activating the Heart: Storytelling, Knowledge Sharing, and Relationship / Julia Christensen, Christopher Cox, and Lisa Szabo-Jones, editors / 2018 / xvii + 210 pp. / ISBN 978-1-77112-219-1

Indianthusiasm: Indigenous Responses / Hartmut Lutz, Renae Watchman, and Florentine Strzelczyk, editors / 2020 / x + 252 pp. / ISBN 978-1-77112-399-0

Literatures, Communities, and Learning: Conversations with Indigenous Writers / Aubrey Jean Hanson / 2020 / viii + 182 pp. / ISBN 978-1-77112-449-2